T0339808

THE PATH OF REASON

THE PATH OF REASON

A PHILOSOPHY OF NONBELIEF

Bruce A. Smith

Algora Publishing
New York

ISBN-13: 978-0-87586-579-9 (trade paper)
ISBN-13: 978-0-87586-580-5 (hard cover)
ISBN-13: 978-0-87586-581-2 (ebook)

Library of Congress Cataloging-in-Publication Data —

Smith, Bruce A., 1961-
  The path of reason : a philosophy of nonbelief / by Bruce A. Smith.
    p. cm.
  Includes bibliographical references and index.
    ISBN 978-0-87586-580-5 (hard cover: alk. paper) — ISBN 978-0-87586-579-9 (pbk.:
alk. paper) — ISBN 978-0-87586-581-2 (ebook) 1. Smith, Bruce A., 1961- 2. Spiritual
biography. 3. Atheism. I. Title.

  BL73.S64A3 2007
  211'.8—dc22

                        2007016678

Printed in the United States

For Sharron,
who gives me something to believe in
and reminds me of what is most important.

Acknowledgments

Special thanks to Janna Southworth, Jim Sitton, and my brother, Phil, for taking the time to read my unpolished work and for their valuable feedback. Thanks also go out to Mike Foley for his assistance with proofreading.

TABLE OF CONTENTS

Chapter 1. Faith and Reason Collide

Unexpected Answers

A white dove hovered over the baptistery. It was frozen amid a stained glass mosaic of yellow, red, and blue. The window served as the backdrop to choirs and sermons, and it dominated my view as I sang my heart out, a seven-year-old boy happy to be in church on a Sunday morning. I would be baptized under that window after professing my faith, and for years I would know no other religion than that of the conservative Baptist churches I attended.

My childhood was filled with church bus trips, youth camps, and Bible studies. By the eighth grade, I had decided either to become a minister or to find a way to use my artistic talents to spread the gospel.

A turning point came when I was in high school. One Sunday morning, in my church's youth group, I asked a question. The answer I received did not make any sense at all. The issue was predestination, and I questioned the idea that God already knew what we were going to do. If that was right, then it could not truly be said that we have free will. It would be years before I realized the full implications of the argument. Meanwhile, it opened up a floodgate. Questions poured out of me, and I began the great search for answers.

In college, I learned of possibilities — so many possibilities that I finally came to doubt that the answers could ever be found. I still believed in God, but it was not the God of my childhood. It was a benevolent God, to be sure, but what form this great consciousness took and how he, she, or it interacted with our world were other questions entirely.

Late one afternoon in the family room of a house in England, where I was living as an exchange student, I sat down to write a paper called, "My Philosophy." It wasn't for a class; it was a project I had taken on for myself. While the wind outside swirled snow around the trees, I scribbled words down on paper, trying to make sense of what I believed. My ultimate conclusion was, "I don't know."

I lived for twenty-five years with that mindset, thinking that the universe was so complex, vast, and amazing that although somebody might know the answers, I definitely did not. With each day, it seemed decreasingly likely that I ever would. Still, I continued to hope and look.

Along the way I learned computer programming. I learned principles of logic through computer games. I began to appreciate science and what those who were involved in it did. They were looking for the same answers I was, but their methods were different. I often felt that those methods were so limited that it kept researchers and scientists from seeing greater truths.

In my early forties, I began several writing projects and one of them turned out to be a continuation of the paper I had begun when I was in England so many years before. The conclusion was the same, but I had a lot more to say about what I didn't know. While writing, I challenged myself with a rule that would not only change what I wrote, but would change me as well. It would cause me to undergo the biggest transformation I had undergone since I left Christianity in high school. The rule was quite simple — whatever I wrote about my philosophy had to be consistent. Anything self-contradictory was not allowed.

I made a list of principles that aided me in maintaining consistency. They functioned as guidelines for separating truth from falsehood, and were ideas such as, "Personal attacks upon people have nothing to do with what the truth actually is. What's important is the idea, not the person." I did not realize it at the time, but what I had begun to compile was a list of logical fallacies and what I was learning was critical thinking. As I employed these principles, I found that certain ideas had to be eliminated from my philosophy, and many of them turned out to be pure speculation anyway.

As part of the project, I began researching many issues that had confused me over the years, everything from reincarnation to out-of-body experiences. I studied evolution and the biblical prophecies of the "End Times" that had always frightened me. I learned repeatedly, as if it were being pounded into my head, that I had given far too much credence to unfounded ideas.

But the big shocker came when I reanalyzed the concepts of God and the soul. There were fewer reasons to believe in these things than I had thought. It was only when the number of reasons for not believing in these things far outweighed the reasons I had for believing in them, that the scales tipped, and I found that I — who had once been a boy singing "How Great Thou Art" with such reverence and joy — had become an atheist.[1]

I felt as if I had sat on a mountaintop for years awaiting enlightenment, only to give up, come down off the mountain, and have the answers handed to me by a passerby.

It seemed an unlikely conclusion, even to me, but despite the stigma that the "A" word held, there was something to be said for my newfound philosophy. It had answers to some of the biggest questions I had ever asked, and although those answers were not what I expected them to be, they were satisfying in their own way. I realized, after the fact, that there was no reason the answers should have matched my preconceptions in the first place. Reality doesn't work that way.

Meanwhile, I had a book to finish and this development meant a significant rewrite. The difference was that now I had a conclusion. I had something to say.

In addition to providing philosophical insights and fresh presentations, it is my hope that this book can help those who are seeking answers in the same way that I was. If they have found that religion, ideologies involving the supernatural, and spirituality in general, are in some way lacking or unsatisfactory, perhaps they may find an alternative here that they had not previously considered. If I could have had this book in my hands as a teenager, it could have prevented a tremendous amount of confusion, internal conflict, unnecessary guilt, and wasted time.

Chapter 1 starts with some basics. I explain a fundamental assumption that underscores my philosophy (and any practical philosophy, for that matter) and then I jump right into the issue that is at the center of many contemporary philosophical debates. The issue is whether faith or reason is the best way to understand our world or if, possibly, a compromise can be found. By comparing faith and reason and by exploring how they work, I show that they are not compatible. In many ways, they contradict each other. The result is that a choice must be made. While faith is always an option, the only rational option becomes reason. This is the choice I made, and it is used as the foundation for the chapters that follow.

---

1 The definition of atheist most commonly used in the atheist community (and in popular books on the subject, such as *Atheism: The Case Against God* by George H. Smith, *Losing Faith in Faith* by Dan Barker, and *Natural Atheism* by David Eller) is that an atheist is someone who lacks belief in God, but who doesn't necessarily deny that God exists. Some would call this an agnostic position, but agnosticism covers a wide range of topics besides belief in God, so it is fair to say that one can be both an agnostic and an atheist. My own position on the existence of God varies depending on what version of God is under discussion. The section titled "God" provides the details.

In Chapter 2, I apply reason to some major philosophical questions. The conclusions are not statements of absolute certainty, but there is good reason to think that they are extremely likely. Those conclusions are that there is no God, we don't have souls, and that although life can have great meaning, it is not assigned by any external force. I was shocked that I had reached these conclusions, but once I got over my emotional objections to them, as well as the societal attitudes towards them that had been ingrained in me since youth, I discovered that these ideas could be remarkably liberating.

Chapter 3 provides a cursory review of some of the principles involved in logical and rational thought. Much of the emphasis is on the logical errors that people make while involved in philosophical debate (as well as in their everyday lives). Several of these logical fallacies come into play in other chapters of the book, and an awareness of them becomes indispensable in more ways than one. With the tools of reason (such as science, logic, and critical thinking), one can achieve a better understanding of the world. Without these tools, achieving clear understanding is almost hopeless.

Chapter 4 shows what happens when you take these tools and use them in an examination of many mystical and New Age ideas. This chapter directly addresses the questions and concerns of believers (of many different sorts) that must sometimes be resolved by individuals before they are able to completely accept the conclusions I reached in the previous chapters. This was the case for me as well. When I discarded my religious heritage, I wasn't at all ready to discard faith altogether. Instead, I took a good look at a wide range of beliefs because I was convinced that there had to be something out there that gave me the answers I wanted. It was this process of examination and elimination that spurred me towards my eventual destination. Those who read this book may find that they have gone through (or will go through) a similar process. No doubt, readers will come from a variety of backgrounds and each will have his or her set of ideas about how the world works. It is because of this that I cannot lay out a straight and narrow path that explains how to get from where they are to where I am, but by addressing an eclectic assortment of beliefs and principles, I can provide some examples of how reason can enable one to make sense of it all.

Chapter 5 is brief but important. As I make the transition from New Age and supernatural beliefs to the faith of Christianity, it helps to address two things that conservatives who believe in "God the Creator" have difficulty with — evolution, and how, without a prime mover and without some kind of guiding hand, our universe came to be.

Chapter 6 deals specifically with Christianity. This chapter is akin to Chapter 4 in that it again shows that reason is the key required to solve some tricky problems. Like the individual sections in Chapter 4, the importance of this chapter varies depending upon the reader's background. For those of us who were indoctrinated into Christianity at a young age, it becomes crucial to work through the ideas here, despite the validity of the arguments that take place in the first few chapters of this book.

Chapter 7 does what few if any books on these topics do: it examines the implications of a skeptical philosophy. Having deconstructed many worldviews, it is here that I begin the work of building a new one. Most of the people who read this book will be those who agree with me, and they already know that a philosophy that does not include the concepts of God and the soul can be just as fulfilling, if not more so, than one that does. There are people of religious faith, however, who find it hard to imagine that this could be possible. I can do little more than reassure them that, after all the disassembling is done, there is the proverbial light at the end of the tunnel — a new way of looking at the world that is rich with potential and vivid in its clarity.

Author Robert G. Olson expresses it this way:

> "But no!" the existentialist answers. You were in despair in the first place. It is for that reason you have heard and understood me when I stripped you of your illusions. All that I have done is to make you fully conscious of your despair, and now if you will listen further I will help you master your despair." [2]

Once the illusions are gone, there is a greater reality waiting underneath. In communicating this, I draw upon concepts borrowed from Eastern ideologies such as acceptance and living in the moment. Also explained is the idea that although understanding the world requires reason, when it comes to dealing with the world, we are not confined to a life of strict rationality. A philosophy based on realism by no means has to drown in it. Rather, realism allows for creativity and provides an appreciation of what it truly means to be human.

A Basic Assumption

Let's just get this out of the way. The philosophical issues addressed in this book are based on the assumption that world around us is real and that there is such a thing as an objective reality. It is an assumption, but it is an assumption we largely have to accept as we go about our daily lives. It's fun to play with the idea that we are taking part in a huge computer simulation like in the movie, *The Matrix*, just as it is an interesting game to imagine that the world around us

---

2 Robert G. Olson, *An Introduction to Existentialism* (New York: Dover Publications, Inc., 1962), p. 3.

is nothing more than a dream of God. These are entertaining ideas, but they are not very useful.[3]

I bring this up now because it is often brought up in the middle of philosophical arguments where it does not belong and where it only causes confusion. The assumption that the world is real is, by nature, an underlying assumption and should be shared at the start. If we don't presuppose this, then all of our discussions about the world become pointless. There is no reason to have any discussion at all if nothing we are talking about is of any substance. Claiming that reality is not objective undermines all claims, including itself. Any basis or standard that we might have for future conversation is lost. In short, progress cannot be made without, first, taking reality for granted.

It is common for people to accuse nonbelievers like me of "believing" in many things, which is a point I'll address in more detail as we progress. One of the things nonbelievers are told they believe in is "reality." The confusion here is simple. My assertion about reality is an assumption, not a belief. (I clarify the difference between these two things in the section titled "Contradiction and Self-Correction.")

Members of the school of thought sometimes referred to as postmodernism express a similar viewpoint to those who disagree with the idea of an objective reality. Postmodernists hold the opinion that all viewpoints about reality, as well as other topics, are open for interpretation. They state that there are no "right" or "wrong" points of view; there are only "different" points of view. According to those who think this, everything is relative and the words "true" and "false" have little or no meaning.

Postmodernists are in a similar position to those extreme skeptics who deny reality. Their arguments undermine their own viewpoint. In the case of postmodernism, their idea is equally valid as everyone else's, but that also means that it is can never be shown to be a better idea. If all ideas are equal, then there is no standard or basis by which to judge and evaluate ideas and the world around us. Without that, comprehension becomes impossible, and the mind is doomed to mental chaos.

I have encountered a hint of the postmodernist attitude when the subject of this book comes up. It is the proverbial double-edged sword. The benefit is that my viewpoint is treated with tolerance. It becomes "just another opinion" and is

---

3 By saying that reality is objective, I am also claiming that reality exists independently of our perceptions. If I die, the world would continue to exist, as it would in the case of any of us. The Philosophy 101 question, "If a tree falls in the woods and no one is around to hear it, would it still make a sound?" has a very simple answer. Sure it would. Sound is defined as vibrations at a certain frequencies, and these exist regardless of whether we are around to hear them.

no more challenging than my choice of ice cream flavors or my preference for a certain color. The drawback is that my viewpoint is given no special regard. It is just another of many, none of which holds any special precedence.

Like the subjectivists and the postmodernists before them, the religionists who dismiss my philosophy this way often fail to recognize that they have simultaneously pushed their belief system into an ethereal region where it is also of marginal importance. If all of our worldviews are that arbitrary, then any one belief (or nonbelief) system is in no position to claim superiority over any other, even those that claim to be "the one true religion."

When everything is subjective, the world becomes an ideological twilight zone. In addition, any solid philosophical basis we might have for our decisions and actions is also lost. However, with this kind of subjectivism and the distracting idea of a nonobjective reality out of the way, a lot can be accomplished.

The Heart of the Matter

My interest in philosophy has always been a practical one. I seek to understand the world so that I can get the most out of life and live the best way possible. The better I understand life, the more likely I am to make better decisions. Naturally, I seek out the best possible information so that I can do this.

So how do I obtain that information? In general, there are not a lot of options. There is reason, which is a way of thinking about and understanding the world that includes the formal disciplines of science and logic, as well as critical thinking (which I'll cover in Chapter 3), and logic in general. A second option is faith. There are many who claim that we should use faith in those instances where reason fails, and in so doing they form a worldview based on a mixture of faith and reason. These are our three choices for how we go about understanding the world — faith, reason, or a combination of the two.

This quickly brings us to the core issue at the center of the whole discussion — the value of faith versus the value of reason. I will consider the option of whether there is an acceptable compromise between them, but faith and reason must first be examined on their own before that can be done effectively. The crux of the debate is not an issue of good versus evil (therein lies the confusion for many a religionist). It is an issue of what faith and reason are qualified to explain and how important we hold these two approaches to be.

Before I expand on why this is the central issue, I need to define some terms and explain their usage. Far too many discussions of these issues disintegrate because this is not done first.

In the paragraphs above, I explained what I mean by reason and what it entails. When talking about faith, I will, for the sake of variety, use the word interchangeably with belief. Mostly, I will be referring to belief in the supernatural or belief in things that are out of the ordinary, and which cannot be proven true. Belief, in this sense, only applies to things outside of us. I will not be using the terms faith and belief to mean imagination, trust, confidence, or hope (all of which I highly value, but they are not the topic of discussion). The word "faith" is often used when the words "trust" or "confidence" should be used instead, resulting in a multitude of misconceptions. I will also not be using the word "faith" to refer to an act of will where one continues to believe despite having doubts.

By necessity, I will also be speaking of the two very generalized groups of "believers" and "nonbelievers." There are so many varieties of belief out there that I could never detail the idiosyncrasies of each one, and because of this, I have had to clump them all together. I am sure that there are Christians out there who do not want to be put in the same group as those who believe in alien abductions and that there are those who believe in alien abductions who do not want to be identified with certain Christians. No doubt there are a variety of disagreements between people who belong to these groups.

Still, they all have something in common — that they believe in something — and that is the only commonality I am speaking of when using the term "believers" inclusively. The Christian agrees with the ghost hunter that the soul continues after death. They just don't agree on how and where. Carlos Castaneda[4] and the Christian agree that there is a level of reality beyond what we see. This reality may be inhabited by angels, demons, or vaguely defined entities, but those are not things we normally see, touch, and feel in our everyday lives.

Alien abductees fall into the category of believers because they are unable to show solid evidence to support their notions. All they can report are personal experiences. Thus, their position has to be regarded as belief rather than knowledge.[5]

Similarly "nonbeliever" is used as a blanket term that applies to all those who consider themselves to be purely scientifically and logically minded — the skeptics, rationalists, and the like. I will often substitute the word "skeptic" for nonbeliever.

Because I cannot address all beliefs at once and cannot account for all varieties of individual belief, I am forced to generalize about faith. As we progress, keep in mind that, when I am talking about faith, I am speaking about many types of belief and not just the religious variety. Some readers may be of the opinion that

---

4 See the section, "The Death of Carlos Castaneda" in Chapter 4.
5 See the section "Criteria" for an in-depth look at this issue.

what I say about faith is not true in relation to their own ideology. I would ask such readers to examine their beliefs to ensure this is correct. In Chapters 4 and 6 of this book I will demonstrate that what I have to say remains true in regard to many ideologies.

Fortunately, I have already dealt with the objection that "everyone believes in something." Those who employ this argument might also say that I "believe in an objective reality" or that I "believe in reason." This objection is answered and invalidated when we distinguish between what is believed and what is known. I go into this in detail in the section "Separation of Knowledge and Belief," but it can be addressed very simply here: There's no reason to "believe" in something you know. Once you have convincing evidence of something, it no longer qualifies as a belief.

This returns us to the central issue — the value of faith versus the value of reason. One way we know that "faith versus reason" is at the very heart of this discussion is that if we thoroughly pursue any debate about these topics, it will lead to this point of contention.

An argument between a Christian and a non-Christian may begin with a debate over the meaning of a biblical passage, but that leads to the issue of whether the Bible is valid. From there the conversation goes to whether or not God authored the Bible, then to whether the idea of God is valid, and finally to the issue of belief in God. To say that it comes down to faith does not take into consideration that there is an alternative to faith. Ultimately, it comes down to how faith holds up against reason. A discussion of the ideas of good and evil will lead us to the same place.

In my own personal struggle with philosophical issues, and in discussions I have had with others about these topics, that is exactly where an examination of the issues led.

It can be seen be seen in the accusation lodged by believers at nonbelievers and vice versa.

"You don't understand faith!" the believer exclaims.

"You're so illogical!" cries the skeptic.

The Christian apologist C.S. Lewis acknowledges this to be a central issue at the very beginning of his book *Miracles*, where he separates people into the two groups of Naturalists and Supernaturalists, just as I separate people into the groups of believers and nonbelievers.

Karla McLaren, a former writer of New Age books who is now a skeptic, states that what lies at the center of the debate between believers and nonbelievers is that they have a different culture.[6] I would agree that the two groups have different cultures, but I would add that culture is based upon the ideas a group of people adopt, ideas that are often mutually engaged through unspoken agreement. In the end, disagreements still revolve around the issue of reason versus faith.

These core ideas affect a multiplicity of issues so that, indeed, there are different cultures, cultures that are becoming more plainly visible in today's America. The attitudes of individuals within groups vary from topic to topic, but we do find that generally there are huge disagreements in which the two parties of believers and nonbelievers mean something entirely different when talking about entire categories of words and ideas. They don't have the same basis of meaning when talking about such primary concepts as logic, science, evidence, knowledge, fact, truth, belief, assumptions, theories, investigation, research, proof, morality, and even reality. No wonder there is so much confusion, misunderstanding, and conflict.

In Southern California there is a group called "Atheists United," which meets at the Center for Inquiry in Hollywood. The Center for Inquiry was built by an organization called CSICOP, the Committee for the Scientific Investigation of Claims of the Paranormal. These skeptical and atheistic organizations are associated with each other because they share a common agreement — that science and reason are essential ways of understanding our universe and that any method of understanding the universe that *contradicts* science and reason is incorrect. The skeptic and those who go by the name "atheist" often have similar mindsets.

Two camps have now been established, believers and nonbelievers. The focus of the debate between these groups is the value of faith and reason in comparison to each other. How effective are they when it comes to explaining the world? How good is the information upon which we base our worldviews? By identifying this core issue, it becomes possible to determine if the conflicts can be resolved or if everyone is going to have to "agree to disagree."

IDEOLOGIES ON PARADE

For a moment, I want to take a look at the reputations of, and societal attitudes towards, faith and reason. These, no doubt, change from location to location and from generation to generation, so I will only speak to the attitudes that are prevalent in America at this time (the early twenty-first century).

---

6 From article titled "Bridging the Chasm between Two Cultures" by Karla McLaren, *Skeptical Inquirer* magazine (New York: The Committee for the Scientific Investigation of Claims of the Paranormal, May/June 2004) p. 47.

I would initially note that those who adopt just about any position considered extreme are usually not received well by the general public. Fundamentalists often bear the brunt of ridicule. Atheists are viewed as the opposite extreme and are not held in a positive light, either. This is quite possibly because in any society, an "extreme" ideology is, by default, one that is not held by the mainstream. In a different society, where few people believed in God, an atheist position would no longer be thought of as extreme.

I have been both a fundamentalist Christian and an atheist, although I spent a fair amount of my life as neither. Because I now label myself as both a skeptic and an atheist, I find that there are many who do not regard my philosophical stance as either reasonable or well-intentioned. The biblical summary of what an atheist is and does — and therefore the general Christian attitude towards atheists — is exceptionally negative. The Bible says, "The fool hath said in his heart, There is no God. They are corrupt, they have done abominable works, there is none that doeth good."[7]

While specific faiths certainly don't get much positive attention in the media, belief in general tends to get a warm round of applause. Faith is held in high esteem. This attitude is reflected in many movies where the skeptic says that something — an event, a monster, or a ghost — is impossible and cannot exist. By the end of the story, the skeptic has been proven wrong, or possibly eaten and devoured by the very thing he or she said was impossible. The skeptic loses.

The theme that belief of some sort is preferable to nonbelief is so prevalent that I breathe a sigh of relief when I don't encounter it in a book or movie.

Logic and science are associated with the cold, sterile whiteness of the lab coat and considered to be without heart. People have trouble picturing the skeptic as being imaginative or the scientist at home playing with his children. It is an inaccurate and unfortunate stereotype. There is a deeper conflict here, often described as "heart versus mind." We are urged to "follow our hearts" and "trust our feelings," but the intellect is mistrusted. Yet, what we call our heart and feelings are, of course, the emotions brought on by our thoughts. If the focus is on emotions alone, then the balance between heart and mind is thrown off. In an effort to be kind and good, the steady guidance of the intellect is neglected. The heart and mind should be employed together, not in disregard of each other.

There is the general conception that without belief of some sort, a person cannot be moral or ethical. There are plenty of reasons to behave ethically outside of belief systems, but this is not widely recognized. In a recent headline, the Boy Scouts of America revoked the membership of an Eagle Scout for this very

7 See Psalms 14:1 and Psalms 53:1. All Biblical quotations in this book are taken from the King James Version.

reason.[8] They felt that because he professed to be an atheist, he had no moral standards. Nothing could have been farther from the truth.[9]

The skeptic is often at a disadvantage because he finds himself criticizing things that people have an emotional and personal investment in. It is not surprising that this should make the skeptic unpopular. It does not help the skeptic that he or she must also state the same old skeptical adages repeatedly. Some people find it offensive, but it commits the far greater crime of being tedious.

The skeptic is accused of being a spoilsport, of taking away the mystery, but, in contrast, the skeptic views himself as performing a service — he's solving mysteries. His intent is not to be a naysayer, but rather to separate truth from falsehood and provide answers. He's helping!

I remember solving a puzzle that a friend of mine gave to me. Delighted and proud to have figured it out, I showed the solution to my friend.

"It's not any fun anymore because of you," he said. That's the skeptic's dilemma.

The difference in mindset between a believer and a skeptic is similar to the difference between a person who enjoys a movie for what it is and a person who is bothered by inconsistencies and plot holes. Both parties may find the other's attitude to be irritating. With movies, it's not really a crucial issue, but when it comes to understanding life, it is. The skeptic plays detective with life. Like Columbo, The Monk, or Agatha Christie's Hercule Poirot, they are always looking for details that don't fit.

To add to the distance between reason and faith, faith (especially religious faith) is considered sacred and personal. Those who criticize religious faith are not going to be well received, and often such criticism is perceived as a personal attack. Reason, on the other hand, does not have such an aura of sanctity about it and can be attacked quite freely.

If I could sum up the general societal attitude towards belief and disbelief, I would say it was this: "It doesn't matter what you believe in, as long as you believe in something. Reason is nice, but it lacks heart. Either way, keep your belief or your lack of belief to yourself."

The biggest losers in this battle of image are the nonbelievers. This negative image doesn't help me at all when it comes to communicating what I have to say.

---

8 Associated Press, November 4, 2002. The Scout's name is Darrell Lambert.
9 See the section titled "Dangerous" for an explanation of why ethics do not require belief.

SEPARATION OF KNOWLEDGE AND BELIEF

Knowledge and belief are two different things. If they were not, there would be no reason to talk about them separately, compare them, contrast them, or make any other distinctions. I realize, however, that being different from each other is not necessarily the same as being completely separate from each other, so I need to go one step further to make the point that knowledge and belief should be treated as two separate entities.

I'll illustrate with an example. I have a television set in my front room. I know the TV is there. I can weigh it, take pictures of it, and turn it off and on. If a team of scientists were to show up at my doorstep, they would verify that my television set is real. I can safely say that I "know" I have a TV. But couldn't I also say at the same time that I "believe" I have a TV? Over the years, there have been many philosophers and laypersons who have said that, yes, there are points at which knowledge and belief overlap. I object to defining these terms this way, because when you do, it creates confusion. The differences between knowledge and belief become distilled and de-emphasized.

Technically, I could adopt the more common usage of these terms and still make my case, because my arguments have little or nothing to do with the ways that they supposedly overlap, but everything to do with the ways in which they are different. In his book, *Natural Atheism*, David Eller makes a great (and relatively elaborate) case for treating the notions of knowledge and belief separately.[10] I have to agree with Eller on this one. If I know I have a TV set in my living room, I no longer have any need to say that I "believe" I have a TV set in my living room. Knowledge starts where belief leaves off. The two concepts should not be combined, and viewing them as separate provides a greater degree of clarity.

As we continue, I will outline the differences between knowledge and belief so that we can draw a dividing line between them. (Note, also, that knowledge is not the same thing as reason. Reason is a means by which some types of knowledge are arrived at.)

Failure to recognize the differences between knowledge and belief is the mistake made by those who would accuse me of believing in reason, science, or evolution. The same people might say, "Everyone believes in something, whether they know it or not," or "Atheism is a religion." I think that what people are trying to accomplish with these claims is to put everyone on the same playing field. It is another way of saying, "You can't criticize me because you're doing the same thing," or the reverse: "You're no better than me; you're a believer too." It's

---

10 In *Atheism: The Case Against God* and *Why Atheism?*, author George H. Smith (no relation) uses the "overlapping" definitions of knowledge and belief, but still arrives at the same conclusions as David and I.

another version of the postmodernist game. In some cases, it is the result of the confusion between the words faith, trust, and confidence. Either way, it accomplishes very little, but more importantly, the statement is wrong to begin with.

Some people will claim that they "know" something when what they really mean is they have an exceptionally strong feeling about it. The other day I heard a disc jockey say that he "knows" that his soul will continue on after death. In the sense that I use the word "know" in this book, and in the way that it is used in scientific circles, his statement would be incorrect. He may be convinced that he is right, and he may have strong emotions about it, but he does not "know."

Josh McDowell, author of the Christian apologetic book, *Evidence That Demands a Verdict*, also makes the same error. He does not appreciate what it means to have real evidence. If he had true "evidence," the very nature of Christianity would change. It would no longer be a faith.

Everyone's worldview contains some elements of knowledge and fact, but what confuses the believer is that they do not know where to draw the line between knowledge and faith. Certain facts may contribute to a faith, but they are not the faith itself.

When science and logic discover something, whatever has been discovered is, by default, no longer unknown. Science and logic move things from the realm of the unknown into the realm of the known, or at least to an acceptable level of certainty. The realm of faith gets a tiny bit smaller and the realm of knowledge grows proportionally. When a thing is known, it is no longer an article of faith. Faith must always deal with the unknown.

Those who say, "I can't defend my faith; it's just what I believe. Faith is faith..." are acknowledging (often unknowingly) that faith is separate from any information gained via reason. If it was not, then faith, in any regard that it is considered rational, could justly be attacked via rational means.

By the same token, to try to defend faith by rational means makes no sense. Every time someone tries to defend creationism with science or tries to defend the existence of God with some facet or feature of the universe, they have fallen into the trap of trying to make faith seem like knowledge when it is not. It is an immediate contradiction. There is no point in trying to logically justify something that cannot be logically justified.

There are some believers, however, who readily acknowledge the difference between faith and reason. An Internet posting I recently read referred to them as "sophisticated believers." Indeed, a believer, religious or otherwise, who understands the nature of his or her beliefs, knows that there is no rational defense for them and does not offer one.

CRITERIA AND PERSONAL EXPERIENCE

When I speak of reason, I am referring to the ability to use rational, logical, and analytical thought. Reason also includes the formal disciplines of science and logic, as well as critical thinking. Critical thinking involves using logical thought in verbal and written discourse, and involves principles of argumentation as well as knowledge of logical fallacies.

A main and vital difference between reason and faith is that reason has strict criteria and faith does not. Both critical thinking and the formal discipline of logic require the ability to recognize invalid arguments. Science also has strict criteria so that errors can be avoided. These criteria are often employed through testing methodologies, and if something is found to be inaccurate or false, then it has to be discarded.

(Incidentally, not everything in the disciplines of logic and science, as they are widely perceived, is about "proof" and "facts." In science, the point is to find out as much information as possible and to ensure that the information is as accurate as can be. It would serve us well to replace our demands for proof with requests for acceptable evidence.)

Criteria are necessary because human beings can misperceive the world around them and make mistakes. We are perfectly capable of seeing and hearing things that are not there, and it is easy to make errors in reasoning.

That is not to say that faith doesn't have any criteria at all, but it is to say that the criteria used for faith are not precise. Those criteria are subjective and can change from person to person, topic to topic. As a result, there are a continually growing variety of religious denominations, so-called "spiritual" principles, and levels of New Age thought. How do you know which one is right and which one to choose? You can't, because there are no sound guidelines.

Faith claims to get its information (its "truths") from a variety of sources — personal experience and divine inspiration among them. Persons of faith are usually able to point to certain things that have led them to believe what they do. Some will even claim that they have logical reasons or "evidence" for their beliefs. It is here that a great number of disagreements between believers and nonbelievers occur.

One of the largest disagreements arises over the value of personal experience as a means of knowledge. Personal experience, I am sorry to say, does not qualify as evidence. Many find this to be both surprising and confusing.

The reason personal experience does not qualify is because it is so terribly unreliable. If personal experience did count, then we would have to take every

UFO abductee at his word and every person who reports seeing Bigfoot in his backyard as an authority.

That is why the credibility of witnesses is often brought into question in court. People can lie or make mistakes. It is only when the word of a witness is not discredited, and when it does not contradict anything already known, that what the witness has said is deemed acceptable for use. To be considered scientific evidence, a statement must meet a set of criteria that is even more rigid.

Let's say I go into the woods, see a leprechaun, and then come back out and report it to my friends. They would have good reason to disbelieve me. If I claim to have evidence of the leprechaun's existence just because I saw him, then I am misusing the word "evidence." Evidence would only be the appropriate word if I brought back a DNA sample from the leprechaun or if I (heedless to his offering of a pot of gold) captured him and brought him back in a net.

I might become a believer in leprechauns because of my experience, but I could not claim that I "know" leprechauns exist in any sense that would be accepted by the skeptical community. It would qualify as faith rather than knowledge, and I would have little choice but to accept the skeptic's derision.

As a skeptic, however, I would be more inclined to question my own experience. If that experience conflicted with all that I otherwise knew to be true, it would make more sense that there was something about the one experience that was awry. You cannot throw out everything you have learned just because of a single unexplained incident.

Many people, who have gone through the same philosophical changes that I have, find that they have had to debunk their own personal experiences. People who have had near death experiences, encounters with ghosts, and dreams that came true the next day, have become skeptics. They first doubt these experiences and then they try to account for them in a way that satisfies their own curiosity. It's part of the process.

The words "personal experience," by the way, mean "in the experience of one person." I have to clarify this because there are those who argue that scientific experiments are nothing more than "the personal experiences of a lot of people," and are therefore no more valid than singular experience. The contradiction is that you cannot have "multiple" counts of personal experience because personal experience is defined as happening to only one person. The experiences of many people must be evaluated differently. Confirmation by consensus is sometimes the only way we have of validating information. It's not like we can ask inanimate objects or animals, so our best option is to ask each other to confirm the results of our experiments. We have nowhere else to go.

Because the Christian faith is the one I have the most experience with, and fought the longest inner battles with, this is often what I turn to for examples.

There are those among the Christian faith who would accuse me of never having been a Christian, even though I became a Christian at age seven when all I had was the faith of a child. They would say it is impossible for a Christian to become an atheist. In support of this, they recite I John 2:19, where Paul says, "They went out from us, but they were not of us; for if they had been of us, they would no doubt have continued with us: but they went out, that they might be made manifest that they were not all of us."

In addition to the fact that this is a great example of circular reasoning, those who would quote this verse to show that I was never a Christian refuse to accept my personal experience. If they did, it would prove them wrong.

Fair enough. None of us can use it as evidence.

You will find the plea to personal experience throughout New Age literature as well.

"You'd believe it, if it happened to you," comes the claim from all corners of the believer's world. "Get out there and try it!" they say, "And then make up your mind for yourself."

Skeptics have their own version, a version that is reflective of their desire for verification. "Investigate it!" skeptics say, "And investigate it thoroughly. Get out there and get to the bottom of things."

CONTRADICTION AND SELF-CORRECTION

Reason has another criterion that makes it even more distinct from faith. It cannot contradict itself.

This also answers a question posed in the section, "A Basic Assumption," which was the question of the difference between an assumption and a belief. A proper assumption cannot contradict what is already known to be true. If it is found to be incorrect, it must be discarded, modified, or the prior evidence against the assumption must be demonstrated to be wrong. A belief, though, does not have to meet these conditions. It *can*, but it is not required to.

With beliefs, you can run into contradictory information and keep on going despite it. Some believers may resent what that implies, so I'll explain further.

The principle of self-correction is fundamental to all disciplines of reason and is, just generally, a good rule to live by. When a person reaches an insurmountable obstacle, he or she should find another way around. If we realize we have made a mistake in the past, or are currently doing something wrong, we should change rather than make the same mistake repeatedly. Integrity demands it.

In the scientific world, when a scientist publishes an idea in a scientific journal, other scientists eagerly jump on it, looking for problems and errors. When the idea survives this criticism and scrutiny, it gains strength in the scientific community, but if not, then reassessment is required.

Liberals get accused of being wishy-washy when they gain new information and then change their actions or positions accordingly, but it would be far worse to keep on doing or believing something for the sake of appearing consistent. Sadly, this happens all too often. There is a very human tendency to continue to act in the same manner even though acting that way has proven detrimental in the past. People refuse to change their ways because they consider it an admission that they have made a mistake. They try to portray themselves as steadfast and persistent, when what they really are is stubbornly wrong. If people act this way and their motives are pure, then they may end up doing the wrong thing because they think it is "the right thing."

In my own philosophical struggle, I did this with the idea that nothing was impossible.[11] Even after I had developed cogent arguments against it, I still clung to the idea desperately. When I finally let it go, pathways of thought opened up to me that I had previously been unable to follow, accept, or understand. Concepts that are treasured too highly can become obstacles in one's path, preventing a person from seeing the big picture.

Self-correction is required by reason, but not by faith. With faith, if one has severe doubts and questions, it is regarded as virtuous to continue believing despite them.

Someone (to choose an inoffensive example) may believe that he or she can fly like Superman. We know that humans cannot fly. They aren't built for flight, they don't have wings, they can't defy the laws of gravity by simply choosing to do so, they don't have the bone structure for it like birds do, and they weigh too much. Still, as far as belief goes, none of that matters. I can choose to believe I can fly and you can argue with me all day long, but if I want to continue believing it, there is little you can do.

If, later, I jump out of a second-story window and break my leg, I still do not have to give up my belief that I can fly. I can just rationalize it by saying that I have to concentrate in order to fly and, clearly, I just wasn't concentrating enough.

I can believe whatever I want; but if I use reason, I must follow certain rules.

---

11 See the section, "Possibilities and Impossibilities" for details.

REASON ON THE DEFENSIVE

Circular reasoning is the logical error of using something to justify itself, such as saying "I am not a liar." Throughout this book, I use the principles of reason to justify reason. Am I therefore using circular reasoning and being illogical? The answer is no, because there are things outside of reason that justify it. Outside validation is the escape from circular reasoning.

Reason is validated by the solid and highly visible results it achieves. Science has given us amazing technologies, lengthened our lives through innovations in medicine, and enabled us to go places and see things we never could have experienced without it. Logic has helped us to develop mathematical theories and solve problems. Critical thinking can help us figure things out on a daily basis.

Just as the results of reason justify its validity, so do its foundations. The techniques and methods of reason were established through vigorous testing and examination to do exactly what they do — weed out the false, bring knowledge to light, and show that the rest is inconclusive.

Without reason, the only other option we have is the chaos of irrationality. It's one of the most clear-cut, either/or situations there is.

***

The last two sections make it clear that reason is much more strict than faith. This is the source of many complaints lodged against reason.

Few will question reason's usefulness or its results as expounded upon above. There is a huge debate, though, about whether reason is enough to answer the big questions that supposedly lie outside its domain. How do we know that the criteria of reason do not rule out things that are possible but are just not scientifically or logically verifiable? Can reason give us a complete understanding of our universe?

The answer, from many, is a resounding "No!" Reason is not enough, they say; it is far too limited. Reason and our meager human minds are inadequate to deal with the great mysteries. To understand those, reason must be transcended! This is the claim of the religionist, the mystic, the Taoist, and a multitude of others. It unites the believers in single opposition to the nonbelievers. The skeptic who refuses to accept anything outside the bounds of reason is then labeled as "narrow-minded" or "too scientific."

In dealing with this complaint, the nonbeliever must walk a fine line. It is unreasonable to assume that reason can and will explain everything. That is too big an assumption. If I were to claim that, then I would be guilty of "scientism," and those who accuse me of "believing" in reason would be justified. Reason would have gone from being a tool to a religion.

There are some things, even though they are not contradictory to reason, that reason may never be able to explain. Take, for example, historic events that we will never be able to re-create. There may be things going on in other parts of our world or the universe that we can't see or get enough information about to ever fully explain. There is much that the individual discipline of science does not know and may never know. There is no need to assume that it will. Let's just wait and see.

Reason is also limited in its predictive abilities. There are too many free and random variables that prevent us from knowing what is going to happen in the future.

Reason may be able to explain the causes of human behavior, but it will never be able to fully explain the motives and behaviors of the individual if the individual is irrational. If their mental processes are chaotic, they become just as inexplicable as the mysteries of the past and future.

Those who crave mystery need never worry. There is no shortage of the unknown and there will always be plenty to speculate about.

(I would also say that even if we do show reason to be the perfect tool for *understanding* our world, I do not think it is the ideal tool for *dealing* with the world. Dealing with the world requires an entirely different skill set. We'll get to that in Chapter 7.)

Meanwhile, the debate over the limits and usefulness of reason continues. Are its criteria its strength or its weakness? Does the strictness of reason prevent it from recognizing certain possibilities?

It should not be overlooked, however, that certain beliefs, once they are adopted, can be narrow in scope and eliminate possibilities as well. They might even rule out completely feasible possibilities! The problem of being considered narrow-minded is not restricted to the nonbeliever.

We will soon see that this leads us to a choice, but first we need to understand a little more about how faith stands up in comparison to reason.

WHY SPECULATE?

Many people contend that their faith, whatever it may be, does not contradict reason. Faith, as such, is not irrational but non-rational. According to this description, faith takes over where reason leaves off and fills in the gaps that reason is incapable of filling. Reason is deemed inadequate to the task of answering our questions and it is thought that something else must do the job. In such a scenario, reason deals with the known, and faith deals with the unknown.

Because faith deals with the unknown, it must, by definition, be speculation and therefore a guess. It might be a guess based on what someone has told you, based on the teachings of a church, or based on personal experience, but it remains a guess. Whatever the reasons for a faith are, they are not substantive reasons according to the definitions provided by the discipline of reason. This is an inevitable result of knowledge and faith being separate.

The question then becomes, why bother with belief at all? Why is it so important to have faith and to make a huge personal investment in a poorly substantiated idea?

When I considered myself an agnostic,[12] this was the stance I took. Why speculate? Why not just stay with what you know and wait for the answers to become available? I felt as if there was this huge pressure to believe.

"You must believe in something!" came the command.

"No!" I responded, "How about if I suspend judgment until I have actual answers?"

I often felt like I was playing the children's game in which someone hides a present behind his back and insists that you guess which hand it is in. All I wanted was for him to show it to me.

I understand that it is human nature to speculate. We love to make theories, guess, postulate, and place bets, when we have no idea what the truth is or what it will turn out to be.

When I was younger, my philosophical premises were riddled with speculative thought — ideas about what could be, what might be, and what the possibilities were. I found these ideas to be fascinating. They were, but they were also pointless.

What happens is that, when people's philosophies are incomplete, they sometimes fill in the gaps with speculation, and then they turn around and treat this speculation as fact or as all the explanation they need. It's dangerous, because if one wants, he or she can build an entire belief system on speculation. I call it "building a tower of maybes."

Speculation becomes a problem when people build such elaborate mental constructs and then say, "It makes sense, so it must be true." Truth requires a lot more than just internal cohesion.

Science fiction authors create worlds with geographies, histories, peoples, cultures, and even languages that seem to make perfect sense. These authors even manage to keep it all internally consistent. But it is fantasy. As with all speculation, it doesn't mean a thing.

12 At the time, I preferred the term "I-don't-knowist" because it more clearly expressed my position.

Speculation even tempts the skeptic, and when we try to guess at explanations for things we do not have enough information about, we can look silly as well.

So where's the need?

There are myriads of answers to this, especially in the religious arena, but the most common of them can immediately be addressed by using critical thinking.

In the upcoming section, "Dangerous," I address the argument that without belief of some sort, we would not have moral guidelines. The main point is that this argument is irrelevant. The consequences of not believing have no bearing on whether belief is correct or, for that matter, on *which* belief is correct. The truth is independent.

In what is known as Pascal's Wager, the philosopher Blaise Pascal proposed that you should choose faith over disbelief because that way you could be sure you weren't going to Hell. Pascal made the mistake of thinking it was an either/or situation. He did not realize there were more than two options to choose from. There are plenty of faiths out there. According to some of them, members of all of the other faiths are going to Hell. If I choose Christianity, the Muslim religion might turn out to be correct, and then I would die and go to Hell as an infidel. There are even Christians who say that other Christians are going to Hell because of specific doctrines they believe in such as "once saved always saved."

Belief guarantees nothing.

Many people find faith to be a source of comfort or they find the notion of reality without the assertions of their faith to be so unpleasant that they refuse to discard their beliefs.

"I could not live in a world where unfairness exists, where the good are not rewarded and the bad are not punished," some say.

"I could not live in a world where there is such cruelty, if I did not know there was a God," comes a similar argument.

What such statements mean is, "I could not cope without my faith."

Again, the relevancy of this needs to be called into question. To set reality aside because one doesn't like it is denial. If the truth isn't comforting, but believing in something that isn't true *is* comforting, is it worth being in denial to feel good? Some feel it is, but, as I will discuss in Chapter 7, faith is not necessary in order to feel good about one's self and one's place in the world. We can stand face-to-face with reality and not be unnerved.

***

What believers also often miss concerning religious faith is that reason has already given us the answers we need. There no longer exists a gap that faith needs to fill.

When science began investigating the nature of things, some religions encouraged it because it was felt that science would confirm the truths behind religion. Instead, science discovered explanations that did not agree with what religion had presupposed.

Science has explained how the universe came into being, how the planets were formed, and how human beings came to be on the earth. The things that faith once proposed explanations for have been explained differently by science, and with methods that have more accuracy and validity.

In some cases religion adapted to what science discovered, but in many others, it flat out refused the answers that science gave.

The philosophical period known as "The Enlightenment" was the period when mankind discovered that the answers to many major philosophical questions could be found outside of religion and in reason alone. It was this that caused Nietzsche to declare that God was dead. It was not a spiritual enlightenment. It was an enlightenment of the mind. Humankind discovered that the world of the spiritual was neither real nor needed.

Reason had provided new answers. Believers just don't like them.

The questions posed by faiths other than the religious variety may also be answered by reason. Investigation and research, as painful as they may sound, are far more likely to yield solid answers than guesses will. When reason cannot answer questions, speculation, and clinging to speculation as if it were reality, are of little value.

Faith is overrated. When it comes to understanding the world around us, there is no need for it.

Coming to Blows

The last major point to be made when comparing faith and reason is the one that proponents of reason often begin with: that faith contradicts reason. This is where everything gets ugly. It is a strong point of contention for many believers, while many nonbelievers consider it obvious.

There are many reasons people are unable to see that faith and reason are at odds. For the longest time, I suffered from this problem myself. I did not recognize contradictions within my own belief system or the contradictions between my beliefs and reason.

In the mind of the believer, these contradictions are re-labeled as "mysteries." They are not seen as contradictions but as problems that (if they are to be resolved) will be resolved later, possibly via divine revelation. To the believer, it is nothing to worry about.

What such people fail to see is that they are facing a contradiction in the present. The principles of logic will never change and what is now a contradiction will always be a contradiction.

The believer also claims that certain things "transcend" reason, but in every case where they are said to do so, those things must also *contradict* reason. This changes the argument. Reason is no longer just inadequate when it comes to explaining the universe. It has supposedly become *wrong* in its explanations. Those are two very different things.

Many people fail to understand the full extent of how reason and faith contradict each other because they do not understand exactly what science, logic, and critical thinking entail.

While researching this book, I visited many atheistic and skeptical websites and read the comments of their many detractors. I visited the sites of believers and read their commentaries. I even read some of the books they recommended. Every single instance of belief was erroneous in some logical or scientific way. This holds true for every religious faith I have encountered throughout my life.

In Chapter 3 of this book, I examine certain critical thinking principles in detail. When these are taken into consideration, logical errors made by claimants of the supernatural leap out like a three-dimensional image against a flat background. Chapters 4 and 6 of the book are filled with examples of how belief and nonbelief conflict with each other. The conflict between evolution and fundamentalist creationism is the most prominent example, but just one among millions. By the end of these chapters (if it isn't clear already), it should be obvious that there is a vast chasm between faith and reason through which a river of muddied water flows.

A Choice

The statements below provide brief summaries of the previous sections comparing faith and reason. Let's perform a quick review of what I've established so far and see the results.

Reason is thought of as useful, but without a heart.
Faith has a better reputation than reason and is often considered sacred.

Reason and faith are separate. Something we *know* is not simultaneously a belief.
By the same token, what we believe should not be called knowledge.

Reason has strict criteria to determine whether it is correct.
Faith does not have strict criteria, which makes faith exceptionally vulnerable to error.

Reason does not allow personal experience as a criterion because it is too unreliable.
Faith does.

Reason is based on what we know and must not contradict itself.
Faith can be based on anything and can contradict itself.

Reason has built-in mechanisms for self-correction.
Faith does not.

Many aspects of reason, especially its foundations, are self-evident.
The results of reason demonstrate its validity.
Without reason, we cannot make sense of things.

Reason is accused of being so strict that it rules out potential possibilities.
Faith is so lenient that it can allow anything to be true.

Faith is often based on, and justified by, speculation.
There is no need for faith.

With very few exceptions, faith contradicts reason.
To choose faith when it contradicts reason is, by definition, irrational and illogical.

With all of this in mind, one is faced with a choice — reason or faith. Choosing any belief that contradicts reason is a choice to be irrational. It's inescapable. People can choose belief if they want, but they are being dishonest with themselves if, after this explanation, they fail to recognize the inherent irrationality of their position. They would be like the philosopher Kierkegaard, who knew it was illogical to believe in Christianity but chose to do so anyway. One of the few existentialists who believed in God, this was the source of much of his angst. Kierkegaard had reached the point where he and I would have had to disagree. We would both agree his choice was illogical and that he had just made a different choice than I.

If someone chooses a belief that is not contradictory to reason (if he or she can find or invent one), then they are doing nothing more than indulging in speculation. There is nothing wrong with that unless they are making decisions based on it. Then, I would think, they would want better information.

While the information that reason provides may not have 100 percent certainty (which I discuss in the next section), it is much more reliable than what we can obtain through faith. This is why it only makes sense to utilize reason, especially when it comes to the big questions about the nature of our world and the universe.

LEVELS OF CERTAINTY

Epistemology concerns itself with the nature of knowledge. I have already offered some epistemological premises by stating that reality is objective, by stating that knowledge is often obtained through reason, and by providing some of the criteria for knowledge.

Knowledge is not 100 percent certain. I do not know of anything that we can be completely and totally sure of. This was implicit the minute I started my philosophy with an assumption. Certainly, the many varieties of knowledge are not equal. Knowledge, therefore, comes on a sliding scale, ranging from just below 99.999 percent all the way down to "likely, but without any evidence." Below that point, when we reach "unlikely and without any evidence," things fall off the scale and become belief.

It would be a mistake to say that knowledge can be ranked on some sort of precision scale, and it is hardly necessary either. All we need is a rough estimate of how reliable our information is. The crucial point, in regard to the philosophy I present here, is one I've already made: that the information provided by reason is far more reliable than that provided by faith.

At the time of this writing, "certainty" is a popular buzzword. I have seen it lodged as a criticism against atheists and fundamentalists alike with the implication that "if you're absolutely certain, then you have adopted an unrealistic attitude." It is also sometimes meant to imply that if you are absolutely certain, you are probably wrong. I would agree with the first implication, but I am wary of the second. Regardless, I have already made it clear that a rationalistic position by no means necessitates an attitude of certainty.

However, it should be noted that certainty and 100 percent certainty are two different things. A person can be confident of his or her worldview, and even be "convinced of it," without being guilty of the crime of "certainty." The rationalist has good reason to be confident of his viewpoint, especially when it is based on education, intelligence, discipline, and intense scrutiny of the questions involved. If the rationalist or skeptic errs at all, he errs on the side of caution. Meanwhile, reason provides him with an excellent set of tools to prevent him from being gullible.

A question that is commonly asked of nonbelievers is, what if you're wrong? When this question comes from the religionist, it is sometimes meant to imply that if you are wrong, you are going to Hell. It leads to Pascal's Wager, which I have already covered. But, in a more generalized sense, it's a good question. It's a question that keeps you honest, and it's a question that the skeptic and the scientist are very familiar with, because they continually ask it of themselves.

If skeptics or scientists are wrong about something, they are supposed to do what they can to learn where they went wrong and do what they have to do to get back on track. They learn from their mistakes, incorporate the new information, and adapt. On the other hand, if religious believers are proven wrong, their whole belief system may be in danger. They may have to rebuild their worldview from the bottom up and deal with the emotional consequences of the change in ideology. They are less flexible and far more vulnerable that non-believers. The "What if you're wrong?" question goes both ways. Moreover, when it is posed, we learn whether people are merely confident in their worldviews or if they are demonstrating an unwarranted certainty.

KOANS

The Tao is a concept central to much of Eastern philosophy. It has had millions, if not more, words written about it, yet it is said to be above all words. It cannot be described, captured, encapsulated, or explained. The Tao just is. It can easily be said to be the Eastern equivalent of a New Age, non-personal God, and in some ways, it is treated much the same. It is said that logic and reason are not enough to understand it and, even more than that, are hindrances to understanding it.

The koan was developed as a teaching tool to help those who meditate to transcend logic and gain enlightenment. The Eastern religions do not describe enlightenment or tell us exactly what it is — if it is a continual transcendent state, a single mystic experience, or what — but it is made clear that those who have attained enlightenment must still live in, and deal with, this reality.

One way to achieve enlightenment is to meditate on koans. Koans are self-contradictory riddles, created with the intent of moving people "beyond" logic. The most common and frequently quoted koan is "What is the sound of one hand clapping?"

Zen literature is full of such riddles and equally contradictory stories. Reading stories of how people attain enlightenment can be taxing. Their stories seem crazy, and in many senses, they are. That's the whole point.

After reading a book of them, I sat down and wrote one of my own as an example:

> A master talks to his student and asks him to report the next day with the one word that sums up all existence.
> The student spends the afternoon and following morning meditating on his master's question. He shows up the next day and says to the master, "Zen."
> The master shakes his head, and the student walks away.

The next day at noon, the student appears before the master and says, "Light."

The master again shakes his head. This continues for months. The student tries many words, "love," "emptiness," "joy," "Buddha," "sparrow," "death," "experience," and so on.

One day the student does not appear before the master. The master finds the student and approaches him. The student is sitting and meditating. He looks up at the master and then, quietly, resumes meditating.

"You have done well," the master says, and walks away.

The message is simple — reason is inadequate when it comes to ultimate understanding.

When you cross the Pacific from America to the Orient, you will find that the issues of contention over philosophical questions remain the same. It is still faith versus reason. At least the Eastern mystics were one big step ahead of Western thinkers. They realized that it was futile to try to logically justify a belief.

Chapter 2. Reason Applied

The Path of Reason

Throughout my life I have heard that I should give faith a chance. But I already have, and I lived with the vagaries of faith for years. But how about the reverse? Why not give reason a chance?

By demanding consistency of myself while writing about my philosophy, I had, almost accidentally, chosen reason. As I progressed, however, it became conscious. I looked at it as an experiment. I wasn't sure how it would turn out. I took reason and applied it evenly across the board to everything in my philosophy and to all the religious, New Age, and philosophical ideas I had encountered during my lifetime. I took those ideas from the compartment of my mind where they were governed by their own set of rules and treated them like I did everything else in reality.

I began a period of frantic activity where I pored through books, scoured the Internet, and wrote and rewrote hundreds of pages in an effort to sort out my thoughts. I was driven by the feeling that I was close to comprehending a mystery that I had once given up on trying to understand.

There was no verbal combat with anyone and there were no dramatic external events that accompanied it, but internally, I was in turmoil. It wasn't something I could do all at once. There was too much involved. Belief systems are complicated webs of ideas, built up over the years, where concepts, stories, and experiences are all linked together in an elaborate structure. It takes a while to untangle them.

Bits and pieces of the solution came to me, and the structure of my internal network of ideas flexed and reformed, sometimes hourly, sometimes daily. I could never re-create the order in which the information came to me, or the order in which I sorted it all out. I'd come across an idea, consider it without accepting it, and then move on to other ideas. Then I would come back to the original idea and finally see its validity. This happened many times.

I could not have made it through without the right tools. I chipped away with logic here; I learned some science there. So much of it was a process of elimination. I even healed some wounds by applying critical thinking. I felt like a sculptor who, taking a chisel to an overgrown statue of a barnacle encrusted whale, carves away at it and discovers an elegant and graceful dolphin underneath.

So many concepts I previously held to be true failed miserably when held up to the standards of reason. Once I was freed from those concepts, answers I had been looking for came running up to greet me, and I welcomed them with open arms.

Through it all, reason demonstrated its usefulness in every instance where it was applied. I had learned to trust it, and I felt confident adding a new assumption to my philosophy, the assumption that reason is a valid tool for understanding our universe. While it could not explain everything and answer every question, reason was perfectly capable of answering the major philosophical and religious questions that I had. If I ever found this assumption to be incorrect, I would have to discard it or revise it.

When I first gave up my beliefs, I did not discard them entirely. Instead, I slowly placed them off to the side in a mental filing cabinet. In many cases, I did this one by one, labeling them as "interesting, but no longer useful." If new evidence appeared that validated them, then they were still available to draw upon. Yet this never happened, nor have I needed to discard reason as my main means of understanding the world. It proves to be stronger and more resilient with each passing day, while the paper passions I filed away grow increasingly yellow and brittle with age.

POSSIBILITIES AND IMPOSSIBILITIES

The skeptic gets the reputation of being a spoilsport because he is always debunking and disproving things. When he says that certain things are impossible, he is regarded as narrow-minded.

It used to be that, as a believer, I hated this trait of the nonbeliever.

"Everything is possible," I insisted. To believe otherwise seemed far too limiting. I had always been a dreamer. It was easy for me to imagine the fantastic, and

I insisted stubbornly upon doing so. I was banging my head against an invisible wall of my own creation. When I finally figured out that some things had to be impossible, and gave up my own personal insistence on being "right," a whole realm of things that had been incomprehensible finally made sense.

For the longest time I had been working on a fiction story called "The God Club." It was based on the premise that there was a group of people who were omniscient and omnipotent. I intended to use the story to show how everything was possible.

It presented some problems. What if two or more members of the club were in opposition and wanted to do the same thing? Supposedly, the "gods" in the club could obtain a state of complete peace and unity with the universe. Why would they leave that and return to the drama and separateness found in the life of an individual? How did these gods accomplish the impossible, when what they wanted to accomplish was, well, impossible?

I spent many nights on that idea. I never got much of a story out of it, but in the process, I learned a lesson I needed to learn. The following is a bit of dialogue from the story that shows I was slowly getting a handle on an important idea.

> "Everything is possible," said Jordan.
>
> "Oh yeah?" David challenged, "Fly to the moon and back within the next three minutes, without help from anyone else, without supernatural aid, and without changing your present knowledge of the world in any way."
>
> "It's possible."
>
> "Do it!" David demanded in response.
>
> "But..."
>
> David stared at his watch. When three minutes had passed, he looked at Jordan and said, "Well?"
>
> "I could have done it," came the timid response.
>
> David shook his head and walked away.

I was learning that certain things were impossible. Reality constantly reinforced the lesson.

At an engineering firm where I worked, I was assigned to a committee in charge of expediting the release of a product. Everyone on the committee knew that it would take several months to get the product ready. Management gave the committee the task of coming up with a way to get the product out the door in one month.

When we received the assignment, we went around the room and each of us (in his or her own way) said that, without greatly sacrificing quality, there was no way possible the product could be ready to ship as soon as management wanted. In the time frame given, the product might not even work at all. We could double the size of our staff, work twenty-four hours a day, and it still would not get done. Too much specialized knowledge was needed and only certain people could do the work. Management had requested the impossible.

The committee put together a recommendation that outlined ways the project could be speeded up, and we were able to push the project completion date up by two weeks, but not by two months like management wanted.

Management pushed back. Our proposal was unacceptable, they said. The project had to be done in one month.

We went over it again. We brainstormed and thought of new ideas. None of our ideas changed the fact that the project would not be ready when management requested. The best we could do was express this more clearly to management, which we did.

Several days later the manager of our department called a meeting with the committee. He explained how he had recently been to a leadership conference where the speaker had explained that employees become obsessed with limitations. They aren't able to think outside of the box or to see what they are capable of. Employees, the speaker had said, need to know that they can do anything and should be encouraged to do so.

"With that in mind," our manager told us, "you need to find a way to do what I have asked you to do."

I have never seen an angrier group of people in the workplace than I did that day.

"I'm about ready to quit," was one of the first things expressed right after the manager left.

"It can't be done!" someone else said, "What about 'can't' don't they understand?"

We knew, at that point, that going back to management would be futile. I guess we shouldn't have been surprised, since this was the same management team that often told us we should give 200 percent. So we put together a proposal with our best ideas, left out the fact that we knew it wouldn't work, and submitted it.

We never heard back from management, and it was three months before the product was shipped.

The ideal I valued, that nothing was impossible, was proving to be more counterproductive than useful.

I gained an even deeper perspective on this issue when I learned that in order for some things to be possible, other things must be impossible.

This is what the conundrum of the irresistible force meeting the immovable object ultimately teaches us. One of them has to give in order for the other to be true. One, if not both, have to be impossible. The irresistible force cannot exist in the same universe with the immovable object because then you have an irresolvable paradox.

This is not as limiting as it might first seem. It is just the opposite. It turns out that laws, rules, and limitations are what give us possibilities in the first place. The skeptic is saved from becoming a spoilsport.

If the universe did not have rules, all would be random chaos. It is only because of the laws of nature and physics that we have order and that our world is possible at all.

Robert G. Olson says it like this:

> If we want to kill someone, laws and police are obstacles which limit our freedom. But if, as is more often the case, we want to walk without fear down the streets, these "obstacles" liberate us. Freedom to achieve chosen goals thus implies, not the absence of obstacles, but the existence of the right kinds of obstacles in the right amounts.[13]

It even holds true for relationships. The single man is often so enamored with all the possibilities (all the different women he could be with) that he prevents himself from experiencing a long-term relationship. The depth, security, and intimacy of such a relationship remain off limits to him until he is ready to give up on all the alternatives. It is only by removing a range of possibilities that a specific possibility becomes available.

The same goes for career choices and so many of the other choices we face in life. You must pick a path. If you stand at the crossroads, in awe of all the possible avenues and undecided where to go, you make no progress.

What I discovered on a personal and philosophical level was that when I eliminated the fantastic impossibilities of my worldview, I opened up a world of real possibilities. My inner Don Quixote had died in the dungeon, but his song was remembered. No longer obsessed with unachievable and over-the-top dreams, I was able to focus on getting things accomplished in the real world.

The Soul

The biggest piece of information that undermined my belief in the soul was the fact that near death experiences (NDEs) and out of body experiences (OBEs) could be re-created by injecting patients with the drug ketamine. The subjects experienced the white light, the tunnel, reunions with loved ones, and visions of Heaven. This test was conducted by researchers at UCLA[14] and has been re-

---

13 Robert G. Olson, *An Introduction to Existentialism* (New York: Dover Publications, Inc., 1962), p. 126.
14 From "Antimatter" article by Ronald K. Siegel, *Omni* magazine (New York: Omni Publications International Ltd., January 1991), p. 73.

created many times since then. Others who have experimented with that drug and various hallucinogenics in non-laboratory settings have reported similar experiences.

Ketamine blocks the receptors to certain areas of the brain. When the brain has no access to the area of the brain that tells a person their location in three-dimensional space, a person feels as if he is everywhere. He attains a feeling of oneness. When the edges of perception are dimmed, one perceives a tunnel. Without the stimuli that normally cloud the mind, there is a feeling of peace. It could be that the ketamine experience is reflective of what happens to the brain at the time of death. The brain shuts down bit by bit. It flickers like an old TV set being turned off, there is a bright light in the center, and then everything goes black.

What this research reveals is that the most common experience used as a defense of belief in the afterlife may all take place in the brain. When people have these experiences, the white light is a commonality, but what they see and whomever they meet on the other side is not. Relatives, Jesus, and religious figures from numerous beliefs have greeted the persons who have had these experiences. The religious figures always correspond to the person's personal ideologies. If these were objective occurrences, then it would seem that this would not be the case. The believer explains this away by stating that what people see on the other side is merely symbolic and represents a greater truth. Perhaps, they claim, someone who is nearing the afterlife may not yet be able to deal with all they will encounter there.

You don't have to do drugs if you want to achieve an NDE. It was found that when pilots and astronauts in training are put through a centrifuge test (spun around in circles at high velocity), they can pass out and have these experiences as well.[15] It happens when the blood is cut off from parts of the brain.

Ghosts, too, have been used to show that the spirit continues on after death, and therefore as supposed proof of the soul, but the evidence for ghosts is even weaker than that for NDEs.

Science is not able to disprove the notion of the soul, but what science can say is that wherever consciousness has been shown to exist, there has been a mechanism to support it, specifically the brain.

With this knowledge, I no longer had anything but purely subjective reasons to believe in the soul.

I wanted to believe that someday I could be reunited with loved ones, like my mother and my sister who have passed away, but that was based on desire and nothing more.

---

15 Penn Jillette and Teller, Episode titled *Death, Inc.* from *B.S., Season Two* (Showtime Networks, Inc. 2004)

I would like to think that my personality is a good one, a kind one, and a creative one. I would also like to see it continue. But the things that make me what I am originate in the material world. The experiences, the memories, the thought processes, and the DNA are all explained physically. Is there a core essence of these things that can somehow be extracted and carry on without any visible means? The more I considered it, the more unlikely it seemed.

I began to think about the question of how important it was that I continue on after my death. I wanted to do so, but what did it mean to the rest of the universe either way? Why should it care? Is there anything amazingly special about me that must be preserved?

In spiritual circles, the concept that you must give up yourself to discover yourself is common. We need to put aside our ego and our own sense of self importance to gain enlightenment or to evolve spiritually. When I put aside my own ego and sense of self importance, I came to the realization (although I was opposed to it) that there was no hugely imperative reason for the continuation of my personality. I discovered a new sense of humility and, with that, the last reason I had for believing in the soul vanished.

God

When I began questioning the Christian idea of God and left the church, I did not do as some have done and instantly become an atheist. Rather, I considered the possibility that God existed in some other form than the one I had been taught for so many years. I took comfort in the fact that I knew my motives were good. I reasoned that if God knew what was in my heart and mind, and he was a kind and just God, I could not be condemned.

Along the way I drafted a poem which expressed one view of God, although it said more about what he wasn't than about what he was.

> My God is not confined to a temple.
> My God doesn't avert his eyes.
> My God doesn't live in a church.
> My God is not stuck in the skies.
> My God doesn't have his own office.
> My God doesn't care about cost.
> My God is not an accountant.
> There's nothing gained. There's nothing lost.

Let the white light surround you.
Breathe in the air.
Feel the power that connects you
with everything, everywhere.

My God doesn't judge you.
You know what you've done.
My God forgives you
without the blood of his son.
Unconditional love is unconditional;
don't even ask and it's yours.
Open your eyes and you've found it.
Don't have to open any doors.

Let the white light surround you.
Breathe in the air.
Feel the power that connects you
with everything, everywhere.

I continued to contemplate the idea of God until, in an earlier draft of this book while I was still an "I-don't-knowist," I created a list possibilities of what God might be like. There were quite a few.

God could be all powerful, but there was a chance that he was just extremely powerful instead. God could have created the universe and left. Maybe he was evil or a crazy old man. God could be a woman, although it made more sense to me that God didn't have any gender at all. I had become more inclined to think that God was a vast ocean of consciousness that we all return to when we died. Another possibility was that God was the equivalent of "The Force," which, as described in the *Star Wars* movies, permeates and connects all things.

At the very bottom of the list, I added one other consideration, just to be fair, to make sure I accounted for all the options. I knew it would be ruled out easily anyway, so I added the idea that there wasn't any God at all.

I then started going through the list, and began adding arguments for and against the many varieties of possible Gods. Once I started applying critical thinking principles, a surprising number of them were ruled out. The Christian version of God had the most arguments against it, and they were extremely convincing. I finally felt that I could rule that one out, but that same thing happened with the other versions of God as well. I continued to review the list until the one consideration that I had deemed the least likely — that there was no God — was the one that won out.

This can't be, I decided, and I went back to the list and started over again, reviewing the arguments and assumptions I had made. The second time through, the outcome was even more in favor of there being no God. I put the list aside. There had to be something wrong. I left the list alone, but it wouldn't leave me alone; and in the end, I came to the conclusion that of all the options, the option of there being no God was the one that seemed most likely. My observations of the world confirmed that the world was the kind of place you would expect it to be if no God existed.

An accusatory question that is sometimes aimed at atheists goes like this: Do you know everything? The answer is, of course, "No," prompting the follow up question, Then how can you say that God doesn't exist?

These questions assume that you have to know everything about the universe in order to address the question of God. This isn't true at all. The question of God can be answered by dealing with specifics relating to the description of God. Of course, if you don't assign any attributes to God then there is nothing really being proposed and so there is nothing to argue with. Some people, whom I would describe as atheists in disguise, call God by other names, saying that God is love or God is nature. All they've really done is substitute some other concept for God. They've changed the word "God" around so much that it can mean whatever they want it to.

In this discussion, I am first going to deal with the Christian description of God and then I'll cover the idea of God as a supreme consciousness, which either encompasses all other conscious beings or is greater than any other conscious being. The main characteristics required for such a God is that he/she/it does not have a body, and is both conscious and aware. By dealing with these two descriptions of God, I will have addressed the most common notions of God, as well as the majority of ideas about God. Descriptions of God that fall outside these boundaries are either irrelevant (as in the case of God being defined as nature) or inconsequential, because the God described has no sort of interaction with the human race that is meaningful to how we go about our lives.

The Christian description of God is a lot more vulnerable to criticism because it is so specific. The characteristics of this God, as presented by the church I attended as a child, were what first prompted me to ask some tough questions.

Sitting in my junior high Sunday School class, I heard something that I could not believe. The lesson touched on the subject of predestination[16] and we were told that God already knows if we are going to be saved. He has to — he is omniscient.

If God already knows whether we were going to be saved, I thought, then we don't have any choice.

In a manner uncharacteristic of myself at that time, I spoke up and asked about it. How could we have free will if our choice was already known and therefore set in stone?

The teacher told us that it was a matter of perspective. God sees everything at once and knows the end result, but we don't. We make our choices without knowing the consequences.

I objected. If it is only a matter of perspective, then it is an illusion. If our choices are already known, then they cannot be changed, and we can never truly have free will.

This was the first time that something I had heard in church struck me as completely ridiculous. It just could not be true. No matter which way you worked the logic, human beings did not have free will. The verses we were reading at the time made it sound even worse, as if the choices were made for us beforehand.

The realization I had in that Sunday School class was a major turning point of my life. It would trigger the release of many more questions that had been forming in the back of my mind. If I had realized the full significance of what I expressed that day, I could have resolved a lot of issues, but instead it took me twenty-five years to figure it all out.

I had pinpointed a problem that theologians have wrestled with for far longer than I did. If God is omniscient, then mankind does not have free will. If you choose to accept logic as an arbitrator of truth, as I do, then any religion that says God is all knowing, and that mankind has free will, is wrong. By logical standards, this disproves the Christian version of God, as well as a few other versions. Logic does not set out to disprove that the concept of God, but the claim that God is all knowing automatically falls under logic's domain.

The same thing happens when you claim God is all powerful. Instantly, based on what was explained in "Possibilities and Impossibilities," we know something is wrong. If God is all powerful, then nothing should be impossible to him. That won't work because we know that some things must absolutely be impossible.

The question, can God make a rock so big that he can't lift it? makes this point. Those who say "Yes, but he would never try to do such a thing," or "Yes,

---

16 See Romans 8:28–30, Ephesians 1:4–5, and Ephesians 1:11 regarding predestination.

but he would never break his own rules," are not answering the real question and are missing the point. The God they claim to believe in is an impossibility.

So now we find that logic disproves both the idea of an all-powerful God and the idea of an all-knowing God. Don't even try it with the idea of omnipresence; it will make your head hurt.

What I have just covered has huge implications. It very simply and straightforwardly disproves the existence of the Christian God. If you refuse to accept it, you must take an illogical stance.

It is because of this, that in regard to the Christian God, I am a hardcore atheist. It is not just a matter of nonbelief. I deny the existence of such a God on logical grounds. But we are not through with the Christian God yet.

Science, like logic, never set out to disprove God. It merely tried to answer questions as reliably as possible. In the process, though, it discovered things that stepped on God's conceptual toes.

Nonbelievers spend a lot of time criticizing miracles that the Christian God is reported to have performed in the Bible. Christians see no problem with miracles because they believe that God transcends the laws of the universe, can alter them temporarily, and can do anything he wants. Meanwhile the nonbeliever tries to make the point that miracles are scientific and logical impossibilities. It forces a choice: rationality or irrationality. There is no in-between.

The significance of the Big Bang theory and evolution is not that they disproved God, but that they showed us that God is no longer necessary. How the universe came to be, how we came to be on this planet, and how things got to be the way they are, have all been explained by science and history. People use their faith in God to fill in the blanks, but there really aren't any big blanks that need to be filled in anymore. The concept of God has become irrelevant.

There are further problems with the common religious conception of God. If God were perfect and complete within himself, there would have been no need for him to create man or to act out the dramas that he has supposedly initiated and involved himself in. What's the point? God does not need anything. Why is he striving, creating souls, and then trying to win them over? Why would he require worship or praise, especially from puny little humans? It's baffling.

Then there is the long-discussed issue of pain and suffering. The pain and suffering that we experience on this planet are often used to demonstrate that if God exists, he is a cruel God.

This is an argument that is going to fly right past just about anyone who believes in a personal God. It is pointless, and usually counterproductive, to even attempt using it. The main reason for this is that in many belief systems, pain and suffering are not attributed to God. They are attributed to man, his sin, and his free will (even though Christianity itself undermines free will).

Secondly, the pain and suffering we experience are temporary and, according to the faith of the believer, will come to an end some day. This "happy ending" mentality says that someday we will no longer be concerned about the pain and suffering we are going through now because God will fix it all.

With the above explanations, the question is not if pain and suffering are necessary, or of how they makes us feel, but of what God's intent is. Does God allow pain and suffering with sadistic intent or does he want us to learn from it? Is he a torturer or a teacher? Pain and suffering may in some way be "good" for us and are not inherently bad or cruel. To the believer, the point of the biblical story of Job is that pain and suffering allow us to demonstrate our faith and help us to become stronger spiritually.

It is because of this point of view that arguments regarding pain and suffering as evidence against a kind and loving God lead us to a dead end. But for those who believe in a God that allows people to suffer in an eternal Hell, there is an immensely serious problem. With eternal punishment, there is never any mercy, never any spiritual growth that results in change, and never a happy ending. Most importantly, there is no amount of wrongdoing, no matter how terrible (let alone any choice of faith) that can justify eternal punishment. Therefore Hell becomes a measure of God's cruelty and it cannot be claimed that he is a fair, just, and good God.

A friend of mine grew suspicious of the idea of God when attending an art history class. He saw that, over the years, the paintings and sculptures of what we think of as God had changed. It became apparent that God was a construction of the human mind rather than an objective reality. Humans molded God into what they wanted him to be, and they did so differently at different periods of time.

A non-artistic historical perspective of God can bring this to light as well. Take a look at Karen Armstrong's *A History of God* and you can see how the idea of God evolved over time. Even with a small knowledge of history, it is easy to see how man began worshipping nature and the Sun, and these became his gods. Varieties of belief emerged, and in Western culture these ideas evolved into gods that demanded certain forms of worship, including human and animal sacrifice. The human sacrifice grew less common, but, in Christianity, the notion that some sort of sacrifice to God is necessary has carried through to the present. God is a product of society, not the cause of it.

This idea of God persists even though we can explain everything that God was once given credit for doing. In our unwillingness to give it up, we accept an outmoded idea.

The concept of God discussed up to this point is the mainstream version of God, often associated with the church. Many people, as I once did when I left the church, envision God in other ways. God may be a sea of consciousness from which we came and to which we all return. God may be the sum total of the consciousness of all living beings that somehow connects us all. Permutations abound.

In all these instances, and according to the criteria of possessing a conscious awareness, the concept of God faces the same dilemma that the concept of the soul presents, the question of exactly what form it takes, and of how it can exist without something physical to support it.

The result is that, as long as the God under discussion is a higher consciousness that is neither all powerful nor all knowing, we cannot prove or disprove God's existence.

God is sometimes thought of as the prime mover, as the force that initiated our universe. While I do not see how such a God could exist without also being a conscious entity, I address the description of God as prime mover in the section "Marbles in a Frisbee." A brief summary of my position is that when you start with God, you start with a being that must necessarily be complex, whereas if you start with the big bang and the laws of physics, you start with basic rules and work upwards towards complexity. Adding God to the mix adds an unnecessary complication that only prompts further questions.

When talking about a God that fits these descriptions and not the Christian one, I am an atheist of the "nonbelief" type. I cannot deny it, but I do not believe in it either.

Yet the probability of such a God existing seems low to me.

When speaking of Pagan gods and their behaviors, C.S. Lewis says, "What raises infinite difficulties and solves none will be believed by a rational man only under absolute compulsion."[17]

"Exactly!" I said to myself upon reading this quote. That is my main argument *against* the God of C.S. Lewis and against every other version of God as some sort of conscious entity or force.

There is an overwhelming lack of evidence for God and the idea of God presents the puzzling questions listed above. But if you get rid of the idea of God, all is solved. The questions go away. You no longer have to deal with the vagaries

17 C.S. Lewis, *Miracles*, 2001 ed. (New York: HarperCollins, 2001) p. 217.

and inconsistencies of faith. Suddenly you realize how many mental calisthenics you have had to perform to keep the idea of God alive, and all the justifications and rationalizations become apparent for what they really are.

It was when I reached the point, where my objections to the idea of God outweighed my reasons for believing that I became an atheist.

MEANING

If there is no God, then there is no entity or consciousness that can assign meaning to the universe. Fortunately, this does not mean that life is meaningless. It just means that meaning is not externally assigned.

There are two aspects to the concept of meaning — the past and the future, or the cause and the goal. To illustrate what I mean by this, I will use a situation I often encounter in the workplace. When they have to issue refunds to clients, employees are asked to provide a "reason for credit." There are two ways that this question can be answered. Either the employee can say something like, "the shipment was not delivered on time" or the employee can say, "to refund shipping charges." One of these is the cause that happened in the past, and one of these is the goal that they are trying to accomplish. If the employee does not provide the cause, I often have to go back to them and say, "No, I mean the *other* reason."[18]

When talking about the meaning of life, a view from both perspectives reveals that there can be no answer to either question.

To examine the issue from the perspective of the past (or the cause), all we have to do is ask the question why, which naturally leads us backwards.

Trying pursuing it and see what happens. Any two-year-old will be glad to be of help.

> Why do I have to eat my vegetables?
> Because they are good for you.
> Why?
> Because they supply nutrients for your growing body.
> Why?
> Because the cells in our body need certain substances in order to function their best.
> Why?
> Because that's how our bodies work as a part of nature.
> Why?
> Because that is how life on this planet works.
> Why?
> Because we are part of a universe that has physical rules, which determined how our planet was set up.
> Why?

---

18 A similar problem occurs when people say that "everything happens for a reason," which I talk about in the section called "Illusions."

> That's just how it is.
> Why?
> That's it. There is no further explanation.
> Why?
> That's just the way it is!

Even if there is a God, the question of meaning presents the same problem. Can the religious or spiritual person answer the question, what is the meaning of life? Not always, and if they do, the answer will be superficial. Let's see what happens if we play "the why game" with a question about God.

> We're going to church.
> Why?
> Because we want to worship God.
> Why?
> Because God made us and we love him.
> Why?
> Because he loves us and wants us to be happy.
> Why?
> Because he's a good God.
> Why?
> Because that's just the way he is.
> Why?
> God is what he is.
> Why?
> There's no more to it than that. That's just the way it is.

No matter how you approach it, if you ask the question *why* enough times, you will end up at a point where you can go no further. The final point is always "That's just the way it is." There can be no other ultimate meaning.

In the words of Joseph Campbell, "There's no meaning. What's the meaning of the universe? What's the meaning of a flea? It's just there. That's it."[19]

Examining the question of meaning from the other perspective, in which "meaning" refers to the goal or purpose of the universe, yields the same results.

If such a goal existed, its very existence would present a problem. Everything leading up to that goal would be rendered less meaningful than what happens at the moment when the goal is achieved. And once the goal was achieved, then what? What would the purpose of the universe be then? If we say that one thing is the "meaning," then we diminish the importance of everything else.

But if we say there is no meaning, then everything becomes equally significant. The journey becomes as important as the destination. Belief in an afterlife implies that, in order for something to have meaning or purpose, it must last forever. I find it preferable to think that things are important regardless of how long they last.

---

19 Joseph Campbell, *The Power of Myth* (New York: Doubleday, 1988) p. 5.

With no single goal or destination, life becomes open-ended. We no longer have to fret over the destiny of the universe. We can pick our own paths, work towards making the world and our lives the best we possibly can, and enjoy the show as the future is revealed.

The absence of an externally assigned meaning does not mean we have to plunge headfirst into existential angst[20], give up, or stay in bed all day. It's just the opposite. If you want meaning, you can have all of it you want. Find the things in your life that you think are most valuable, and you will have found your own meaning. Don't fall prey to the idea the meaning and purpose must necessarily come from one single source. They can change from moment to moment. They can come from anywhere at anytime. Nor must meaning and purpose be found externally. You can create them for yourself.

DANGEROUS

There are those who are concerned that atheism is a dangerous idea — that without the moral guidelines of a belief system, or without the fear of God's judgment, people will become wicked or try to get away with things they would not otherwise do.

This is sometimes expressed as an argument against atheism but fails completely because it is irrelevant. Regardless of the consequences, the truth remains the truth. Whether an idea is correct has nothing to do with what might happen because of it. Even if it did, Ethics, by definition, must be based on the truth. If the truth is that that there is no God, then an ethical position should incorporate that idea rather than reject it. Morals cannot be based on a lie.

We could stop the argument right there if it were not for the fact that we have not yet allayed the underlying fears that remain.

To assuage those fears, all we have to do is turn to the real world. There are numerous atheists in the world and they have already proven to be no more dangerous, immoral, or irresponsible than believers are. If they were, the world would be much more chaotic than it already is. I suspect that if you were to compare a random sampling of 1,000 atheists against 1,000 believers, you would not find that the atheists were committing all sorts of terrible crimes and the believers were exhibiting exemplary behavior. You might even find the opposite to be true.

---

20 Webster's dictionary defines existentialism as "A philosophy that emphasizes the absence of supernatural authority and the freedom and responsibility of the individual in a universe that lacks essential meaning." This definition suits our purposes just fine. The sense of despair often associated with the existential position is commonly referred to as "existential angst."

Many believers have a problem with the idea that a person can be ethical without a belief system. Part of the confusion lies in what is deemed as acceptable behavior by various belief systems, as opposed to what is deemed as acceptable behavior by those who do not subscribe to beliefs. There are disagreements over what are considered morally ambiguous or highly controversial areas among believers themselves, as with the issues of abortion and the death penalty, or even the use of obscenity or birth control. One person may consider these things immoral while another may think that they are either the proper ethical choices or, quite possibly, none of anyone's business. Questions surrounding sex often make it evident that there is no such thing as a "standard" objective morality. If there were such a thing, even the religionist would have a tough time proving he possesses it.

Incidentally, if you say that atheism does not provide a basis for morality because it is not a religion, then you cannot turn around and use the argument that "atheism is a belief."

Having a belief system in no way guarantees moral behavior, as evidenced by people across the globe who believe in a God while committing terrible crimes including murder, rape, and child molestation. Religious people commit lesser crimes on a daily basis without ever acknowledging they are doing any wrong and their beliefs never stop them. People who have a destructive or inscrutable nature are going to behave badly regardless of their belief system. They may even hide behind one. However, there is no correlation between "goodness" and belief.

When Martin Luther supported the idea of salvation through faith alone in his 95 Theses back in 1517, people attacked it for the same reason they now attack atheism. "If moral behavior is not mandatory, then why do it?" they asked. The complaint doesn't work against Christians *or* atheists.

There are plenty of reasons to act ethically regardless of whether we have a personal faith. The law is one of them. Human beings police each other and will do what they can to prevent extreme negative behaviors.

Society influences us through its attitudes. Many people do not act in destructive ways simply because they do not want to be disliked, or even hated, by society at large. This remains true even if a person does not have a belief system.

There are exceptionally practical results to being moral as well. People are more likely to like you when you are nice. The person who loves his or her fellow human beings, and who is loved by them in return, is happier than the person who does not. The person who can get along with other people, and who chooses to act with integrity, has a better life. People who don't get angry very often have better blood pressure. People who don't pick fights avoid physical injury, have better relationships, and stay out of jail. Smart people know that certain behaviors, thought of as moral, yield positive results. Being good, as they say, is its own reward.

If we think of both the short-range and long-range consequences of our actions, we are less likely to do destructive things. We should take care of our planet so that it is a good place to live for everyone around us, as well as ourselves, and so that it will be in good shape for future generations. We should be nice to people so that people are nice to us and so the world is a more pleasant place overall. We have many good reasons not to steal if we consider the long-range effects that stealing will have upon the price of items, on insurance rates, on the economy, and on whether or not we have to have our receipts checked as we leave the stores we shop in.

But the biggest reason of all that those of us without faith act morally is that we still care. We care about our loved ones, our children, our spouses, our family, our friends, and humankind in general. A large number of atheists prefer to go by the title "secular humanist" because their first priority is contributing to, and helping, humanity. The humanist knows that without God, all we have is each other.

People should want to be good of their own free will, and for the sake of being good in itself, not because they fear the consequences of Hell or because they are simply being obedient to a higher power.

There are no reasons left to object to atheism as a "dangerous" idea, but we now have more reasons to instill positive ethical values in our children as well as in those adults who have not learned them yet.

There is no need to fear that atheism breeds anarchy. It may even prove to be beneficial.

Why Bother?

When I first identified myself as an atheist, I faced the difficult question of how outspoken I should be about it. If life had no pre-assigned or ultimate meaning, and we had no idea what the outcome of mankind's existence would be, then why would it even matter if I said anything?

The answer to that came to me rather quickly. The reason was the same as one of my reasons for behaving ethically — I still cared. Regardless of what infinity had in store, what meant most to me was what happened in my lifetime and what happened to humanity.

My friends and I used to tease a college buddy who professed to be an atheist. We blamed his philosophy on his "weird" European background. Fortunately, he had a great sense of humor about it. Shortly after I "converted," I called him up and we were able to laugh about it from a different perspective.

Telling people who agreed with me about my new ideology was no problem, but how about the rest of the world?

I remember the sinking feeling I used to get in my gut when I heard someone say that he or she was an atheist. "That poor person. They simply do not understand," I would say to myself. There was some crucial point the atheist was missing, or they just did not know what it was to have faith. I thought that, above all, an atheist overestimated his or her own thinking.

There are some who are far less kind and forgiving in comparison to the way I once thought of atheists. For them, the word "atheist" conjures up images of an inhumane, immoral monster roaming the countryside looking for innocent villagers to kill. An atheist is downright evil, wicked at heart, spreading lies — a corrupter of innocent minds.

Now that I was an atheist, I knew they might think that of me. My skeptical stance, which was entwined with my atheist one, would not earn me any social points either.

My philosophy presented a problem for my personality. I did not want to engage in any arguments or confrontations because, generally, I hate that sort of thing. I definitely did not want to be obnoxious about expressing my views. Nor did I want to stand in the mall and hand out atheist pamphlets like I had done with Christian tracts when I was in my teens.

Maybe, I thought, I should just keep it to myself.

Ah, but that too was frustrating. More strongly than ever before, I felt that I had something to offer. When I became an atheist, it was as if someone had just let me in on the biggest secret in the world. It was one of those secrets that you miss even though it is right in front of your face. I hadn't discovered anything that thousands of people didn't already know and so I didn't feel that entirely brilliant to have figured it out. In actuality, I felt somewhat silly because it had taken me so long.

The thing is... there were elements to my new worldview that were practical and helpful. I felt myself torn between the desire to share it with people and my desire to be liked.

I wondered whether it would do me any good to share my philosophy with people anyway. It was commonly said that arguments about philosophy and religion get you nowhere. You can't convince someone to change his or her beliefs, can you? If people have irrational beliefs, came another argument, then you can't use rationality to convince them otherwise.

It's a good thing I was already in the habit of questioning people's assumptions. I knew, for one, that *I* had been converted. I did most of the work on my own, but not all of it. The words of various authors and the stories of former believers had influenced me. People could change their minds and other people helped them to do it.

Dan Barker, author of the book *Losing Faith in Faith*, was once a minister but then became an atheist. He lost his wife over it. She was never able to understand why he had changed. In contrast, Dan was able to explain it to his mother, who eventually did convert.

The idea that people's minds cannot be changed is a generalization. Whether or not a person can be converted depends upon the person and upon how ideas are presented. There are some who are set in their ways and with whom there is nothing you can say that will change their minds. You can frequently identify them just by talking to them for a minute or so. It would be foolish to try to affect their thinking. But there are thousands of other people who just need information, a nudge in the right direction, or who would really appreciate some help. Some good could be accomplished by expressing my thoughts. What I needed to do was use discretion. Say a word here. Keep quiet there.

I was in an odd situation. I was proud of something about myself that others held in complete disdain. Normally, when you are proud of something you've done, like winning a football game or accomplishing a great goal, you can tell people about it and they'll be impressed, if not envious. On occasion, you'll get accolades for it. It's a nice bonus, added to the fact that you have done what you set out to do. Not so with the results of my philosophical struggles. I fought the battles. I came out on the other side. Now that I had done so, people would be eager to express just how wrong I was. They would say I hadn't accomplished anything and that, instead, I had gone backwards and was a philosophical failure. They would want to save me when I, in turn, wanted to save them.

What overrode my reservations about expressing my conclusions was the importance of the issues at stake. These are issues that can impact all levels of our lives and that underlie all else in the human experience. We desperately need to understand these things more clearly than most of us currently do. Our understanding affects the choices we make and the way we interact with each other. During our lives, doors remain closed to us and we never realize it because we have made poor choices and sacrificed personal empowerment to our beliefs. Some of us remain unaware of just how greatly our beliefs affect our actions, not to mention how profoundly negative the consequences of belief can be. An unrealistic worldview can turn into a cop-out. It can result in greater delusions.

How is it that people, even the oldest and supposedly wisest of us, fall for the simplest of cons and believe wild and crazy superstitions? For the same reason.

Our ideas about religion and God find their way into politics and world affairs where misunderstandings of such important concepts can, and do, result in disaster. On a global scale, and on a daily basis, there are people on this planet who kill or are killed for religious reasons. Political leaders who make decisions based on unfounded premises, and without understanding the philosophical basics of how this world works, run the risk of inadvertently doing more harm than good.

Without proper understanding, people make poor decisions. In a country where decisions are made through democracy, those decisions affect me personally, so I both want and need people to be smart. I live in fear that committees (like city councils and school boards whose members lack the skills to make the right decisions) will have a negative impact on my life. I fear this because I have seen in happen, at places where I have worked and in the government. Detrimental policies and laws have been passed down by those who do not understand the reality of how things work at the most fundamental level.

Like the person who winds up on welfare because of his laziness, people who are ignorant or weak-willed also inadvertently have a negative affect on society as a whole. They pass those values down to their children as well. When we educate people, we counteract that and help society as a whole.

In short, there is a need for the knowledge I have gained.

Within the context of this book, it is difficult to fully express why lack of this knowledge is harmful and to give examples in relation to the philosophy or belief system of each and every reader, but in Chapters 4 and 6, I am able to show the problems with a wide range of beliefs and explain why there is a need for reassessment.

I do feel that everyone does, and should have, the *right* to believe what they want. The question I have asked throughout this book, though, is whether believing in something is the best possible way to think about the world.

Above I give reasons why beliefs may come under attack, and in some instances, why they *should* come under attack. In scientific, atheist, and skeptical circles I have noticed a common sentiment that we have been too timid in expressing our views. Believers have not been shy, but many nonbelievers have been. This has happened because beliefs are treated as sacred, while reason and knowledge is not.

One of the reasons people cling so strongly to their beliefs is because they think it is the right thing to do. But if those beliefs are wrong, it's not the right thing to do. A second reason that people hold on so tightly to their beliefs is that they find comfort and strength through them. Often, in order to deal with the irrationality of life, people turn to faith. The death of a loved one, for example, may be so traumatic to them that they feel they cannot deal with it any other way.

"What's wrong with that?" people ask. "Why shouldn't we be able to believe whatever we want to believe in order to help us cope?"

I would lodge no complaints against belief at all if I felt there was no other way to deal with life. However, in Chapter 7, I will explain that there are other, and far more preferable, ways to deal with the problems of life. If we can raise the standard and encourage people to be the best they can without believing in something false, then it is all for the better.

When belief can be shown to have negative consequences, there is a larger dilemma. The skeptic is faced with a problem similar to that of the person who does not know whether to tell their friend that their spouse is cheating on them. Delivering the news could have a positive or a negative effect depending on how it is delivered and who is receiving it. Is it worth it? Should we bother?

It requires a certain amount of discrimination. My own solution to these problems was, of course, to write a book.

CHAPTER 3. CRITICAL THINKING

SIMPLE THINGS OF PROFOUND IMPORTANCE

I'll start with an example.

I frequently hear people say, "Change is good." Now, to me, this is obviously wrong. Change, like many things, is neither good nor bad in and of itself. Change is simply when things go from one state to another.

Change is not always for the better. Death is change. Finding out you have cancer is change. Getting stabbed in the eye is change. I would say that change is not, by definition, "good."

But here come the arguments. "We learn from all these things," people say, "When someone dies, they go to heaven and that's good. If someone has cancer, that person learns to value their life, adjust to life's realities, and look at it in a new perspective. That's good. Whenever we get hurt, there is an opportunity for us to grow as people and that's good too!"

But see, it's no longer the change that is being talked about. It's the possible consequences of the change and how you react to the change. It's the silver lining that someone made up, not the change itself.

To say that all change is good is to say that every single thing that happens in the world is good. If you extrapolate that one step further, you have to assume that the world is constantly getting better by leaps and bounds because change is happening every second.

Many who say change is good say it because they have not thought much about it. Others say it as a generalization, aware that it isn't always true. Their error is simply one of imprecision.

There's another reason this phrase is repeated, and it has to do with the misinterpretation of the popular book, *Who Moved My Cheese?*, by Doctor Spencer Johnson. In his book, Doctor Johnson talks about those who have trouble adjusting to change and the trouble it causes them. He makes some extremely valuable points, but, unfortunately, his message is sometimes misused by those in the business world. It is twisted to mean that if an employee doesn't deal well with change, then it is the employee's fault and has nothing to do with how a manager implements change. It suddenly becomes a management cop-out.

Scott Adams expresses this brilliantly in a Dilbert[21] cartoon where the boss approaches an employee and tells him that an absurd policy is being replaced with an equally absurd policy. When the employee objects, the boss says, "Well, it looks like someone doesn't like having his cheese moved."

As it often does, the cartoon reflects real life. Employees have become afraid to object to bad management decisions because they will be labeled as "resistant to change." Employees cave in and walk around saying, "Change is good. Change is good."

What has happened is that misunderstanding a relatively simple concept has resulted in real world problems. The failure to think for ourselves, question things, and make distinctions can hurt us. At the very least, when we fail to think clearly, we make ourselves look silly. At the worst, we make ourselves victims.

This is where critical thinking skills come in. Critical thinking is a way of thinking that, among other things, includes problem solving skills, knowing how to ask the right questions, understanding methods of argument, recognizing legitimate and invalid forms of argument, and identifying logical fallacies that can cause us to make errors. Critical thinking provides us with useful tools to troubleshoot thought processes and keep them from going awry. There's nothing spectacular about them, in and of themselves. Sometimes we recognize them and use them automatically. A critical thinking skill can be something as simple as being careful to use the right words. But what often goes unrealized is the tremendous impact these seemingly insignificant principles can have.

I have already demonstrated this by making the distinction between reason and faith. Much of what I accomplished in Chapter 1 was simply a matter of taking the time to be clear about what these two words actually mean. When you follow the implications through to a logical conclusion, the results are astound-

---

21 Dilbert is a trademark of, and copyrighted by, United Features Syndicate, Inc.

ing, especially considering the meager beginning. This is the power of critical thinking. People assume that using a poor analogy or a cheap personal attack to make their point is no big deal and doesn't make much of a difference, but it's these very same logical errors that can prevent a person from understanding the world as it really is. It shouldn't be called "critical" thinking; it should be called "crucial" thinking.

A person's entire worldview can be changed simply because he or she uses (or fails to use) critical thinking. That worldview, in turn, determines how a person acts and makes decisions. These might be small decisions or life changing decisions. In the case of political leaders, they can even be world-affecting decisions. Logic and critical thinking principles turn out to be incredibly far-reaching. The purpose of much of this chapter is to spell out some of these principles in detail. A few of them may seem perfectly obvious, at least, I hope so. Several of the principles I cover may seem to have nothing to do with the larger philosophical questions I address in this book. Don't let that trick you into thinking that these things are irrelevant or trivial. They're not.

FALLACIES AND CRITICAL THINKING

Most of us like to think that we know what it is to be rational, but it is not an innately human skill set. Logical thinking does not come naturally. It usually has to be learned and it often takes discipline. It is not uncommon for people to make critical thinking errors in their everyday lives — in the break room at work, in business meetings, and at the dinner table. Turn on the TV or watch a political campaign and within minutes you will probably see a good example of illogical thinking. It's everywhere.

Failure to understand the world is merely a symptom of a larger disease, the inability to examine thoughts and ideas with the discipline that reason requires.

What follows is a list of what are mainly logical fallacies. Lists like this are nothing new — Aristotle provided a list of nine fallacies in his *Rhetoric* — but they are extremely useful.

My hope is that as you read the examples below and in the next two sections (which are, in essence, a continuation of this list) you'll recognize commonly used, illogical arguments and be more aware of them so that they can be avoided. Many of the arguments against what I say in this book are prone to these types of mistakes.

For me, critical thinking was the one of the last things I needed to figure out my personal philosophical quandaries. The principle of non-contradiction and an awareness that arguments and questions were often posed in illogical ways were what it took to get me on my way. For those who are not accustomed to it, critical thinking may take some getting used to. Step one is to understand how important it is and to be aware of it.

It should be noted that critical thinking is not always accomplished by following certain formulas and there is no singular definitive list of critical thinking skills.[22] Sometimes it requires that you draw information from different sources or approach ideas from creative (albeit logical) angles.

The list below and the next two sections should give you a feel for what it is all about.

Proper Word Usage

Changing a dot or a single quotation mark in a computer program can cause it to crash or to behave entirely differently. The act of changing the punctuation in a sentence can dramatically alter its meaning. Changing a word can alter it even more so. Again, we see that simple things do have profound importance.

When the meaning of a word is changed, but not the word itself, the change may go unnoticed, but it still has great repercussions. Changing the meaning of a word in the middle of a conversation can be like changing the value of a symbol in a math equation. The overall meaning or the overall result can change significantly. The flexibility of words is great for poetry, bad for clarity. If you point this out, some may accuse you of nit-picking, but clear understanding is impossible without such precision.

The Use of Analogies

Analogies, like the one I used above about a word being similar to a symbol in a math equation, are a commonly used tool in verbal reasoning. They are extremely useful because they give us another way to look at something and picture it with more clarity. As with words, it is important to exercise caution in how analogies are used. Misused analogies can cause more confusion than they alleviate. They then become faulty analogies, which misrepresent situations rather than provide clarification.

In Chapter 6 of this book, we'll find several examples of poor analogies that are used to support religious ideas. Crazy notions and crackpot theories are often accompanied by poor analogies.

---

22 If you would like to learn more about critical thinking, I recommend the following books:
   The Demon-Haunted World by Carl Sagan. See the chapter titled, "The Fine Art of Baloney Detection."
   Informal Logic: A Handbook for Critical Argumentation by Douglas N. Walton
   The Philosopher's Toolkit by Julian Baggini and Peter S. Fosl

To see the flaw in an analogy, you have to note the differences between the things compared, but only — and this is important — in relation to the specific topic under discussion. It should be obvious that two different things are not going to be the same in all respects and that, consequently, analogies have their limits. Yet it isn't, because there are also those who carry analogies too far and refuse to accept any legitimate comparisons that analogies afford. It may require careful thought to determine if an analogy is accurate or not.

Straw Man Arguments

Straw man arguments often utilize faulty analogies. A straw man argument occurs when someone constructs a description or analogy that inaccurately represents his or her opponent's position. The person who has constructed the "straw man" then turns around and knocks it down. This gives the illusion that he has successfully dealt a blow to their opponent's position.

Generalities

It is very easy to make generalities about ideas, things, people, or groups of people. All it takes to avoid a generality is to qualify it, by adding the word "some" or identifying the generality for what it is. I have heard many an argument that could be resolved this way. One side says, "People are this way," while the other side says, "No, people aren't like that. They're another way." All it would take to settle the dispute is the simple acknowledgment that a portion of the population is one way, and that other portions are different.

The woman who assumes, for example, that "all men are pigs" may prevent herself from recognizing that there is a nice guy out there with whom she could have a mature and fulfilling relationship.

Generalities, all too easily, can blur our vision of the world.

Correlation and Causation

When two things happen at the same time (or within the same data group), it does not mean that they are connected or that one of the things caused the other. To say that they do is to confuse correlation with causation.

I once overheard a mechanic arguing with a customer about this concept, although neither of them realized that this was what they were debating. The customer had brought in his car to have the starter replaced and was complaining that now he had trouble with his carburetor.

"My carburetor was working before I brought my car in here and now it's not!" he complained.

"But I didn't touch your carburetor," the mechanic answered. "It has nothing to do with the battery or the electrical system."

"All I know is," the customer continued, "that when I brought my car in, the carburetor was working, and when you guys were done with my car, the carburetor wasn't working."

"But they're not connected!" declared the mechanic.

They went around in circles.

The customer had confused causation and correlation. The carburetor just happened to go out while the car was in the shop. It was ready to go bad at that time. The mechanic had not sabotaged it, and there was not anything the mechanic did with the battery that affected the carburetor. The two things had happened simultaneously, but they had nothing to do with each other.

When I worked as a computer support person, I often faced the same problem. I would be blamed for things that went wrong with a computer just because I had been working on the computer at the time when other problems occurred. Try as I might to explain, there were people who refused to believe that the problems were not connected.

Sometimes survey results are interpreted with the same imprecision. If fifty percent of households have lettuce in their refrigerators and fifty percent of households include someone who has athlete's foot, it does not mean that lettuce causes athlete's foot.

Aristotle included this type of fallacy as number seven in his list. (The Latin term for it is *post hoc ergo propter hoc*.)

Black, White, and Between

In the section "Why Speculate?" I dealt with Pascal's Wager, which suffers from the problem of being a black-and-white description of a multiple-option scenario.

Some situations are clearly either/or scenarios, where if one thing is true, the other must be false. It's a basic tenet of logic. But many situations have other options and a black-and-white mentality prevents us from seeing them.

The ability to discern when a situation is "either/or" and when it is not can prevent us from making huge mistakes. This is especially the case with issues of morality. Those who think that all things are clearly right or wrong, and that there are no in-betweens, are making a serious mistake. The statement, "If you're not for us, you're against us," often comes from the same kind of misplaced mindset.

It is ironic that those who are stuck in black-and-white thought patterns can accuse others of being narrow-minded.

The secret to avoiding this type of error is to make sure that all valid options are accounted for.

Absolutes

One of my college professors told our class that whenever a true-or-false question on a test said that something was *always* true or *never* true, we should mark the question false. Nothing was always true or always false, she claimed. Our teacher was not aware that she had broken her own rule by creating another absolute. If what she had said was on a test, I would have had to mark it false. Absolutes are rare, but they do exist.

You'll notice throughout this book that I qualify many statements with words like "usually," "sometimes," "often," and "many." It would be much more dramatic to say "always or never" and to make statements without the use of qualifiers. It would also be far less accurate. Take the following statements for example:

- Never say never.
- Everything in moderation.
- Every rule has an exception.
- Nothing is impossible.

If we want to be accurate, here is how the above statements should read:

- Rarely say never.
- Do most things in moderation.
- Most rules have exceptions.
- Many things that you think are impossible are not.

We have already used this understanding of absolutes in the sections about impossibility and God.

Circular Reasoning

A thing should not be used to justify itself.

When I was a young Baptist boy in junior high and was taught how to share my beliefs, I was told always to refer to the Bible. I was encouraged to memorize the verse Timothy 3:16, which says, "All scripture is given by inspiration of God, and is profitable for doctrine, for reproof, for correction, for instruction in righteousness."

"What if people don't believe in the Bible?" I asked.

"Always answer with the Bible," was the response, and then Timothy 3:16 was repeated again. *Wait a minute,* I thought, *there's a loop there.* If people don't accept the Bible as true, they have no reason to believe the verses I quote from it.

I was being taught to use circular reasoning, to justify something with itself. It doesn't work. In the section, "Criteria and Personal Experience," I gave another example of circular reasoning from the Bible where it says, in effect, that I was never really a believer, because if I had been, I could have never become a nonbeliever. The path of thought (it can hardly be called logic) goes around in circles.

This example gives us a hint of just how confusing circular reasoning can be and how difficult it can be to decipher. It is one of those things that seem obvious to those who understand it, but completely mystifies those who do not. Sometimes you feel as if you need to chart the trail of reasoning out on paper in order to see what's going on.

The issue is complicated by the fact that some things are so basic that they are self-evident. A rock is a rock. A = A. Logic and our understanding of reality are based upon these simple ideas.

It is important to note that I am not committing the mistake of circular reasoning when I say that something is self-evident. What makes something self-evident is that there is no deeper level at which it can be explained. In logic, such things are referred to as axioms.

If, instead of saying that a rock is a rock or A = A, we say that a rock is an igneous rock or that A = B x 92, then we are no longer making self-evident statements, and we need to find another way to validate them.

The way to identify circular reasoning is to find out if something is being used to justify itself. If that thing is not so basic as to be self-evident, then another way to establish the truth of it needs to be found. If another way cannot be found, then nothing can be concluded.

There will be plenty more examples of circular reasoning to come, especially in Chapter 4 where I examine the Bible.

An understanding of the above principles not only helps us to think logically, but, if employed in our daily lives, it would improve our communications (and therefore our understanding of each other). Critical thinking would compel us to take a more fair and reasonable approach to our social interactions. It certainly couldn't hurt.

THE INDEPENDENCE OF TRUTH

I can touch on several facets of logic and critical thinking by examining the idea that the truth is independent.

It does not matter where the truth comes from, who says it, how they say it, or why they say it. It does not matter if the truth is something you don't like, you don't believe, or you don't want to hear. Truth is truth regardless. The truth is independent in and of itself.

***

One of the most common logical fallacies that people indulge in is the personal attack. The personal attack gives psychological leverage to those who wield it. Those who use it may undermine other people by picking on a personal characteristic or a past mistake. The personal attack is used in the politics of the nation and in the politics of relationships. Sometimes the combatants involved have no idea they are being unfair. At other times, they are perfectly aware of it.

The Latin term for this kind of thinking is *ad hominem*, meaning "to the man." A person is being attacked when an issue should be under scrutiny instead.

The personal attack is not always easy to recognize. It may be veiled, hidden in another statement. A criticism that I have heard of atheists is that "most atheists are people who have had bad relationships with their fathers." The implication is that because people have emotionally rejected their fathers, they have projected the same feeling upon God — the ultimate father figure — and rejected him as well. It's a personal attack because it suggests that atheists are what they are because of an emotional or social defect. Yet the atheist could use the same sort of distorted logic. They could say that many people who believe in God do so because they have bad relationships with their fathers and have created an imaginary father figure to make up for the lack of fatherly love. Both of these arguments are logically invalid, but if you go online or just listen to people talk, you will hear these types of statements from those who think they are being both logical and insightful. Neither is the case.

***

The truth remains the truth regardless of who says it.

A murderer can say that people should not commit murder and still be right despite his hypocrisy.

My stepfather always used to say, "consider the source." By this he meant that you should take into account the motives and background of whoever is presenting an idea to you. Yes, it is sometimes advantageous to consider it, but you should not take that information as an automatic indication that someone is wrong.

Keep in mind that we all make mistakes (an obvious truth, to be sure). It is part of being human. What the personal attack manages to do is to take advantage of this. "You made mistakes in the past," the argument goes, "so why should I trust you now?"

There may be some validity to the argument if the accused has made many mistakes in the same area, as with the case of a cheating lover who has repeatedly betrayed your trust. But in general, especially when it comes to dealing with the expression of ideas, it is a very weak argument. For the sake of logic, it should be understood that even the compulsive liar must sometimes tell the truth.

The silliness of the argument that anyone who has erred in the past can no longer be trusted becomes apparent when you take into account that if everyone who had ever made a mistake was forced to stop talking, the world would be a very quiet place.

It is especially unfair to criticize someone for past mistakes of an ideological nature when they have already acknowledged and corrected them.

Science is often attacked in the same way that the individual is. Attempts to denigrate science will frequently consist of lists of things it has been wrong about in the past, is if this undermines everything about science all at once. Every discipline, religion, or person has been subject to error at some point, and this is not necessarily a weakness. On they contrary, it is often the most successful individuals who make the most mistakes. This is because the successful are out there trying things and taking chances, thereby discovering what works and what doesn't work. The process of experimentation, in its many forms, shows us that mistakes are sometimes necessary if we are to make any progress. Moreover, they are inevitable. Mistakes should be used as learning experiences and not as weapons.

Just as we might *disbelieve* people for the wrong reasons, we may also *believe* people for the wrong reasons. This is the other side of the *ad hominem* argument. We might believe a person based on his authority alone. We may trust our parents when they are completely wrong about something. It's quite natural to do that, because as children it is necessary to rely on our parents. Regardless of our belief, what is true or false is separate from who says it.

To be fair, an argument should not be supported because a particular side makes it. Those who do not understand this will react with incomprehension or anger if someone fails to take their side when they present an illogical argument. To them, the person who is only trying to be fair may appear to be changing loyalties. The actuality is that the person who does not adopt an illogical attitude is showing loyalty to higher principles — those of reason.

***

Sometimes we believe what people say simply because of their tone or the way they say things.

I used to have a boss who would make statements with such conviction and authority that I did not even think to question them at first. But after he turned out to be wrong a couple times, I started thinking, *What's going on here?* On those occasions when I state things authoritatively (which happens more often in this book than it does on a daily basis), I try to make sure that I have a great deal of backup and know what I'm talking about first. When my boss said something with such surety, I thought he must have expended the same amount of effort to make sure he was right. Not so. Once I figured it out, it was amusing to watch him in action. He could have been guessing, yet what he said seemed as definitive as if he were saying the ocean had fish in it.

The opposite happens when people are disbelieved because of their attitude, their tone, their facial expression, or even because someone perceives that they are having certain thoughts.

For example, an accuser might say, "I know you're lying because you're so defensive and angry."

Sometimes people's attitude does give away their motivations, and then such a statement is accurate; but it's not dependable. People may just as easily get angry and defensive because they know they are right and are offended that anyone would question them.

The same potential for misinterpretation exists when people use the Shakespearean line, "Methinks thou dost protest too much." This quote is used to imply that a person's guilt is evident because of how strongly he objects to whatever accusations are made against him. If a person is unfairly accused, of course he will object! The reverse happens as well. People are sometimes said to be guilty of an accusation because they don't defend themselves *enough.* Evidently, to avoid being thought of as guilty, a person has to protest or not protest in just the right proportions. Or perhaps we can be smart enough to figure out that the way a person reacts to an accusation is not a clear sign of their innocence or guilt.

A common social trick used these days is to assign emotions or thoughts to another person. It is done commonly as a joke, sometimes out of ignorance, other times out of malice. On occasion, it is valid.

Imagine a party scene where a man, we'll call him John, is seen blushing. A friend might say, "John is blushing because he likes that girl at the bar and we're making a big deal out of it," when in actuality John's face is red because the alcohol just hit him.

Expressions and motives are often misread. Unless you are clairvoyant, you do not know for sure what another person is thinking.

The situation here is similar to another loose assumption that is often made. I frequently hear the comment that only those who are guilty run from the scene of a crime. The comedian Chris Rock says that whoever came up with that must not have been a black man.

Point taken, Chris. There is more than one reason to leave a crime scene. Maybe you're afraid that a racist cop is going to beat you. You might be concerned that, although you are not guilty, being at the scene of a crime will make you look like you are. Panic alone can make one flee the situation. At a highly-charged crime scene, it is natural to act without thinking first.

All of these examples illustrate that truth is distinct from tones, attitudes, emotions, and appearances. These things may give us clues to the truth, but they are hardly clear or precise indicators.

Conservatives, moderates, and liberals, fundamentalists, agnostics, and atheists, all make passionate claims at times, investing tremendous amounts of emotion in what they say. Ignore the exclamations and the invective, disregard the cheap shots, and get down to the issues. The content itself must be examined to find out if it is true.

***

Another argument I commonly hear (and that strikes me as odd) is that something cannot be true because a person does not like what would happen if it were true. Regardless of whether we like the truth, where it comes from, or how it is delivered, it is still to our advantage to be aware of it.

I compare it to balancing my checkbook. I don't like doing it. I don't like finding errors and discovering that my balance is a couple hundred dollars less than I thought it was, but I do it anyway. If I want to buy computer games and DVDs before I go to the grocery store, I need to know my balance.

Knowing the truth about life is vastly more useful than knowing the balance of a single checkbook, even if the conclusions are not to your liking. The effort expended in gaining that understanding is worth it.

QUESTIONS AND THEIR PURSUIT

As I started to employ critical thinking skills, I learned that there was a tremendous amount of information being fed to me during the day that was flat out wrong — from the trivial to the extremely important; from the urban myth to second hand "facts"; from generalized clichés to widely held cultural ideologies.

It is important to question things rather than to accept them blindly. There is nothing wrong with doubts or questions. They simply reflect the desire to know the answers. The truth should have nothing to fear from close examination.

This spirit of thoughtful inquisitiveness was not present in the religious community in which I grew up. Usually, inquisitiveness was discouraged. When I finally realized that this curiosity about life was what the skeptical and scientific communities embraced, I immediately gained a new appreciation for these people. They were doing what needed to be done. They weren't afraid of questions. They encouraged them and were digging deep, looking for answers. It was so refreshing!

Volumes could be written about the sentiments and clichés that pass from people's lips without any consideration of their merit. The statement "change is good" that I looked at earlier is a perfect example. It is necessary to think and ask questions in order to avoid the problems that such blind acceptance can cause.

But asking questions is just the beginning. When asking questions, there are several things that must be done in order for the questions to yield effective results. These fall under the category of critical thinking principles.

Improper questions can cause as much trouble as improper answers, so before a question is asked, it should first be examined itself. Some questions presuppose things that are not true, and therefore the questions are at fault and need to be revised before answers can be found. Questions that contain hidden assumptions are used by the media all the time. The example my mom always used was the question, do you still beat your wife? There is no way a person can answer this question with a yes or no answer and come out looking good. When aimed at someone who hasn't even so much as called his wife a name, this type of question is unfair. It implies that that person has done something in the past that he never did. The only way out of the predicament the question presents is to identify what is wrong with the question or to throw it out entirely. I recommend the latter.

I often wish that those who are questioned by the press in such a manner would call them on it. The media gets away with many attacks by disguising them as questions. For the sake of drama and entertainment, the media continually propagates an antagonistic and illogical approach that has an impact on all of us.

Such questions are often used in philosophical debates to make another side look bad. It is both irritating and unnecessary.

Once questions are asked, especially in the search for philosophical answers, the questions should be followed to their conclusions. One of the common causes of misunderstandings about the world is the simple failure to put everything together. When all it would take to achieve understanding is to add A + B + C, people add A + B and stop. Crucial answers are missed due to a lack of persistence.

So very often, people simply lose sight of the point that an argument or train of thought began with. Being sidetracked causes them to reach an irrelevant answer. People consciously and unconsciously change the subject when they near a conclusion they do not like. Intentionally dancing around an issue or sidestepping a point is a disservice to the truth and to one's self. When one begins to take notice of it, this pattern turns out to be alarmingly frequent.

I would go so far as to say that one of the many reasons people fail to see the conclusions I have reached in this book is that they are swimming in a sea full of red herrings, which exist in the form of a preponderance of supernatural and religious ideas. It is only when these ideas are passed through the fishing net of reason that the red herrings can be caught and filtered out.

While it is important to pursue a question to its conclusion, it is also necessary to recognize when a dead end has been reached. Some arguments cannot be resolved, and rehashing an issue that cannot be resolved is unproductive. When questions can go no further, they should be consciously put aside.

It is also important to be careful not to accept poor answers. Often, people are not so discerning. It seems that any answer will do, regardless of its quality, as long as there is an answer out there somewhere. All that matters is that the answers agree with their conclusions. Certain "answers" seem so flimsy, fabricated, unconvincing, or not to the point, that I have difficulty understanding how people can take them seriously.

Another problem occurs when a satisfactory answer to a question has already been given and yet people continue to ask the same question. Dismissing an answer this way (by acting as if the question has not been resolved when, in actuality, it has) is interesting psychologically. In some instances, it reflects how people can ignore, be in denial about, or refuse to accept answers they do not like. It is illogical to disregard good answers and intellectually dishonest to ignore them when one knows they have been provided.

The journey that is begun by asking questions can have unexpected and interesting results. It is worth taking the steps, but those steps sometimes require a certain measure of precision.

THE BURDEN OF PROOF

When a scientist comes up with a hypothesis, he or she does not then rush out into the scientific community and say, "Here's my idea. If you can't prove it wrong, I must be right!"

A scientist who did so would be ridiculed, and rightly so. It is an absurd way to present an idea. Whoever proposes an idea, whether it is a new idea or an idea that has not yet been accepted as valid, must provide the evidence for it.

In the first place, no one else cares about the idea. Why should they? It wasn't their idea; they didn't come up with it, and they aren't out promoting it. Secondly, there are plenty of things that are untrue that cannot be disproved. You can make anything up, but in order for something to be meaningful, it must be test-able. Otherwise it is just speculation and, as I have already established, specula-tion has no significance. It is meaningless in any scientific sense or in any sense that can accurately be described as knowledge.

When you place the burden of proof upon the nonbeliever, you make an un-reasonable request. You might as well ask the nonbeliever to refute a random ridiculous claim. When a claim (ridiculous or otherwise) cannot be disproved, it does not gain validity. Yet it is not uncommon for a believer to say, "Prove me wrong!" and when no one can, the believer acts as if he or she has achieved some great victory.

The name for this logical fallacy is the "appeal to ignorance." It is sometimes based on the misconception that the scientific and logical worlds revolve around the ideas of proof and disproof, which is not the case at all.

The skeptic is often faced with challenges from the believer to prove some-one wrong or to explain some unusual occurrence. For the reasons stated above, it is an unfair challenge. Regardless, it is understandably tempting to try to rise to such challenges, although it is not always a good idea. The skeptic's explana-tions are often dull, dry, or consist of arguments that have been heard before. The believer's response to these may be little more than a nose wrinkled in dis-agreement. In the eyes of the believer, the attempts at explanation are complete failures and the skeptic probably would have been better off if he or she had not ventured their guesses.

When skeptics do not know an answer, and there is not enough information available to get one, the best response is often, "I don't know. I don't have enough information."

Sure, the believer claims this as another victory, but there is nothing much the skeptic can do about it but continue to try to educate the believer. Carl Sagan said, "Extraordinary claims require extraordinary evidence,"[23] making the point that if the believer wants to make his case, not only is he going to have to provide his own evidence, but it's going to have be remarkable.

Skeptics also try to make it clear that it is impossible to prove a negative. For example, if I send you a letter and then I turn around and say I didn't, then you can prove that I sent it by showing the letter to me — postmark and all. How-ever, if I say I sent you a letter, but you claim I never did, you cannot prove it. (Neither can I.) The letter could have easily been lost in the mail.

Here's another example: you cannot prove that there are no alternate uni-verses. If they existed, you might be able to prove it by opening up a passage to

23 Carl Sagan, *Billions and Billions: Thoughts on Life and Death at the Brink of the Millennium* (New York: Random House, 1997).

an alternate universe and taking people there, but it would be difficult, indeed, to show that alternate universes do not exist.

The less defined the claim, the more difficult it becomes to disprove it.

When someone makes a statement such as, "Prove that ghosts don't exist," or even "Prove there is no God," they are making an unreasonable request. Skeptics have not failed in any way by not disproving something. When they cannot, the believer is wrong to think that they have scored any "points," as it were. The skeptic cannot do the impossible, whether it is disproving something that cannot be tested or convincing someone that he or she is claiming a false victory.

Where Did All the Logic Go?

One of the questions that is commonly asked in the skeptical, atheistic, and free thought communities, especially by those who have been skeptics since birth, is the question, how can people believe the things they do and not see how illogical they are? The question is repeated in a variety of tones ranging from the simple desire to know to incomprehension and frustration. Many skeptics, because they cannot perceive any other alternative, assume that many believers are being dishonest and really do not believe what they claim to believe.

I see no reason, though, why the tendency to believe illogical things should be considered mysterious. There are a great number of factors contributing to it. When you stop and look at all of them at once, what becomes amazing is that we can overcome our human failings and see the world clearly (or, at least, relatively so).

You need go no farther than basic human psychology to explain the human propensity for belief. I know of two people who, as nonbelievers, turned to psychology because they figured that if answers were to be found about why we are the way we are, that was the best place to look. I think they chose correctly.

As humans, we make numerous conceptual errors on a daily basis. It happens to Christians, Muslims, atheists, New Agers, agnostics, doctors, lawyers, scientists, firemen, dentists, cheerleaders, runway models, schoolteachers, and stock analysts. Our views of the world are tinged with biases and predispositions. This is true in general, not just in regard to how we think about philosophical issues.

Psychologists have identified numerous biases in the ways we behave, make decisions, act socially, and form our beliefs. There are over a hundred of this "cognitive biases" that have been identified, tested, studied, and documented. Although many of us have probably observed these biases and behaviors in our daily lives and don't need studies in order to know that they exist. Listed below are seven of them.

- The clustering illusion — Seeing patterns where there are none.
- Confirmation or "My side" bias — Seeking out information that confirms one's ideas, beliefs, and preconceptions while avoiding information that does not.
- Endowment effect — Valuing something more when it belongs to you. (It is because of the endowment effect that I do not hold garage sales. No one ever wants to pay me the amount that I think my possessions are worth.)
- The Lake Wobegon effect — Rating one's own characteristics and attributes as better than those of others.
- The planning fallacy — Underestimating how long it will take to complete a task (despite past experience).
- Rosy retrospection — Viewing past events more positively afterward than one views them at the time they occur.
- Self-serving bias — Taking responsibility for successes but not for failures.

Our psychology is tied directly to our physiology, and many have speculated that we are "hardwired for belief." Scientists have identified a gene (or genes) that, if all connected genetic factors are conducive to it, will make a person more likely to have mystical experiences, and therefore more inclined to believe in "something more." This genetic coding has been mislabeled as the "God gene," but it has little to do with God per se, and it does not mean that people are "programmed" by their DNA to believe. All it means is that their brain chemistry is more susceptible to certain kinds of experiences. The way that those experiences are interpreted depends upon the individual. But this is only one factor in a much larger equation.

The part of the brain that plays a primary role in processing our emotional reactions (the amygdala) has a very strong connection to the part of our brain which controls the higher brain functions such as thought, reasoning, and memory (the cortex). But the connection the other way, from the cortex to the amygdala, is much weaker. This suggests an explanation for why it is so hard to override our emotions and why emotions so often invade our thinking, even when we try to avoid it.

All sorts of mood-affecting drugs are created by our bodies and pumped through our systems in response to sights, sounds, smells, and experiences.

There are evolutionary reasons for all of these things. Our minds and bodies are built around the simple principle of survival. Because of this, we have defense mechanisms that make us feel better about ourselves. They may give us undeserved but still useful optimism. They can be advantageous because they affect our attitudes that, in turn, result in the brain sending helpful chemicals through our bodies.

So many of the cognitive biases that occur in human beings are there because they usually work. We are constantly deluged with all types of information and the mind needs to have simplified strategies for dealing with all of it and processing it, otherwise we would be so overwhelmed with data and decisions that we would not even be to function. Sometimes, even though these strategies and defenses are usually beneficial, they fail. These mechanisms are fallible and that is what we need to be on guard for.

Knowing all this, and being aware of my own faults, makes it a lot easier to be forgiving of others and the mistakes they make, but these psychological and physiological factors are just the beginning.

Our ability to be rational is also hampered by a number of social factors. Social interactions are rarely based on reason. A night at the bar with friends may be filled with poorly reasoned arguments, innuendoes, and laughter, but rarely does reason enter the mix. There is nothing wrong with this, except when people do not realize that social discourse often lacks the characteristics that would make it reasonable and logical. The same techniques that are successful socially will often result in failure when applied during reasoned discourse. This is because the goals of the two types of interactions are usually not the same. Clear and productive thought, as well as reasoned philosophical discussions, demand a much higher level of discipline and fairness than our everyday social encounters do. A comedian can use a poor analogy to make me laugh, but if he tries to do it in the middle of a serious debate about the meaning of life, it will have the opposite effect.

It takes all the effort I can muster to sit through any television talk show in which the audience is allowed to shout out questions or yell accusations at the guest. The goal in these situations is often to "win" — for one side to outmaneuver or out yell their opponents; but when that happens with no regard for reason, then true fairness can never be obtained. Everyone loses and no one wins. When emotional reactions and unfair arguments reign supreme, it is the rare individual who seems to know that there is something wrong.

It is for the same reasons that I dislike debate. Despite the appearance of structure, principles of reason are often violated in formal debate by means of improper word usage, attacks upon irrelevant issues, and personal attacks. The speakers' demeanor, emotional tone, looks, whether or not they can make people laugh, and how they make people feel, all have a dramatic effect in verbal debate. A clever quip or the group dynamic can cause a perfectly good idea to be disregarded. Someone who is absolutely correct can easily lose a debate because he couldn't think of the right words at the right time. Verbal debate requires quick thinking and does not allow for reflective thought, which is sometimes necessary to arrive at correct conclusions. Arriving at a well-founded conclusion should be the goal, but even in debate, the rules and goals of social behavior interfere.

In these scenarios, another source of frequent misunderstandings comes to light, and that is the nature of communication itself. Communication fails because people have different frames of reference, because they come from different cultures, because they think they're talking about the same thing as someone else when they're not, and because of mistrust — to name just a few reasons.

I have had communication fail because I have simply been too diplomatic. As a part-time auditor, I have found that when I try to phrase things in such a way that the other party does not end up looking too bad, he will, on occasion, fail to see that he has made a mistake. In order to communicate, one must sometimes be direct, even at the cost of people's feelings. But when you do that, the other party's emotions may prevent them from hearing what you have to say. Can you win? Not always.

In addition, questioning and doubting the world around us requires an effort that we may not have the time or the energy for.

> We are credulous creatures who find it easy to believe, easy to doubt. The problem is that we believe things to be true as a matter of course... Of course we are not burdened with our gullible beliefs forever, or even for very long. However, it is only with some mental effort that we can decide they are untrue. Our natural urge (our default position) is to believe. This may be because, in general, people speak the truth more often than not. It's therefore more efficient to assume that things are true unless we have reason to think otherwise.
>
> But there is a problem with this system. If your brain is too busy with other things to put in the necessary legwork to reject a doozy, then you're stuck with that belief. Advertisers and car salesmen will be delighted to learn that incredulity really is hard work for us, or so research suggests. If your brain is distracted or under pressure, you will tend to believe statements that you would normally find rather dubious.[24]

When I read the above passage, I immediately thought of a gentleman I used to work with. He had the habit of saying things that were untrue but that you had no reason to disbelieve. He might say, "Hey, the stoplight on Fourth Street is out, so you'll want to take New York Avenue."

When I would say, "Thanks," to such a statement, he would respond by laughing at me and saying, "Ha! You believed that? You sure are gullible."

"Why would I have questioned that?" I would ask, because there was no reason I should have. Of course, I believed him. That's how we function in everyday

---

24 Cordelia Fine, *A mind of its own* (New York: W. W. Norton & Company, Inc., 2006), p. 121. Quote does not include footnotes referencing studies, which are provided in the original text.

life. Soon, I learned to distrust everything that came out of his mouth, no matter how mundane, but I had to remind myself, "Don't believe anything this guy says."

I mentioned before that we, as humans, make errors in a plenty of non-philosophical areas, but another problem occurs when philosophical questions get sequestered off into their own arena. This is similar to the suspension of disbelief that occurs with movies and fictional books. Reason is thought of as ideal for solving math problems and answering scientific questions but not much else. In the educational world this problem is referred to as "transference." When students are taught skills in a classroom environment, they may not automatically think to apply them to problems they face in everyday life, which is exactly what they need to do. In the same way, many, who are perfectly aware of critical thinking principles, and may even be aware of the cognitive biases that humans have, suffer from compartmentalization of thought and fail to use this knowledge where it is most needed — in the philosophical world.

In the chapter about critical thinking, I touched on a few of the many errors that people often unknowingly make in their thinking. In the section titled "Popular Myths," I talk about how myths are perpetuated. Counteracting such an onslaught of myths is an uphill battle. Later, in the section "Brainwashed," I will provide a series of pressures that are sometimes put upon individual, causing them to continue in believing irrational things. Put all of theses together with the psychological, physiological, and social factors, as well as with poor communications and compartmentalization of thought, and we see that there are plenty of obstacles preventing people from seeing the flaws in their belief systems.

To overcome all of this requires work. It requires attentiveness, awareness, discipline, and knowledge.

At my day job, I often have to ask people to make corrections to credit card refund request forms. I am frequently amazed (I shouldn't be, but I still am) by how often people will only follow one of my instructions and skip the rest. This is true regardless of whether I put the corrections in paragraph form or provide them as a list. Sometimes they will do something in the middle of the list and skip the rest. My wife has the same problem in her classroom. She will ask students to put their names and the date on their papers, and the students will do one of the two — or neither.

In some cases, this type of errors are perfectly understandable. People are in a hurry. They have a lot on their minds. I know that the people at my work are buried in phone calls and other demands, so they get distracted and they don't finish what they started to do. There is a lot to worry about that keeps them from doing things right. If this is true at work and at school, then it is even more applicable when it comes to how they think about philosophical issues that do not seem to have the same pressing immediacy.

Understanding does not come naturally to us. It is something that has to be learned and executed despite a large number of obstacles. Rationality is a skill, and we should be proud of ourselves when we exercise it effectively. It means that we have taken our ability to be self-aware and put it to good use. We have risen above our animal instincts and origins. It is unreasonable for people to think that they can achieve an understanding of the world with a minimal amount of effort, and yet many do. Sometimes we all need to slow down, put our names and dates on our papers, read the instructions, and do the work.

Chapter 4. Skeptical Specifics

A Few Examples

The sections in this chapter cover a diversity of topics that one might not intuitively think of as connected. The common theme is that they are all varieties of belief. Examination of them reveals that beliefs, of all shapes and sizes, share similar defects. At the very least, they are speculative and unfounded, but they can also contradict reason outright.

This chapter serves many purposes. The first is to demonstrate, again, the power and value of reason. In disassembling New Age and supernatural ideas, I have occasion to use principles that were established in previous sections.

The second purpose of this chapter is to serve as a warning. That is one of the services that skepticism provides. It tries to prevent us from being fooled. From my own experience, I know that such warnings are rarely heeded. Tell me something is a fantasy and I have to be first deceived and then disillusioned before I acknowledge that you were right in the first place. Tell me the stove is hot, and I have to burn my fingers on it before I believe you. We all learn slowly sometimes, but regardless of how they are learned, these lessons are valuable.

For me, and others like me, dealing with these subjects is part of the process of ridding ourselves of superstitious and mistaken ideas that we have incorporated into our worldviews over the years. That's the third purpose of this chapter, to help those who are going through a similar process.

The fourth is to answer some of the objections from those who oppose a skeptical outlook. Even after explaining why belief fails and why reason supplies knowledge we can trust, skeptics often find themselves dealing with the kinds of issues I look at here. "What about this?" the believer asks, "And what about that? What about Edgar Cayce and therapeutic touch? What about 21 grams, the Bermuda Triangle, and Electronic Voice Phenomena?"[25] There is no limit to the number of questions about "the unexplained" that can be presented, other than the number of people who can think of them and the amount of time they have on the planet to do so.

Entire philosophies are often based on several, or maybe one or two, of these types of things which come to us via the media, from stories we hear, and sometimes from personal experience. The extreme number of them that are reported is often enough to convince people that there must be something to "at least one of them." But the number of claims is irrelevant. What matters is the quality. Invalid claims remain invalid, no matter how many of them there are. It is because of this that we need methods for testing their validity, which is where reason comes to the rescue.

I found that when I continually applied reason and science to the supernatural in the quest to find something to believe in, I was continually disillusioned. What first seemed to be an innumerable number of claims becomes a limited number of seemingly legitimate claims. With further investigation, these also began to dwindle until there was nothing unusual or supernatural that I was willing to acknowledge as true without first having good reason to do so. This was an end result for me, but it should have been the starting point.

This chapter provides some examples of how to go about applying reason to specific issues. In total, it will reinforce earlier points, answer some questions in a world where there are far too many, and, possibly, prevent some fingers from getting burned.

---

25 For the record, A) Edgar Cayce's predictions, medical remedies, and reincarnation claims have been thoroughly debunked elsewhere. B) Therapeutic touch takes advantage of the placebo effect, which I discuss later. C) 21 grams is supposedly the amount of weight a body loses when a person dies, suggesting that something, presumably the soul, leaves the body at the time of death. This is based on experiments performed by a man named Duncan Macdougall in the 1900s. The conditions of his tests were highly suspect and the results remain unverifiable. A larger point can be made, though. If the soul is substantial enough that it can be weighed, science would be able to detect it easily, and the whole issue would have been resolved a long time ago. D) The Bermuda Triangle has more shipping lanes running through it than any other area. Proportionally, there are fewer disappearances in the Bermuda Triangle than in areas outside the Triangle. E) Electronic Voice Phenomena (which, like 21 grams, was the topic of a movie) is the phenomenon of hearing the voices of the deceased in the static from electronic devices. It reminds me of when people played records backwards to see if they could hear hidden messages. If you listen hard enough, you will be able to find something, regardless whether it is really there.

THE NATURE OF COINCIDENCE

Philosophies are hung like draperies from the curtain rod of coincidence. Coincidences are pointed to as evidence that some higher power is at work in people's lives, whether it be a force that is beyond our comprehension or a God who is so involved with all the tiny details of reality that he orchestrates events at an incredibly precise level. According to some New Agers, if we are in tune with the universe, coincidence will happen more often. Carl Jung heaped piles of significance upon coincidence when he called it synchronicity. All too often cosmic significance is attributed to it. When coincidences occur, people are stunned, and in a voice filled with incredulity, they say, "What are the odds of that happening?"

But there is a problem right from the onset. When those who have conflicting philosophies embrace coincidence as justification of their personal belief, then who are we to believe? A one-on-one correspondence between coincidence and any particular ideology does not exist. The events that individuals are claiming to be unique, special, and validating are nothing more than common occurrences that happen to, and are observed and remarked on by, a vast number of people.

My perception of coincidence seems to be out of line with the average. I am not amazed when I think of a friend and then see him on the street, or when I draw an inside straight several times in a row in a poker game, or even if the lyrics of a song playing on the radio are in sync with what I am doing. I am not startled when I blindly guess things right or when the parking space right in front of the pharmacy is open for me when I most need it.

My sense of intuition tells me that the improbable will occur frequently and that I will see patterns in the events around me. I play the long shot on occasion because my gut tells me that the long shot pays off now and then. The universe does not look down upon me with any special favor. It happens to everyone. I am sometimes surprised that things of this nature don't happen more often. There is nothing weird, bizarre, or supernatural about it. There are such a tremendous number of events happening in our lives on a daily basis that coincidences should happen. The odds are that they will.

The many interpretations of coincidence as meaning something significant are the result of problems of perception and a misunderstanding of probability. It is a mix of faulty math and human emotions.

I was sitting at a birthday party and a good friend of the birthday boy said, "We were born in the same month. Isn't that weird? What are the odds of that?"

One in twelve, I thought. *There are only twelve months...*

That's the main problem. We do not understand the math. There are six billion people on the planet. The number of possible coincidences that could occur between them are so numerous as to be incalculable — especially when it comes to random, unpredicted coincidences.

There's something to note, right there. When a coincidence is not predicted, the odds of it happening are not the same as they would be if someone *had* predicted it. Calculating odds after the fact is misleading. When we ask, "What are the odds of that?" after something has occurred, we are asking the wrong question. We should ask, "What were the odds that something coincidental in nature *should* happen?" Surprisingly high, actually.

No doubt, we would have remarked on *anything* coincidental (and assigned it meaning if we were so inclined).

The human mind tries to make sense of things. From the moment we are born, we start doing it. We have to figure out what all those blurs and funny noises are. We figure out the difference between real people and stuffed bears. We identify shapes and learn colors. We categorize. In our adult lives, we don't stop doing this. We continually look for order. It is no surprise that we should observe patterns around us. It is only a mistake when we assign meaning to these things when there is none.

It is frequently noted that when psychics attempt to predict or reveal information, people have a tendency to remember the hits and forget the misses. This is known as selective observation. The same thing happens with coincidence. If one notices coincidence, but doesn't take into consideration all the times that coincidences do not happen, then proper perspective is lost. If all the misses are taken into account then it becomes apparent that the odds against "coincidence" are not as extreme as they are frequently imagined.

It is not uncommon for people to tell a story about something that has happened and make it seem amazing by listing the string of events that led up to it. When they do this, they stress the fact that if certain things had not happened, the result would never have taken place. It usually sounds something like this: "If Jill's microwave hadn't broken that very day, she wouldn't have gone to the restaurant and met Bob, who later became her husband!"

It is key to recognize that *every* event in our lives has a cause and effect sequence leading up to it. When we report that sequence, it can make any event seem more remarkable than it would if it was reported without the backstory.

Our backward perspective on the story makes it sound even more incredible. We act as if everything was designed to lead up to a certain goal, when it wasn't. That's just what happened. It sounds a lot more impressive when we say, "If such and such hadn't happened, another thing *wouldn't* have happened," rather than, "This happened and it caused another thing to happen."

When things are described in these ways, they appear to be much more than they are and the coincidence myth is perpetuated. I like to express it this way: If I had not been raised in a church and had not attended certain philosophy classes in college, I would have never have been driven to understand philosophy. If I had been more successful in any of my other creative pursuits, the path of my life wouldn't have led me to where I was deeply involved in my writing, and I would have never combined it with my philosophical interests to begin the project of this book. Without that, it seems highly unlikely that I would have come across the lists of critical thinking skills, which were repeatedly drawn to my attention by various sources in my research, as if I was *meant* to find them. Without all these things coming together as they did — the principles of logic, my personal understanding of faith and reason, the various arguments for and against so many abstract subjects — I would not have come to the realization that coincidence is meaningless. What are the odds of that?

ILLUSIONS

Richard Bach, who at one time was my favorite writer, has often used coincidence in his work as justification of his worldview. In examining how he has done this, we can see the mistakes that many people make.

I remember my eighth grade teacher, Mr. Pribenow, reading the words of Richard's bestseller, *Jonathan Livingston Seagull*, to our class. It filled me with inspiration and the growing sense of possibilities that I cherished as a young boy. I doubt that Mr. Pribenow, who attended my church, would have read the book to us if he knew where Richard was going with his philosophy. With the next incarnation of his work, a book called *Illusions*, Richard would expand on the theme of possibilities to say that everything was possible. He would do so in a way that would be offensive to many Christians, by telling the tale of a reluctant messiah.

Richard Bach's love is flying. His earlier writings focus mostly on his adventures in airplanes, but it is there that we see his philosophy forming, and there we see the errors he makes, which seem small and innocuous at first, but that eventually led him down a road of muddled New Age confusion.

In his book, *Nothing by Chance*, Bach details his adventures as he flies around America charging people to ride in his biplane. Part way into the book, he lets his friend Paul use the biplane for flying practice. When Paul brings the plane in for a landing and wrecks it, he is forgiving. Generously, he gives his friend a break. "Nothing happens by chance," he says to his friend.

Bach expounds, "No such thing as luck. A meaning behind every little thing, and a meaning behind this. Part for you, part for me. May not see it real clear right now, but we will, before long."[26]

According to this philosophy, somehow, in some way, and in some fashion, there are powers behind the scenes in our lives manipulating events so that *everything* has significance. Every event in our life is another cog on a gear in a giant cosmic clockwork, ticking away towards some mysterious end.

This idea creates far more questions than it answers. Who runs the clockwork? What is the ultimate goal? If things are this intricately intertwined and intermeshed, then how does the whole thing keep from being so tangled that it comes to a grinding stop? There are too many gears in the clockwork, too many strings on the puppets.

Bach's idea is often expressed in the phrase, "Everything happens for a reason." What he (and others like him) are wrong about is the reason. Things happen because of previous events and because of our choices. They don't happen because of some unknown intentionality in the universe. That's completely backwards.

People fall into this trap with their interpretation of their experiences. They take the little coincidences and the natural progression of events in life and they turn them into hugely significant events that their philosophies revolve around.

Let's take a look at how it happens in Richard Bach's world. In *Nothing by Chance*, after Richard's biplane is wrecked, he needs to get it fixed. The flight began and ended at a small landing strip by a hangar. Not surprisingly, the owner of the airfield is an airplane enthusiast. He witnesses the accident, and because he has been working on airplanes for years, he has the parts necessary to repair the plane. There is nothing incredible about that, but Richard manages to turn it into a minor miracle.

> This was beyond any coincidence. The odds against our breaking the biplane in a random little town that just happened to be home to a man with the forty-year old parts to repair it; the odds that he would be on the scene when the breaking happened; the odds that we'd push the airplane right next to his hangar, within ten feet of the parts we needed—the odds were so high that "coincidence" was a foolish answer.[27]

Only, where else are airplane parts going to be but in an airplane hangar? The odds that an airplane is going to land on a *landing* strip by an *airplane* hangar are also good. It certainly isn't remarkable enough to deserve the attention it gets

---

26 Richard Bach, *Nothing by Chance* (New York: Avon Book, 1963) p. 67.
27 Ibid., p. 69.

here. The situation is nothing more than a natural sequence of events. If this is the basis of a philosophy, you need to back up and start over.

But Richard persists. Another mishap occurs near the end of the book. When hauling his airplane down the freeway on a flatbed trailer, the trailer starts to swerve, and the trailer separates from the truck that's towing it, ripping the hitch right off. This causes the airplane to be damaged beyond immediate repair and brings Richard's barnstorming adventures to a close. "I was disgusted," Richard says, "The lesson escaped me entirely. If there is nothing by chance, just what in God's name was this all supposed to mean?"[28]

It should be clear that it does not mean a thing, but like many of us, Richard misses the obvious and keeps digging. He gets lost in his own misunderstanding of how things happen and what makes them happen: "What were the chances of this happening, on the one time I had ever put the biplane on a flatbed trailer, on the only time she had not been able to fly herself out of a field, with a truck and a trailer that had been designed for hauling airplanes? A million to one."[29]

Later, Richard discovers that the hitch was welded into rusted iron on the truck. Well, there it is. The second you put the weight of an airplane on a trailer that is welded onto weak metal, it is likely that an accident is going to occur. But not according to the author; to him it is a million in one chance. Maybe some math lessons are in order now that he has completed his pilot training. After already explaining the weak hitch connection, Richard still refers to the trailer accident as "strange."

Sitting on the side of the road with a beat up airplane, a pilot with a truck comes along and offers to tow them. Yes, that is a good bit of luck, but certainly within the realm of possibility. Here is how Mr. Bach describes it:

> About that time I came awake to what was happening. Again... What are the chances of this guy coming along this road in this month in this week in this day in this hour in this minute when I have no possible way to tow that trailer, and him coming along not only in a truck, not only in an empty truck, but in an empty truck with a trailer hitch on it, and he happens to like airplanes but he is an airline pilot and he has days to spare? What are the chances of a lucky coincidence like that?[30]

Do you see what he has done? He has, unconsciously or not, thrown in little details that are irrelevant in order to make the whole thing seem more improbable. When he says, "In this day, in this hour, in this minute," he might as well say, "in this second, in this millisecond." With each division of time, he makes the whole thing seem more unlikely. There is nothing incredible at all about somebody driving a truck, of the truck being empty (most trucks are), or of the

28 Ibid., p. 187.
29 Ibid., pp. 187–188.
30 Ibid., p. 188.

truck having a hitch (most trucks do). An airplane pilot is exactly the kind of person who is going to take interest in a torn up airplane at the side of the road. If a veterinarian who didn't give a whit about airplanes stopped by and saved the day, that would be a little more remarkable, but not much. Let's not get carried away.

Soon after, Richard says, "I still don't know the why of the wreck, but some day I would."[31] To Mr. Bach's credit, he proposes an answer in the final paragraphs of his book. Unfortunately, the answer is unsatisfactory. Here are the relevant excerpts:

> At last, the answer why. The lesson that had been so hard to find, so difficult to learn, came quick and clear and simple. The reason for problems is to overcome them. Why, that's the very nature of man, I thought, to press past limits, to prove his freedom. It isn't the challenge that faces us, that determines who we are and what we are becoming, but the way we meet the challenge, whether we toss a match at the wreck or work our way through it, step by step, to freedom.
> And behind it, I thought... lies not blind chance but a principle that works to help us understand, a thousand "coincidences" and friends come to show us the way when the problems seem too hard to solve alone.

We have been waiting for the big answer. In the final reveal, Richard says that we have problems so we can overcome them and learn from them.

Mr. Bach's conclusion is the same conclusion as that of two other authors, Suzanne Northrop, author of *Everything Happens for a Reason*, and Mira Kirshenbaum, author of the similarly titled book, *Everything Happens for a Reason: Finding the True Meaning of the Events in Our Lives*. All three of these writers say that we have problems so that we can learn from them, and, allegedly, these lessons are part of the progress of our souls in the overall cosmic scheme of things. It seems that "everything happens for a reason" has become a religion all its own.

I do agree with one thing. We should take the events of our lives, learn from them, and make the best of them. We can take some of the worst tragedies and come away from them with something of value. We can learn what our strengths are and learn to become stronger. We can learn not to take things so seriously and thus reap many unpredictable benefits. Human intelligence and ingenuity enable us to do this. I would hope that it is what we would always try to do. However, when we learn from the events in our lives, it does not show that the universe is benevolent or that it has plans for us. It just shows that we are adaptable.

Bach, Northrop, and Kirshenbaum have all made the same mistake. They have taken the effect and called it the cause. It's easy to do this because of the ambiguity of the word "reason." It can refer to everything that led up to an event or it can refer to what is supposed to happen after an event (the goal, as it were).

---

31 Ibid., p. 190.

But it is much simpler than our New Age authors make it. Things happen because of the series of cause and effect events that lead up to them. There does not have to be any other "reason."

Even if these events were designed towards an eventual higher purpose, we are never told what it is. What is the *real* reason? What is the goal of all this so-called learning and spiritual evolving that's taking place? What's the point? What will become of us once we learn everything we need to know? That's the answer we need in order for any of this to make sense. All we are given is the promise, or maybe just a hint, of an eventual answer. It's the self-help equivalent of saying, "The check is in the mail."

In his book *Jonathan Livingston Seagull*, Richard Bach took these same ideas and elaborated on them. In subsequent books, Bach reveals more about his personal life. In one of them, Bach expresses that he really does not like practicalities. People give him advice, but he doesn't want to hear about how to manage his finances. He wants to hear lofty philosophical ideas.

When I first read this, I couldn't have agreed more. Now I wish I had thought otherwise. It would have helped if I had paid more attention to practical details in my earlier years.

Perhaps Mr. Bach should have paid attention, too, because when he got his money from *Jonathan Livingston Seagull*, he didn't take care of his taxes, and he trusted the wrong person to manage his finances. Soon, his financial situation had turned ugly. He explains in his books how it took his fiancée and future wife, Leslie Parish, to save him. She buckled down and dealt with the practical matters he had been overlooking.

There then, is the lesson. No matter how high you fly — pilot or seagull — reality cannot forever be ignored. If we interpret cause and effect as something more than what it is, we run the risk of losing sight of it. It is then that we become lost in the clouds, and our sense of direction is continually obscured.

THE GENERALITY TRICK AND PSYCHICS

The way that coincidences are interpreted is not very different from the way that generalities are interpreted. With both, significance is given to something that does not deserve it.

Even skeptics are tired of hearing themselves say it, but, despite how dull it is to hear, it remains true. Vague generalities play to the weaknesses of the gullible and work in the favor of those who practice prophecy, fortune telling, the I Ching, horoscopes, tarot readings, psychic readings, and spirit readings. Practitioners of all of the above know that if you are vague, people will read meaning into what you say. It is the age-old standby of the trickster, not to mention the guy at the party who just wants to impress you without saying anything of substance.

The tendency to attribute personal significance to a generalized description is known by several names: the personal validation fallacy, the Barnum Effect (named after P.T. Barnum), and the Forer effect, named after psychologist Bertram R. Forer.

The astrological sign is a perfect example of this. In my case, I identify with the zodiac sign of Gemini because there is a duality to my personality, just as there is with everyone else on the planet. I also fit the description of the Gemini because I value the intellect and am creative as well. But I'm also a Taurus because I am determined, patient, and persistent. I can relate to something about every astrological sign and could claim many of them for my own. There's nothing of cosmic import to it.

Psychics can use vague generalities to their advantage by making statements like the following:

"You often feel like people don't understand you."

"You wish you could achieve more."

"You feel removed from your body as if you and it are two separate things."

"You find yourself frustrated with everyday events."

"You wish you had more time to do the things you like."

"You often feel alone or unappreciated."

If someone said any of these things to me, I would be tempted to think that they were very perceptive or that they knew me well, despite the knowledge that these statements are generalities that can apply to a large number of people. Most of them appeal to things that are common to the human condition.

If a generality applies to just a tenth of the population, that's a tremendous amount of people to whom it is going to apply. Make the generalization flattering and the number increases. Psychics love to tell people that they, too, have psychic abilities. It is an appeal to the ego, and those who believe in psychic abilities are not likely to argue the point.

Psychics, it appears, are everywhere. They can be heard on the radio, seen on TV talk shows, and their books can purchased at any local Barnes and Noble. Among such today are John Edward, Sylvia Browne, and James Van Praagh.

The question is, do they offer anything of value and, more importantly, are they really doing what they say they are doing?

John Edward, who had once gotten so famous as to have his own TV show on the Science Fiction channel, is perhaps one of the most successful of these. A look at what he does can give us some insight into the techniques used by all psychics. Years from now, John will have faded from view, but there will probably be someone in the public eye who claims similar abilities. No doubt, much of what applies to John will apply to them as well. In the psychic trade, certain techniques are recycled in slightly different forms throughout the years.

John's TV show was called "Crossing Over." Armed with the generality trick, the general public's misunderstanding of probability, and a studio audience filled with people who very much wanted to believe, John Edward would step onto the stage and, supposedly, communicate messages from the dead.

Watching a recording of the show, one could see that John had several routines that he went through to establish who was communicating from the beyond. Once he identified someone in the audience who associated with the person who "passed," John made note of some commonality between them, and then, only rarely, would he pass out a tidbit of advice from the dead. Usually it was something along the lines of "watch your health" or "take care of your heart" — good, safe advice that is not going to hurt anyone. The audience members responded positively, feeling that their lost loved one was okay and in a safe place. Then the whole process would repeat. After a few shows, it wasn't even interesting enough to watch, unless you were observing technique.

Consciously or not, John is a skilled cold-reader, which means he is able to pick up clues about people's personality from their appearance, and he is able to judge from their reactions whether he is going in the right direction with his comments.

The reactions of audience members were crucial to John's performance and they were encouraged. The website where people went to get tickets for the show said, "Validation is important! Since John does not know your friends and relatives, it's very important you give feedback. A simple nod of the head, a yes or no answer, goes a long way in a reading. Please don't give more information than John asks for." These instructions were provided on a page called, "The Rules." The last sentence about not giving too much information was frequently ignored.

I saw one show where John did a celebrity reading for Gene Simmons, former front man for the band KISS. The reading did not go well. Gene did not react much and this made John's part very difficult. John expressed his frustration and nearly walked off the stage.

Another interesting bit of instruction found under "The Rules" said, "Don't get 'psychic amnesia.' John coined this phrase to describe what happens when he goes to someone in the audience and they all of a sudden forget their family tree. Bring a copy of your family tree to the show, just in case."

The upshot of this was that if John named a name and it didn't ring a bell to an audience member, John blamed the audience member. Could it be that John was guessing a random name and it wasn't the name of somebody the audience member knew? Absolutely. But it was always made to look as if the audience member was forgetful and that John was always right.

On occasion John would say something to an audience member and get a blank response. From the expression on the audience members' faces, you could tell that they did not have any idea what John was talking about. In these cases, John often said, "That's okay; take that with you." Again, the implication was that it was not John who had made an error.

I watched quite a few episodes as the show progressed and it seemed that, as it did, John became increasingly assertive, coming across with the attitude that whatever he said was completely correct and the audience members just couldn't remember all of their relatives' names. Sometimes they did forget, and when the audience member suddenly remembered, the rest of the audience laughed and John appeared to be vindicated for all of his mistakes.

It was, and is, a fascinating psychological game.

When John started a segment, he would often start by naming a date or an initial that he hoped would ring true with a member of the audience. More often than not, it did. With any initial the odds were no less than one in twenty-six (there are twenty-six letters in the alphabet) that the initial was going to match up with somebody. If he used a common letter, the odds in John's favor got even better. From there the guessing game continued.

Audience members often filled in the blanks with their own information and stories. Afterwards they reported that there was no way that John could ever have known about what was mentioned, having already forgotten that they were the ones who told the story and that John only gave them a word that triggered it.

An interesting fact is that each half-hour show was created from a six-hour taping. With six hours of material, there should be a lot that John could use on the air, even if he was just guessing.

It was odd to watch John interact with the audience while supposedly communicating with the dead. Usually the "passed" appeared to be communicating in single letters, words, or images. It was like John and the audience were playing charades with the dead.

One wonders why the information was communicated this way. If the dead were communicating from beyond the grave, why didn't they have more important things to say? Sometimes the dead issued apologies or they wanted their loved ones to know that everything was okay. While this is always nice, it would seem that someone on the other side might have access to a lot more valuable and intriguing information.

When you know everything involved, *Crossing Over* was not very impressive, especially for what it pretended to be.

At the very end of John's show, a disclaimer was flashed on the screen so fast that it was difficult to read. The last part of the disclaimer said that the material in the show was "not meant or intended to be...a factual statement in any way whatsoever." That is quite a concession.

Did John actually communicate with people who have died? No way.

Did he think he communicated with the dead, or was he taking advantage of the bereaved so that he could make money on books and a TV show? I don't know. John has an aura of sincerity about him that serves him well. Given the fact that human beings are masters at deceiving themselves, I think it is quite possible that John, from the age of a child, has convinced himself that what he does is real.

When speaking about all psychics in general, there are psychics of both persuasions — the intentionally deceptive and the self-deluded. As part of my research into this subject, I went online and looked up the phrase "confessions of a phone psychic." There were some very interesting results. In some "confessions" the psychic fully believed in his or her psychic abilities. Others did not. These two kinds of people sit side by side at the phones of psychic hotlines, answering people's questions, giving them advice, and, often, just listening to them, because sometimes that is all that the callers want.

Performing the "psychic" aspect of the job didn't seem to be truly difficult for any of the phone psychics whose confessions I read, but it was a great source of confusion for the one woman who had a strong belief in her powers. She noticed that, on some days, her abilities seemed fairly accurate. At other times, her predictions and intuitions were entirely wrong. Such days, she ascertained, were days when she was being "reverse-psychic." She was always "psychic," but somehow the magnetic poles of her ability would get swapped around and her predictions were the opposite of what they should be. What really confused her were the days when her ability seemed to flip-flop from minute to minute, hour to hour. She would be right, then wrong, then wrong, then right again. It was almost like there was no pattern to it.

What, she inquired of the psychic community, would cause this? What made these fluctuations in ability happen? Was there a way to get control of it?

Never once did it occur to her that what she had identified was the randomness of guessing. That is all she was doing, but her belief in her own abilities required her to find some speculative answer to an unavoidable situation. Her web page should have been called "Confusions of a phone psychic."

She also remarked how she could not understand how the man who sat beside her could do what he did without believing in what he was doing. How unethical it was!

Either way, we are foolish to give these people our money. If we are not smarter and savvier about such things, we are doomed to live our lives in confusion, and we run a much greater risk of being taken advantage of.

THE DEATH OF CARLOS CASTANEDA

Just as Richard Bach's work inspired me and fueled my interest in things beyond the everyday world, so did the writings of Carlos Castaneda. Carlos Castaneda is deemed by many to be the father of the New Age movement. His series of books, beginning with *The Teachings of Don Juan, A Yaqui Way of Knowledge*, catalogued his adventures and lessons with Don Juan Matus, a Yaqui Indian sorcerer.

These books were my introduction to the New Age movement. I was immediately drawn in and intrigued by Castaneda's work. He asked questions that were academic and that questioned the very nature of the mystical experiences he soon began having upon meeting Don Juan. Don Juan would laugh at his questions and then answer them with vague generalities.

Soon the old man had Castaneda taking peyote and mushrooms. The mystical experiences got wilder and the poetry more vivid.

It was here where I first encountered the possibilities of the New Age movement, although, at that time in 1979, it was not yet called that. I loved Castaneda's books because they made me feel that, if I wanted to, I could walk through walls, and I could transport myself to different worlds. All of reality would be mine to manipulate, instead of the opposite where reality held me down under its big oppressive thumb.

Castaneda, and the authors I read after him — Shirley MacLaine and her collage of UFOs and afterlives; Dan Millman's *Way of the Peaceful Warrior*, and James Redfield's popular *Celestine Prophecy* — all filled me with this notion. I was on a search for the tiny crack, the hairline fracture, between our world and a world beyond. If Shirley MacLaine could catch a glimpse of the other side, I had to have a chance.

I had a big problem with Castaneda, though — his use of drugs. How could he claim to be objective about anything or examine his experiences in a light that we could understand, if he was tripping on peyote? The hallucinogenic nature of the drug ruined his credibility.

The other New Age authors I read did not share that particular problem, but they shared a trait with Castaneda that began to bother me — they were vague. He starts off asking good questions, but Don Juan never provides solid answers. Castaneda seems to hang around just so he can figure out what the crazy old Indian man is trying to tell him.

But all of the books I read from this genre shared one maddening problem. When I set them down and walked down to the store, reality was still there. If I didn't eat, I would get hungry. If I didn't pay rent, the manager would throw me out. If I walked in front of a car, I would be injured or killed.

What was it the New Age authors weren't telling me? Where was the key that would allow me to somehow shift to an alternate or better world?

It was twenty years after I had read the first in Castaneda's series that I started searching the Internet for information on things I had not thought about for some time. Castaneda was one them. I was surprised to find that he had died. He died in Westwood, California on April 27, 1998, not far from where I lived.

I learned much about Castaneda. When I had first read his books, the Internet was not available. I did not know that he was extremely reclusive. I also did not know that there was a tremendous amount of controversy over his books. Many people said he had fabricated Don Juan.

I read the debates over these issues. Some postings claimed Castaneda was absolutely brilliant. The others said that his works were just a hoax. Not surprisingly, many of the arguments boiled down to a squabble over the objective reality of this world.

One of the most interesting works about Castaneda is called *A Magical Journey with Carlos Castaneda* and was written by Margaret Runyan Castaneda, his one-time wife. Of anyone, she had the most insights into his attitudes, behaviors, and writings. It became clear from reading her work that Castaneda had always had a weak grasp on the truth, that he was a compulsive liar, and that his main character Don Juan was a composite character, if not a fictional one.

The most revealing sentence to me, though, was one in which Margaret describes Carlos as going to work at the Mattel Toy Company and driving an old Chevrolet to get there.[32] Carlos Castaneda, like every single guru, prophet, messiah, and rock star we hear about, turned out to be a human being, nothing more, nothing less.

I looked back, and I saw what Castaneda and his merry band of New Age bandits had done to me. They had sent me chasing red herrings. On their cue, I had scrambled off looking for shortcuts that would somehow get me past the

---

32 Margaret Runyan Castaneda, *A Magical Journey with Carolos Castaneda* (Victoria B.C. Canada: Millenia Press, 1996), p. 69.

very real obstacles that stood in my way. Like the man who spends his life looking for a get-rich-quick scheme when he could be making hard-earned cash, I was so obsessed with the New Age sense of "what could be" that I wasn't taking care of what really was.

Okay you guys, I get it now, but the false hope you gave me — that was a cruel trick.

Carlos Castaneda died of liver cancer. He was roughly seventy years old. By example, and in a very human fashion, he had finally shown us the only way we can ever truly escape this reality.

POPULAR MYTHS

Throughout this book, I have been dealing the subject of how to recognize myths that have gained far too much credence and become beliefs that people are emotionally invested in. Even as I dispel these myths, new ones are being born.

You can see the myth-making machine in action. It clatters away in the office break room. It is the bid for attention. It is the exaggeration thrown in to get a gasp from the fellow employee. It is the conversation starter made to escape an uncomfortable silence. It has its roots in personal drama and in psychology.

At my day job, I audit the work of other employees. Occasionally an employee will start doing something that is against company policy and will pass it on to others; their incorrect method will spread like wildfire. When this happens, I have to send an email to the department explaining the correct way to perform a task and refer everyone to the policy and procedure. It is very similar to what I am attempting to do in this book: to fix misconceptions that have been innocently (and sometimes, not so innocently) perpetuated. What is fascinating, though, is how quickly falsehoods gain both acceptance and momentum. In the everyday world, we are surrounded by falsehoods because the human race does not have enough auditors.

If you want a quick reality check on how many things you believe to be true that really are not, take a close look at some urban legends. They are the kinds of stories that come from a friend of a cousin of an acquaintance, the stories that clutter our email in boxes. They are repeated so often that we think they are true, regardless of whether they are. An examination of them can be very revealing.

In *Curses! Broiled Again! The Hottest Urban Legends*,[33] Jan Harold Brunvand lets us know that the Mrs. Fields cookie recipe was never sold to a customer for the amount of $250 and then passed around on the Internet. (The test of this story

---

33 New York: Barnes & Noble Books, 2003.

is to bake the cookie from the recipe.) We also learn, just so you know, that a female earwig has never crawled into a person's brain and laid eggs.

Another common urban legend is that a lady killed a poodle, or some other small animal, by putting it into a microwave to dry it off. It never happened.

We have been told a vast number of things that are in fact false, but which we take for granted.

George Washington did not chop down a cherry tree and then admit to it. This was a story made up by a parson named Mason Locke Weems in the 1800s. It was published in his book, *The Life of George Washington*. The cherry tree story is often used to encourage young children to be honest, which is ironic, considering that the story itself is not true.

Hair does not continue to grow after we die.

When it comes to relationships, opposites, in most cases, do not attract.

There *are* snowflakes that are alike, in both shape and pattern.[34]

Studies show that sugar and sweets do not make children hyperactive. Sugar merely gets the blame for normal childlike behavior.

Nor does a full moon affect anyone's behavior.

The list goes on and on.

These minor misconceptions are fun to hear about, but, unfortunately, the same forces at work that perpetrate them are also at work in the larger arenas of religion and philosophical belief. Misconceptions and lies are unwittingly perpetuated on a daily basis and ignorance feeds on itself.

I would encourage us all to think, question, and examine a little more often. I have been surprised at how fun researching these things can be. It would not hurt if now and then we took off our rose-colored glasses and replaced them with microscopes, telescopes, and magnifying glasses.

REINCARNATION AND KARMA

Once I eliminated the idea of consciousness surviving death, I was forced to give up on the idea of reincarnation, as well as karma, but I did so reluctantly. I actually liked the idea of reincarnation better than the idea of immediately going to Heaven when I died. In the long run, reincarnation still offered a heaven-like goal. In the case of the Eastern religions, it was Nirvana. If I accepted some New Age thoughts on the subject, it was a union with all life forces and consciousness in the universe.

The idea of living past lives was fascinating to me. Just wondering about who I might have been and what I might have done was enough to engage my

---

34 Stephan Wolfram, *A New Kind of Science* (Canada: Wolfram Media, Inc., 2002), p. 992.

imagination and make me want to consider the possibility. Reincarnation poses intriguing questions. What might have happened to me? How could it explain the person that I am now? Reincarnation gives one the sense that he or she has played an ongoing role in the events of history.

When reading the works of authors who put down their words in print hundreds of years ago, I was often struck by how markedly their thoughts reflected my own. It was as if my own self had reached out from the past, put a hand on my shoulder, and said, "I know exactly how you feel." How could it be, I wondered, that those authors had so aptly expressed feelings and ideas I thought no one else but myself had ever felt and thought? Maybe they were earlier incarnations of me. That could explain it!

The possibility of reincarnation made the dramas of my present life seem even larger. It also gave me an out. If I messed up my life this time around, I would get another chance. Reincarnation is suited to the idea (prevalent in various mystical ways of thinking) that lessons learned are what life is all about, rather than simply being a fact of life.

As often as I entertained the idea, reincarnation was never something I could fully embrace or believe. When I noticed that living authors gave me the sensation that they knew exactly how I felt, just like writers from centuries ago had, I knew that there was a better explanation for my ability to relate to writers from the past than reincarnation. They were doing what good authors do. They were capturing elements of the human condition.

Investigation into reincarnation further dimmed my view of it. All of the evidence for it was anecdotal and a large proportion of past life remembrances came from people who were under hypnosis. People under hypnosis, as you can see in any stage show put on by a hypnotist, are notoriously subject to the subtlest of suggestions. They will try to say or do what they think will please the hypnotist. The result is that hypnotherapists who believe in UFOs have many patients who suddenly remember their abductions. Hypnotherapists who have an interest in multiple personalities have patients who suddenly discover hidden egos and patterns of past sexual abuse that they did not even know about. There is an unfortunate pattern there.

Karma, in which all wrongs and all good deeds are punished or rewarded appropriately over a series of lives, has its own set of logistical problems.

Say a person commits murder. In the next life, the person who was murdered is given a chance to get retribution, so he kills the person who in a previous life murdered him. Is that okay? Can the person who killed his murderer go into court and say, "I know I killed this person, your honor, but he murdered me in a previous life, so I don't think I should be punished?" How would one even know if he had been murdered in a previous life? If he doesn't know it, then isn't his act also an act of murder? If so, then where does it all end? Do the people involved continually kill each other over a series of lives?

Maybe karma is not so specific. The universe might arrange it so that we eventually pay for every unkind act we perform, but not at the hands of the one we initially wronged. Supposedly, according to the proponents of karma, somewhere in the cosmic computer, there is a massive database of every deed committed by everyone who ever lived. The cosmic computer arranges lives and incidents so that each and every one of these is paid back in kind, while cleverly avoiding gridlock. Believers in karma say the universe is capable of pulling this off and that it manages to escape endless cycles of retribution while doing so.

While there is a certain satisfaction in the idea of an eye-for-an-eye, tooth-for-a-tooth kind of justice, it seems highly unlikely there is a sequence of perfect movie endings in which every bad guy pays for his crimes. We will not all get to see the day in which the hero confronts the killer, and the killer (after having his life spared by the hero) falls from the cliff into a chasm of boiling lava.

Belief in reincarnation and karma originated in the East, but the New Age movement has taken these beliefs and made them its own. They have been glamorized, modernized, and mixed up with a grab bag of concepts so diverse that it is difficult even to know what to make of them now. Early Buddhists might have been taken aback by the idea of being reincarnated as an alien in a distant galaxy or as an entity from another dimension.

Although they have taken new forms, reincarnation and karma still have a strong appeal. In addition to offering interesting speculations for us to consider, they also attract us for the same reasons that the ideas of Heaven and Hell do. If reincarnation and karma were true, they would provide resolution for two of the most common complaints regarding the human condition. With reincarnation, there is the possibility of eternal existence and freedom from death. Karma can provide the justice we long for when we witness unfairness in our lives. As untruths, reincarnation and karma tell us that people so vigorously resist injustice and our mortality that, if they cannot see these things defeated, they will willingly believe in something that gives these things the illusion of defeat.

SKEPTICAL AND SCIENTIFIC

As with the previous sections in this chapter, there may be some point in the lives of those who are searching for answers that certain subjects become particularly relevant or when an understanding of the skeptical position can provide a needed insight. Below, I provide short commentaries on several topics related to science and skepticism that may be important in this way and that are commonly the source of disagreements between believers and nonbelievers.

***

The word "energy" is often abused. Psychic communication, the activities of ghosts and spirits, and many other alleged phenomena are ascribed to "energy." But when this is done, no one bothers to explain what type of energy is involved. If it truly is energy, then we should be able to measure it in some way. We should be able to identify it and classify it, just as we identify and catalog the full spectrum of color or the range of sound waves. Energy is not a force that occurs randomly or that operates by rules that someone made up on their own. When it is used as a speculative term, it means nothing.

***

Energy is only one of many scientific concepts that are swallowed and regurgitated in new forms by religionists and New Agers. Quantum physics, the study of physics at a subatomic level, frequently falls victim to this sort of treatment. People point to the Heisenberg principle and other elements of quantum physics to say, "Look, the world is not as it seems. There are things that science cannot explain." Then they extrapolate and postulate, proceeding to fill in any theoretical gaps with their notion of what they think runs the world, anything from "vibrations" to God.

Yes, events at the subatomic level have been described as miraculous, out of the ordinary, and simply contradictory to what we know about how things should work. Subatomic particles have been said to appear and disappear out of thin air. However, quantum physics is a science in its infancy. We really do not know what it will be like when it is fully grown, and we would be hasty to jump to any unfounded conclusions. Meanwhile, it speaks in a language that most of us do not understand and that many of us misinterpret.

The important thing to know is that there have been no discoveries in quantum physics that change the nature of our reality. Some findings may change our understanding of what goes on at a subatomic level, but they do not change what happens in our daily world. Reality has not dissolved around us. It does not become more permeable because we found out that a quark does unexpected things.

Even if things at the subatomic level do work in a dramatically different fashion than they do at larger levels, perhaps there is a threshold of size that cannot be crossed when it comes to the rules that affect our lives. But when I say that, I am venturing into speculative territory, and I am best off stopping there. I'll let the experts take over, and the physicist Alan Sokal will serve as their spokesperson. It speaks volumes when we learn that he has been "personally vexed by the tendency people have to draw philosophical conclusions from quantum theory, which is particularly rash given that even professional physicists find quantum theory baffling."[35]

***

Equally as mysterious as quantum physics, partially because they are even harder to be objective about, are our bodies.

Just as the mind can tell a finger to hit a key on a keyboard or a foot to move forward, it can send chemical and healing agents throughout the body. The mind can make the skin tingle or make a point on the body feel as if it has been touched. In what is called "the placebo effect," the mind, thinking it has taken medicine, can cause (within limits) the body to act as if it has.

> The placebo effect is pervasive in medical science — many people feel better after receiving a given treatment, even though the treatment has no real therapeutic component. In fact, since medical science has developed most of the treatments with a real therapeutic effect in just the last hundred years, it's been said that "prior to this century, the whole history of medicine was simply the history of the placebo effect." Studies have shown that about 35 percent of patients with a number of different types of ailments receive benefit from placebo pills (e.g., sugar pills). Placebos even help about 35 percent of patients with postoperative pain. Their effects are so potent that some people actually get addicted to placebo pills.[36]

The interior chemistry of the body can have a direct effect on the mind and vice versa. At the same time, what is ingested into the body has an effect on that chemistry. Our experiences come to us via this complex and tightly knit arrangement. When the mind and the body are so closely interrelated, it is sometimes difficult to tell where sensations originate.

When our experiences appear to be of a miraculous or supernatural nature, they are highly suspect, not only because they conflict with the substantiated knowledge we have acquired about how the world works, but because they are experienced via a system that can so easily deceive us. It is bad enough that we can fool ourselves mentally, but when our own minds and bodies team up against us, it's a double whammy that is hard to ignore. It is one of the things that make skepticism so difficult.

It is the close connection between the mind and the body that often make it seem as if supernatural and miraculous events have occurred. As removed as they might seem from each other, reports of people feeling less pain because they wear a copper bracelet on their arm, reports of miraculous healing, and reports of people feeling "ghostly presences" brush past them, are related. They all fall un-

---

35 Julian Baggini and Peter S. Fosl, *The Philosopher's Toolkit* (United Kingdom: Blackwell Publishing Ltd., 2003), p. 197.

36 Thomas Kida, *Don't Believe Everything You Think* (New York: Prometheus Books, 2006), p. 59, footnotes omitted.

der the same subcategory of personal experience — mind/body related incidents. These experiences are a frequent source of rationalizations for whatever beliefs people wish to support, but their reliability cannot be trusted.

Sometimes events of this type are described as being examples of "mind over matter," which is a phrase often used to imply that the mind has somehow changed reality. That would be amazing if there were no direct physical connection between the mind and the aspect of reality it has changed (think telekinesis), but when we're talking about the body, the mind is physically connected to it in more ways than one. In this context, the phrase "mind over matter" is misleading.

In order to yield maximum benefits, scientific terms and concepts should be used correctly.

MAGIC

It is no coincidence that many stage magicians become skeptics, from Harry Houdini, who became a relentless debunker of psychics and mediums, to the modern day obnoxiousness of Penn and Teller, who do much the same. Performing magic, learning the secrets of magic, and watching the reactions to it, teaches us a lot about why we tend to perceive things as supernatural when they are not.

As a child, I was fascinated by magic. I wanted to be able to know how it was all done and perform every illusion, from card tricks to levitating women. In high school, I took my allowances and invested in magic equipment — silk scarves, plastic thumbs, ropes, foam bunnies, decks of "shaved" playing cards, Svengali decks, linking rings, and expanding canes — until I had quite a collection.

I lost count of the number of times I saw an illusion performed and even though I knew it was a trick, what happened in front of my eyes seemed impossible. Then I would learn how it was done and be amazed at how much skill a magician must have in order to pull it off — or at how obvious the actual workings of the trick were. At times, it was harder to believe how simple the trick was than it was to believe that the illusion might have been a miracle in the first place. It was very revealing to watch a performance of the trick after I had learned the secret. The experience was transformed. It was still enjoyable, but in a different way.

When I grew older, I visited The Magic Castle, a club in Hollywood where magicians perform for magicians. The Magic Castle makes its home in a grandly refurbished old Victorian house. It has a restaurant, several bars, and stages where magicians regularly perform. The halls are filled with magical memorabilia and in the basement, there is a members-only library of books on magic. One of the highlights of The Magic Castle is a "haunted" piano. The keys on it tinkle away by themselves, played, we are told, by a ghost named Irma who will play just about any song you request of her. The piano typifies the atmosphere of The Magic Castle, which is playful and fun.

The Magic Castle is frequented mainly by magicians, but many non-magicians visit as well. The magicians never seem to tire of seeing illusions performed, even when they know how they are done. They admire the skill and presentation rather than the "magic." There are always new variations on old tricks and, occasionally, there is even a new illusion.

When you know how a trick is done, it is interesting to watch the reactions of those who do not. The sheer amazement they express would be laughable had you not once experienced it yourself. Almost inevitably there are those who want to know how an illusion is done. Magicians usually won't give away their secrets, but watch what happens when they do.

"That's not how you did it," people will respond.

"But that's exactly what I did," the magician will reply, and then repeat the trick precisely as before.

I have seen observers shake their heads and say, "No, you did it differently this time."

Even when they know the secret and have been told that they have just witnessed a trick, people will refuse to accept what they have seen as ordinary. They will remember an illusion as they thought they saw it and not as it actually happened.

I will never forget the expression of fear that came across a coworker's face when one of my magician friends made a paper clip float in midair. My coworker was from Brazil and had a strong belief in demons and spirits. She was clearly terrified. If I recall correctly, my friend felt obliged to show her how it was done.

My experience with magic has reinforced the idea that our reality is as solid as can be.

Not long ago, two friends of mine pointed me to a magic trick on the Internet. They could not figure out how it was done.

The trick was relatively straightforward. You first had to pick one of five cards that appeared on the screen. You didn't click on it. You just thought of it. The cards were all red cards, mostly royalty, or cards with many pips on them, like nines or tens.

After you chose your card, you went on to the next screen where you were shown four cards.

"Your card has been removed," the computer told you, and if you looked for your card, sure enough, it was gone.

I considered the possibility that the computer might be able to sense the movement of your mouse as you chose a card, but the catch was that you never clicked on the card, you only thought of it. Still, I thought, you might be subconsciously moving your mouse. So, I tried the trick again a few more times, moving the mouse in the opposite direction of the card I chose, moving the mouse randomly, and not moving it at all.

The trick still worked, so I tried another tactic. It seemed odd to me that rather than telling you which card you had picked, the program showed you the four cards you didn't pick. When I tried it again, I wrote down the names of the first five cards I chose. After I chose my card, I went to the next screen and immediately discovered how the trick was done.

None of the four cards shown in the second tableau was in the first set. There was no way the trick could fail.

I told my friends how the trick was done and, after having so much fun figuring out that one, I went back online and did a search for Internet card tricks. I discovered another site where a man had posted the trick I just described, claiming that it was genuinely magical. He then asked people for explanations of it. In response, he received pages of emails from people who provided a multitude of fantastic (and some clearly crazed) "explanations." The trick itself was not all that astounding. Human psychology was.

The same friend of mine who floated the paper clip in midair also performs a mentalist act in which he claims to truly read minds. I have known him since high school, and I can assure you that he does not possess a single telepathic skill. Still, people approach his wife and say, "How can you live with a man who can read your mind?"

If you watch his act, you can learn something that can also be gleaned from the card trick described above. If there is ever an extra step involved in deducing information (whether it is "magically" or "psychically"), the fact that there are extra steps is a clue that a trick is being performed.

If there were no trickery involved, a magician would say, "Think of a card." When you thought of it, he would immediately tell you what it was. He could also do it repeatedly, without a problem. Instead, after telling you to think of a card, he goes through some sort of routine in order to reveal the card. In the midst of the extra steps, he are able to glean the information needed to pull off the trick. That is one reason why psychics such as John Edward and others like him are so obviously suspect and why, in many ways, what they do is similar to what a magician does. Their method of gaining information is circuitous. If what they were claiming to do (such as talking to the dead) was genuine, it would be a lot more straightforward.

What we learn from magic applies to the entire world. When we look at the bigger picture analytically, as we would with the performance of a stage magician, we discover sliding doors, black curtains, mirrors, hidden pockets, uses of misdirection, and clouds of obscuring smoke. All about us, there are magicians who have gone unrecognized for lack of a cape and a top hat.

CHAPTER 5. ORIGINS

EVOLUTION

Before I begin an examination of Christianity, it seems fitting to address two things that those who believe in "God the creator" find nearly inconceivable. The first is that humankind has arisen from lower life forms. A study of evolution will reveal that it does not deserve the questionable status that some fundamentalists have placed upon it. The second "inconceivable" notion is that our world, with all of its minute details and grand wonders, came about from an explosion billions of years ago. The following section provides an aid towards understanding and visualizing it.

***

For years, I could not have cared less about evolution. As a Christian youth, I believed what I had been told in church — that the scientists were mistaken, that the Earth was 6,000 years old (but created with the appearance of age), that carbon dating was flawed, and that the dinosaurs had never existed.

Later, when I believed only in a very generalized sort of God, evolution did not seem to matter. If evolution had happened, it was God's method of bringing about the human race. It did not mean that he did not exist. The Catholic Church has incorporated evolution into its theology in a similar manner.

Recently, evolution has come under attack again, this time by the Protestant Christian Right. Now that I find myself on the other side of the fence, where I understand the value of science, I feel as if it is rationality itself that is under attack. This gave me one incentive for investigating evolution. Curiosity was another.

Study revealed that science and this highly debated idea of evolution was not only right, it was dead right. It took highly intelligent and observant individuals to put together the clues, form the theory, and refine it. It took people with courage to get it to where it is today.

We are still learning about specific details of evolution and probably always will be, but the main mechanisms of evolution have been solidly established. Evolution is often attacked as being "just a theory" and not "a fact." One response to this is to say that creationism is "just a faith," and so it is farther removed from "fact" than evolution could ever be. However, there is another important point that should not be overlooked, and that is that evolution is a group of ideas. A group of ideas can never be considered a fact; only single statements can be considered facts. However, the validity of all of the principles that make up the theory of evolution have been repeatedly demonstrated. If evolution is not a solitary fact, there are still tens of thousands (if not more) facts behind it. A vast amount of research has been done and mountains of data have been compiled, all of which support evolution. The general theory is widely and generally accepted in the scientific community because of this. To deny evolution after having studied it is to stubbornly insist on remaining ignorant.

Believers in God will tell you that if you want to see evidence of God, you should look at the world around you. Evolutionists can say the same, but in the final analysis, there is more in the world around us to support evolution than to support the idea of a biblical God. The following paragraphs provide examples.

The DNA of all living things is very similar. The DNA of human beings is not that different from that of insects, indicating a common heredity. We are very distant cousins to the blade of grass, the ant, and the seagull. If you want to feel a connection with all of life around you, there it is.

As it matures, the human fetus goes through many stages that reflect its hereditary background. At one point, it resembles a fish, complete with nonfunctional gill slits.

X-ray the fin of a dolphin. You will see five bones in the fins, as you would in a hand. That is because sea mammals like the dolphins were once land dwelling creatures. Not only did we come out of the oceans, but some of us went back in.

Even the wings of a bat have a five-fingered bone structure and layout similar to that of humans.

One of the principles of evolution is that if you isolate parts of a species geographically from each other, the separated groups will change and become different from the groups they are isolated from. The different races of humanity are a prime example of this.

Contrary to a common anti-evolutionary bumper sticker that says, "Fish can't walk," fish *can* walk. Our example is the snakehead fish. The fish can live out of the water for brief periods, getting around by wriggling short distances and maneuvering on its fins. We shouldn't be too quick to dismiss amphibians, either. They live both in water and on land, suggesting, quite strongly, that a transition between the two can readily be made.

The most edible parts of fruits and vegetables often carry seeds. Men, in their self-centered worldview, have often assumed that fruits and vegetables were created to feed him. From an evolutionary standpoint, the story is different. Plants that have seeds covered with edible material, which animals eat and carry around, are the plants that were more likely to survive. Therefore, seeds ended up being in the fleshy part of many plants. Apples, oranges, peas, avocados, etc., all point directly at evolution's main impetus, which is replication and survival.

A gardener I once knew, who would have been the first to argue against evolution, spent quite a bit of his time crossbreeding iris plants. By performing selective breeding, he had unwittingly echoed many of the experiments Darwin used in *The Origin of Species* to demonstrate evolutionary principles. The genetic code is variable. It can be directed towards specific traits in domestic animals and plants. In nature, it is natural selection that provides the direction.

Go through several days as a teenager or young adult and experience how powerful the sexual urge can be. Is it the result of sin or is it some test from a God who wanted to see how well we could resist temptation? It's neither. It is the result of billions of years of evolutionary programming that is so strong that sometimes no amount of faith can overcome it. Sex is so powerful because of natural selection. Those with the strongest urge to reproduce are the most likely to do so, and so that trait survives and perpetuates.

Watch young boys in line at a movie theater or a fast food restaurant. If they do not have decent supervision, they are likely to jab at each other, roughhouse, and wrestle. Does it look at all like lion cubs in the wild? It is.

Become angry, and adrenaline rushes through your system. Within seconds, you are ready for "fight or flight." Is this useful in most situations that involve anger these days? No. But it has been programmed into us over years of evolution and is difficult to escape. A God who would have designed us this way would have been incompetent.

That is not the only way in which humankind is far from being ideally designed. The eyes of the squid are wired in a way that makes a lot more sense than that of a human. Many structural improvements could be made to our joints, our bones, and our intestinal systems. Anyone who has lived past forty can tell you that the body is hardly designed to last. The number of improvements that could be made and the number of defects cannot all be attributed to "problems brought on by sin." If mankind was created in the physical image of God, then God is far from perfect.

We all know that children (animal and human alike) are not identical to their parents. If there are changes from generation to generation, and these changes occur across species, and you have periods of billions of years for these changes to keep happening, then eventually dramatic changes are going to come about, resulting in new species. One common argument against evolution states that changes can occur within species, but species cannot change and become another species. Well, just where, exactly, does the changing stop? Why should it stop? With continual variations and enough time, it is only natural that populations of creatures come about that are significantly different from their ancestors, enough to be considered new species.

Survival of the fittest is brilliantly illustrated when strains of bacteria become resistant to antibiotics. Because bacteria have short life spans, scientists have been able to use them to demonstrate evolution in the lab. In these experiments, the shorter the life span of an organism, the better, because evolutionary changes can be observed within populations of those organisms over a short period of time, instead of over millennia.

It was the very act of looking around at the world and observing some of the things above that caused Darwin to realize his theory. As a naturalist, wanting to learn more about living things, he had the unique opportunity to take notes on species of animals at points all around the world. Sailing on the English Royal Navy ship, the *HMS Beagle*, Darwin traveled from England across the Atlantic and down to South America, past Rio de Janeiro and the Falkland Islands, down around the lower tip of South America, and up to the Galapagos Islands in the South Pacific. From there the Beagle went across the Pacific Ocean, circled the lower half of Australia, jutted north then south, and made it's way around the Cape of Good Hope at the very southern tip of Africa. The Beagle then crossed the Atlantic (again) for a brief stop near South America and proceeded back up to England on a path similar to the one it had taken years before on its departure voyage. The whole trip took roughly five years.

On the voyage, Darwin carried a book with him titled *Principles of Geology*, by Charles Lyell. This book explained that the earth was very old, had changed over the years, and was continually changing even now. That might seem obvious to us these days, but the idea was revolutionary for its time. The Earth and its geology were commonly thought to be young and unchanging. Once it became evident that this was not true, then it was only a natural step to realize that it wasn't true for living creatures either. Lyell's understanding of geology opened the way for evolution.

The idea of evolution was not entirely new to Darwin, however, as it had been a topic of interest to his grandfather, Erasmus Darwin, who had discussed it with him. In 1802, Erasmus wrote a poem titled, *The Temple of Nature*, which anticipated much of his grandson's evolutionary theory, as you can see in this excerpt:

Organic life beneath the shoreless waves
Was born and nurs'd in ocean's pearly caves;
First forms minute, unseen by spheric glass,
Move on the mud, or pierce the watery mass;
These, as successive generations bloom,
New powers acquire and larger limbs assume;
Whence countless groups of vegetation spring,
And breathing realms of fin and feet and wing.

It was not until after Charles Darwin's trip around the world that he developed his theory of natural selection. Darwin's theory was remarkable, not because of the idea that "higher" species from "lower" ones, but because he explained the mechanism behind it — natural selection. Darwin was reluctant to express his findings because of their controversial nature, but he felt that they were far too important to be left unsaid.

Darwin is greatly misunderstood, just as some of the terms he used. Perhaps two of the most misunderstood terms used in evolutionary theory are "natural selection" and "survival of the fittest," which are meant to say the same thing — that those organisms which possess traits that enable them to survive are the ones who are able to procreate. These external traits (or phenotypes, as they are called) are carried in the genetic code (genotypes) of a population, and those members of a population that survive pass the traits on.

Say there are two bugs on a tree. One of those bugs looks a little more like a leaf than the other one. A bird eats the bug that looks a little less like a leaf. The bug that looks more like a leaf has offspring and so do hundreds of other of the same type of bugs in the vicinity. They all carry the genes that produce the proteins that result in this trait. They reproduce and over a series of generations, you end up with bugs that look remarkably like leaves. That is natural selection.

Far away in another field, the bugs that look more like sticks are the ones that survive.

Meanwhile, among the birds, there are some male birds that have bright plumage and some that do not. The bright feathers attract female birds and the birds with the brightly colored feathers have offspring, while some of the birds without vibrant plumage, do not. The tendency towards a certain trait is reinforced by both the male and the female of the species, the male birds that have the trait and the female birds that prefer the trait. This happens not just to one pair of birds, but throughout the population of birds, greatly reinforcing the trait. The result is a species of brightly colored birds. On it goes in hundreds of thousands of different species simultaneously.

When one looks at a chart of how the various species of animals and man evolved, it appears as if the whole process took place along narrow channels with branches at regular intervals. In reality, as life spread across the planet, evolution was occurring everywhere at once, at different rates. It wasn't a single stream. Rather, it was a vast river with many channels that mixed together, spun in eddies and whirlpools, and split up around obstacles, only to meet up with itself again.

Evolutionary change occurs as the result of simple cause and effect. It does not happen because someone says, "That bug would be safer if it looked like a leaf," nor does the bug decide that itself. People get confused by the word "selection" and think that it implies there is some sort of choice being made. This process is often misrepresented in nature shows, where it is made to sound as if a creature intended to become camouflaged. The deer does not develop a mottled pattern of its own will so that it will be less visible to predators while sitting in the shade of a tree. It is the other way around. It's a weeding out process in which those are the types of deer who survive.

The phrase "survival of the fittest" was developed because of all the confusion caused by the word "selection." Unfortunately, survival of the fittest also brings some confusion with it. Because something is fit does not mean it is superior to another, just more suited to its environment. A fish may be more "fit" in the ocean, but a monkey is more "fit" on land. There are multiple ways to be fit, resulting in many different adaptations.

There are plenty of works that detail the processes and mechanics of evolution, so I do not feel the need to go into all of them here. However, I do need to address some of the most common objections to evolutionary theory, and along the way I can touch on some interesting aspects of evolution.

Of all the objections to evolutionary theory, the objections that hold the least weight are those that say evolution is too brutal or that it is offensive to think that we "descended from monkeys" (or, more accurately, came from a common ancestor with the rest of the primates). These objections are irrelevant because they have nothing to do with the truth of evolution. They also do not take into account that we as humans are greater than our origins. Evolution does not doom us to a savage future or cause us to become "just animals." Our intelligence, will, and wisdom enables us to rise above that.

Similarly, Social Darwinism, which is when "survival of the fittest" is applied to mankind's societal affairs, is silliness. Darwin never intended the idea to be used as anything but an explanation of processes in nature.

When the emphasis is on survival and competition, as it often is in discussions of evolution, cooperation is often overlooked. From the ant to the honeybee, as well as to human beings, cooperation is a survival skill and can be just as important as any trait that makes one creature stronger than another. Such cooperation can be within a species or between two entirely different species. Either way, nature is not all tooth and claw; it also involves working together.

Life, because it is always reproducing, spreads wherever there are the resources to support it. Many forms of life fail to survive in new environments, but with mutation and genetic change occurring, life can relentlessly create new organisms until there is one that works. Then another niche in the environment is populated with life. This is how there is life at the depths of the oceans, in underwater caves, in the deserts, at high elevations, and even in bubbling hot springs. It also accounts for how life made its way from the oceans onto land, which, compared to some of the other thresholds that life has had to cross, is not quite the big deal it is made out to be. Flight, for example, has been "reinvented" many times, with insects, birds, dinosaurs, bats, flying fish, and flying squirrels.

One of the arguments against evolution is referred to as "the absence of intermediate types." The first part of this objection addresses gaps in the fossil record, stating that if species changed so much that they become other species, there should be fossils representing the stages in-between.

Part of the reason this is a problem is because fossils are hard to come by. Many animals exist in places where conditions are not right for fossils to form. Their bodies die, disintegrate, and that's it. There is no record. Meanwhile, the surface of the planet is grinding and churning, crunching up many of the fossils that have formed. Getting access to the rest is not easy either. How do we know where to dig to look for fossils, especially given the massive surface area of the planet and the fact that some fossils are buried where we can never get to them (like below cities, to cite one example)? Regardless, the more fossils we find, the more "missing links" we find. Evidence is building rather than not coming to the surface at all.

Darwin was aware of this complaint and addressed it in *The Origin of Species*. Part of the problem, as he saw it, was that there are few intermediate forms to begin with. When species change in drastic ways that result in new species, the generations between them are often small and die quickly. Species usually establish themselves in large similar groups. That is why the surface of the planet is not populated with a myriad of individually different animals that seem to blend from one form to the next.

Another objection to evolution is often expressed in the question, if evolution is true, why don't we see it happening now? Well, we *can* see it now. The examples at the beginning of this section make that known. We do not see incredibly dramatic evolutionary changes happening around us because those require spans of time longer than the individual lives we have in which to observe them. We are in the midst of evolution, not (as many think) at the culmination of it. Where it will take us and all living creatures on the planet is unpredictable.

One reason people object to evolution is simple lack of imagination. People often have difficulty comprehending how complicated beings such as ourselves could have come to be without some sort of guidance. The computer program called *Life*, which I explain in the next section, can be used to show the kinds of changes that evolution evokes. Computer simulations have been used to dramatically demonstrate the truth of evolution, and I am looking forward to seeing what we will be able to do with them in the future. With the creation of virtual worlds, like you see in online gaming, we will be able to create richer and more vivid simulations where evolutionary scenarios can be acted out. We can create virtual life forms, give them the ability to change and the resources they need to "survive," set up obstacles to their survival and create other species for them to compete with, then let them go.

The path that evolution took on our planet is one of billions of possible paths it could have taken. Objectors to evolution are often guilty of assuming that evolution was meant to lead to the human race. That's not so at all. Had there been tiny changes in circumstances and events on our planet, evolution would have taken life an entirely different way, and our planet would be populated by creatures remarkably unlike us. Computer simulations of evolution would allow us to see it re-enacted in millions of ways that never took place in reality.

My father considered himself an "opponent" of evolution and would occasionally lecture me about how evolution was impossible. He had intended, someday, to write a book about evolution called *Bits and Pieces*, explaining how the organs and glands of the body could not come about by evolutionary means because of their specific functions and because of how they interacted with each other. These organs and glands, my father said, were interdependent and could not have evolved independently. The only way an organism with these parts could function would be if the organism and all its parts were created simultaneously.

If my father had thought about the changes a growing fetus goes through, he might have seen the error in his reasoning. He failed to recognize that individual organs could serve more than one purpose and that they often do. He also missed the fact that organs can get better at what they do and they can even change their function from generation to generation. One fish uses a lung to breathe with while another fish uses it as a flotation device. The snake and other animals smell with their tongues. The frog uses its tongue to catch its food. The elephant's trunk is both a nose and a hand. As creatures evolve, organs and appendages are used in any way possible for survival. Natural selection enables such things to advance in their usefulness. They become interconnected as a natural result of cause and effect. It would be unusual if they remained separate.

We see similar changes taking place in all kinds of systems, not just organic ones. We see it in communities as people become reliant upon the services of others. We see it in language where words and phrases change, develop multiple meanings, and have different usages. Biblical authors did not understand this, so they created (or, rather, recycled an already existing version of) the myth of the Tower of Babel. The Tower of Babel is to language what the creation story is to evolution.

Similar changes are evidenced in technology and in how technologies interact with each other to form new ones. Specialization occurs and dependencies develop. We see this with ideas too. They change, are used differently, and form connections in people's minds. Complex ideas like this are often called "memes."

Even the universe is changing, evolving, and interacting with itself in unusual ways. When one hears about our continually expanding universe and the concept of entropy, it is easy to get the impression that the universe is complete and that it is moving in a straight line towards a cold and dreary death. But that is a misleading impression. As the universe continues to expand, it is very vital within, and going through innumerable cycles.

Before the planet Earth could begin to form, a star had to be born, die, and form a huge gas cloud. The atoms from that gas cloud came together and formed the sun and the planets that we know as our solar system. The elements of helium and hydrogen were present at the beginning of the universe, whereas the elements that make up the Earth were not. It requires the intense heat that occurs in the explosion of a sun to create the elements our planet is made of, which is what tells us that it came from the remnants of a dead star. This process is still going on throughout the universe. Stars are being born. Stars are dying. Solar systems come and go.

Everything that changes, evolves — geology, society, language, technology, ideas, and even the universe itself. It would be an oversimplification, but not incorrect, to say that evolution is a way of showing how change occurs in living creatures, just as it occurs in all other areas of life. Those who deny evolution are denying the reality of change, as well as the nature of change and its inevitably.

MARBLES IN A FRISBEE

I had not moved the bicycle that sat on our porch for several days because a caterpillar had crawled up one of the spokes and made a cocoon. I would have to wait until the butterfly emerged before I could ride the bike again.

Bored, I sat on the patio playing with several marbles that I bounced around on the inside of a Frisbee. It was an odd thought for a boy in the fifth grade, but I remember thinking how there was something significant about the way the marbles bounced. As a child, I could not put words to it. As an adult, I can.

Physicists tell us that matter and energy behave in certain ways in certain situations. Our descriptions of these behaviors are known as the laws of phys-ics. There are other rules and principles that go along with these laws. However, these laws do not exist as physical things. They are formulas that we have de-vised. The question of where these laws came from is often asked, and deists are quick to suggest that God put the laws in place at the beginning of the universe and everything else followed. The mistake is that this treats the laws of physics as if they exist in and of themselves. In fact, it is only matter and energy that ex-ist in and of themselves. So then, the answer to the question, "Where did these laws come from?" is that, technically, the *laws* came from us. The behaviors and properties they describe are an inherent part of matter and energy. They did not have to be "assigned" by an external source.

We often think of the laws of physics as rules in a game in which we came up with the rules and then the game was played out according to the rules that we devised. In the "game" of the universe, the "rules" were built into the shape, structure, and nature of the elements involved.

It is all too convenient to refer to the "laws of physics" as something more than concepts or descriptions because, in most discussions, this does not interfere in getting the desired results. Such is the case with the next example I am going to give.

The purpose of this example is to illustrate the answer to a common problem. The problem is that many people have difficulty understanding how an explosion, "the big bang," could result is the formation of galaxies, suns, stars, and planets, and from there, sentient life. "How can such complexity come from simplicity?" they ask. "How can patterns emerge from seemingly random chaos?"

The answer is that rules were in place. The rules (which, in the case of the universe, are an inherent part of matter and energy) are what make it happen.

Our illustration comes from a computer game that is appropriately called *Life*. It was invented by mathematician John Conway. The game doesn't really have a goal unless you create one. *Life* is more of a toy that one plays with to see what kind of results will emerge (much like real life). It starts with nothing more than some dots on a piece of graph paper or a computer screen. When very simple rules are applied to the dots, and you follow their development from turn to turn, you see amazing patterns emerge. They seem to take on a life of their own.

You can find many free versions of *Life* on the Internet. If you are so inclined, you can program your own. *Life* is often used as a beginner's programming exercise.

It is played out on a grid over a series of turns that are often referred to as "generations." On the first generation you color in some squares on the grid (whether it be on graph paper or on a computer). Each square on the grid has eight surrounding squares (the top, bottom, sides, and corners). The squares can be either blank or filled. In subsequent generations, you change those squares and the squares around them based on three simple rules, which are as follows:

1) If a square touches more than three or less than two squares that are filled, then that square will be blank in the next generation.

2) If a square touches only three filled squares, then it will be filled in the next generation.

3) If a square touches only two filled squares, then it will remain the same (either blank or filled) on the next generation.

From those meager beginnings come remarkable results. John Conway named the game *Life* because "it seems to model the way complex life forms multiply and evolve from both simple beginnings and a few rules of natural selection."[37] When watching a *Life* program in action, it is not hard to envision how random particles can evolve into patterns, systems, and life forms.

Life is just one of many types of cellular automata. Cellular automata gets it name from the fact that it takes place on a grid of "cells" and it continues "automatically" based on an established set of rules. There are hundreds of other variations of cellular automata with different rules and playing surfaces such as

---

37 From "Games" column by Scott Morris, *Omni* magazine (New York: Omni Publications International Ltd., October 1984).

hexagonal graphs and 3D computer graphs. Cellular automata are employed by scientists to simulate events in physics and biology. Some of the patterns created with cellular automata are identical to patterns found in nature, such as the designs on seashells or animal skins.

Complexity comes from simplicity. This can be seen to take place as the intrinsically simple mechanism of natural selection causes startling changes in populations of organisms. Moreover, it can be seen when simple forces such as inertia and gravity result in complicated interactions in the galaxy. It is a natural progression.

If you want a simpler example than the game of *Life*, take several different types of soil, put them into a bottle and shake them vigorously for a long time. The heavier ones will move towards the bottom, the lighter towards the top, and layers will form. When there is consistent behavior among like things, patterns will emerge. Again, it will appear as if order has come from randomness. This principle is behind the existence of solar systems and planets. It makes chemistry possible, and therefore makes life possible, which in turn makes consciousness possible.

In these processes, the concept of God is an unnecessary element. Those who contest that God was the prime mover who put the universe in action, or who assigned properties to matter and energy, are faced with the same difficulty that creationists are faced with. Their argument requires that everything begin with a complex and conscious being — God. It is hard enough to imagine the singularity that became our universe coming from nowhere, if that is, indeed, what happened. But it is even more unfathomable that a conscious entity capable of planning such a thing could have existed forever or popped out of nowhere, and then turned around and created that singularity. Adding any sort of God to the entire process complicates the matter, making it even more counterintuitive. We then have to answer the question, what caused God — something even more amazing?

In comparison to the deist's rendering of the creation of the universe, which begins with complexity, the origin of the universe that the physicist portrays makes more sense by itself because it starts simply and works upwards towards complexity. By adding God, the deist inserts another element that only creates more questions and further confusion.

I do understand that when something is difficult to believe, that doesn't necessarily mean it is false, but those who argue that it requires a lot more "faith" to imagine the origin of the universe without God, rather than the opposite, have got it backward.

Meanwhile, we can see evidence of some of the "rules" by which the universe operates in the physical world around us. Marbles bouncing around in a Frisbee are like the particles in space. Water spinning down a drain, a dust devil spinning across a parking lot, the designs that occur in a randomly stuccoed wall, all reflect the principles, inherent in matter and energy, that brought this world into existence. They illustrate how order can come from seeming chaos and complexity can come from simplicity. To the eye of the human beholder, it seems as if beauty is erupting from randomness. It can even be seen in the turning wheels of a bicycle, pedaled down the street by a young boy — a newly emerged butterfly left fluttering in its wake.

Chapter 6. Christianity Examined

Into the Fray

I am sure there are portions of the previous chapters that will leave some people very unhappy, but it is this chapter that will really get me into trouble. Here I examine Christianity. You probably will not be surprised to discover that I find it wanting. Having already found that Christianity is wrong about the origins of our universe, our world, and our species, I conclude, not too far into this chapter, that Christianity is also incorrect about the cause of our problems and its proposed solution for our problems. As such, Christianity fails from all perspectives, including both the fundamentalist and liberal viewpoints.

From there, I move on to smaller issues, in a path that is opposite to the one that I, and many others, have taken in leaving Christianity behind. Perhaps only those who have gone through the difficult and even grueling process of questioning, testing, and putting aside a belief, can understand how important it is to resolve specific issues with a religion like the ones addressed in this chapter.

The Christian God is the most prevalent version of God in America. Christian believers will most likely turn to the Bible and the works of biblical apologists to support their notion of God, regardless of how clearly I have stated my previous arguments. There are so many common arguments in defense of Christianity that share similar failings that I feel compelled to point out a thing or two.

It is not an easy task to look at the Bible from a vantage point that is free from the forced interpretations that are taught in churches. It is even more difficult when you have been raised with a certain set of interpretations, but in this chapter, that is what I endeavor to do. Just so I get on everyone's bad list, I should note that the same type of evaluation could fairly be applied to other religious texts such as the Koran or the Book of Mormon. To gain a realistic perspective on these works, one needs to treat them with a critical eye, as one would treat any other form of literature in a collegiate literary course.

I intend to show that the Bible does not make sense if you try to interpret it literally. At least the liberal Christian will agree with me on this point. The liberal attempts to avoid many complaints by saying that stories which relate atrocities are historical and are not intended to be morally instructive, while at the same time identifying other stories as mythical representations that we can learn from. But all too quickly, I will again alienate the liberal by showing that the general principles of the Bible are inconsistent. God commands many of the "historical" atrocities that occur, and some of the "mythical" stories have messages that are reprehensible. While it is often said to provide a moral guideline, the Bible actually presents an inconsistent morality.

When quoting from the Bible, I have included some concepts or stories surrounding the quoted verses so that I cannot legitimately be accused of taking the verses out of context.

It is often argued that the social context (as opposed to the conceptual or story context) of the Bible is what makes it so difficult to understand. Certain sections, it is said, were intended for people of a certain time, who were only sufficiently advanced to accept or appreciate certain ideas. According to this view, the Bible was written so that it would best communicate to people of past eras in a way that they could deal with. The theologian Calvin referred to it as *balbutive* or "baby talk."

If that's the case, then this "dumbing down" of the Bible has backfired and caused it to fail at effectively communicating to people in the present. However, it seem far more likely that the Bible conforms to the historical periods in which it was written because it was written by people from those times. Those people were not aware of how societal values would change in the future. Nor did the God, who supposedly inspired them, impart any of this knowledge. More importantly, if the Bible does not accurately depict reality or provide adequate instruction when we are asked to believe that it does, then it is still incorrect.

Justification of the Bible as being written within a certain social context is disturbing. If right or wrong is determined based on culture or a societal norm, then morality becomes relative, not absolute. If that is the case, then the Ten Commandments and the very idea of sin as presented in the Bible become pointless. Take, for example, an issue as straightforward as that of how many wives a man may have. In the Old Testament, the Bible advocates the idea of having multiple wives. In the New Testament, it does not. This was a societal change and has nothing to do with "right or wrong." Yet modern day Christianity has made it an issue of morality and therefore has put itself at odds with the very book that is supposed to provide it with moral guidance.

This division of moralities between the Old and the New Testaments is continually troublesome. The Old Testament says "an eye for an eye,"[38] but in the New Testament, Jesus tells us to turn the other cheek.[39] In this case and in others, Jesus goes against several Old Testament laws.[40] These, let there be no mistake about it, are contradictions. Somehow, what is right and what is wrong has changed. It is said by defenders of the Bible that with Jesus came a new dispensation, an era of forgiveness based on his sacrifice on the cross. I contend that, at least as far as Christianity is concerned, neither this, nor cultural and societal change, should justify a change in what is considered right and wrong or good and evil because it automatically pits Christianity against itself.

A common error of those who advocate the literal translation of the Bible is that they will often refer to the original Greek, Hebrew, or Latin meaning of a word in order to "clarify" the meaning of a biblical passage. Sometimes they manage to change the meaning of a passage with this technique. To do so is to make a concession. This very act indicates that the Bible we have before us is inadequate, that it is not clear enough, and that something of value was lost in the translation from other languages to English. By turning to the original language, a point is scored for those who argue that the Bible is not as strong a document as it is pretended to be.

The Bible has been a book of controversy for ages. I have heard it described as a very "human" book. To me that says that it has many weaknesses and that we have no other choice but to adopt a more liberal interpretation of it. Students in Bible college say that there is much debate about what it means to say the Bible is "inspired" by God. Of that, I have no doubt. A multitude of different Protestant churches has sprung up because of debates over issues in the Bible, from the importance of baptism to the method by which a person gets to Heaven. Each church focuses on different verses to defend its position, but the divisions are a direct result of the Bible's inconsistency.

The devout religionist will say that my criticisms of the Bible are invalid because God is wise in ways that are far beyond my comprehension. I answer this in the section "Smart is Stupid."

---

38 Exodus 21:23–25, Exodus 24:19–20, Deuteronomy 19:18–21.
39 Matthew 5:39, Luke 6:29.
40 See the section "Jesus in Matthew" for examples.

No matter what I say, there will be those who hold that the Christian God is a good and just God. Some believe that God can do whatever he wants, as Paul says (Romans 9:20–21): "Nay but, O man, who art thou that repliest against God? Shall the thing formed say to him that formed it, Why hast thou made me thus? | Hath not the potter power over the clay, of the same lump to make one vessel unto honour, and another unto dishonour?" Unfortunately, a God who acts in ways that are opposite to what you and I would think of as kind and just cannot fairly be said to be kind and just. These words only have meaning when used in a human context with human definitions. By saying that God can do anything and still maintain the qualities of "kindness" and "justness," one renders the terms meaningless. There must be a uniform criterion for what those words mean. Fair is fair. When these conditions are not met, the Christian God instantly has permission to commit any atrocity he wants without question, and any argument against him is casually dismissed.

By pointing out many of the discrepancies and problems with the Bible, I am committing no blasphemy. It is only my conclusions that are blasphemous. The Bible, as we know it, has been under scrutiny and debate for hundreds of years. At any number of Church-approved colleges throughout the country, the issues I discuss here are being debated among theologians and future ministers. On the Internet these questions are openly debated by all types of people.

For what some claim to be a crucially important document, far too many people remain unaware of the criticisms against it. These same people do not know how obvious the problems with the Bible are or how one can discover them with no more than a small amount of reading and a little thought.

It is unfortunate that these problems do not usually make their way down to the general public from those behind the pulpit. Perhaps preachers are trying to protect their congregations from things they think will cause them doubt. Maybe they think that people cannot handle it. They might also think that this is all background information that the average person does not need to know, but with the sin of omission, they have turned their religions into half-truths. When I discovered these problems, I felt as if I had been deceived, as if crucial information had been denied me, as if the truth had been edited and censored so that I would be more likely to conform to Christianity.

Why is it that those who learn this information do not turn away from religion altogether? Well, some do. Others fall prey to the various traps that faith captures people with, including fear, a desire to do right (but a lack of knowledge of how to properly do so), lack of education in areas other than theology (which creates tunnel vision), and lack of critical thinking skills.

Another thing that happens is that people try to extract spiritual lessons from biblical passages and, in doing so, they turn the verses into metaphors and poetic representations. The moment they do this, they lose sight of the factual content and it becomes very easy to overlook any underlying problems of accuracy, factuality, and consistency. In the mind of the believer, these problems become nothing more than distractions, and the seriousness of these concerns goes unrecognized.

Believers should be aware of problems with the Bible and with Christian theology and, if they can, resolve those problems to their own satisfaction or continue to hold them as open questions. To choose the Christian faith without this information is to make a decision without being properly informed about what one is choosing.

CHRISTIANITY DISSECTED

In the following criticism of Christianity, I examine the basic beliefs of Protestant Christianity. While it cannot allow for all versions of Christianity in terms of doctrinal specifics, the principles spelled out here apply to most and show where severe failings arise in Christianity as a whole.

The basic premises of Christianity are as follows:

1. God created the universe, the Earth, and man.
2. Humanity has free will and chooses to sin and disobey God.
3. For this sin, humanity is deserving of punishment, specifically Hell.
4. God came down to Earth in the form of Jesus.
5. Jesus died on the cross as payment for humanity's sins, so that humankind would no longer have to suffer the punishment for sin.
6. To gain salvation (to avoid Hell and go to Heaven), an individual must believe all of the above and ask for forgiveness for his or her sins.

I will examine these premises as I go through portions of the Bible.

The biblical book of Genesis begins with the words, "In the beginning God created the heaven and the earth."[41]

Many ministers like to stop at word four. "In the beginning God." They do this to make the point that everything started with God.

That, itself, is problematic.

---

41 All verses quoted from the King James Version of the Bible. Some verses will be grouped into paragraphs for the sake of readability. In those instances, verses are separated with the "|" character.

God, according to the Christian religion, is all powerful, all knowing, and exists everywhere. He is the most complex and amazing being that ever has or ever will exist.

Some who tell you this will then turn around and tell you that mankind must have been designed. They'll tell you that mankind is so complex and amazing that he could not have appeared or emerged without a creator or a guiding hand. Immediately they have contradicted themselves. They have no problem believing that the most complex and amazing being of all has always existed and was not designed, but they insist that a less-amazing being — man — must have been designed.

The Bible was written a long time ago by authors who did not know what we now know about the universe, so they recorded what had been established via oral tradition, the biblical story of creation. To take that literally, when we have evidence to the contrary, puts the fundamentalist believer at odds with science and reason. The liberal is willing to accept that the description of God's creation is a metaphor, and he thereby escapes such a contradiction, but instead is left in a no man's land. Now he is faced with a predicament that the fundamentalist finds unbearable: if we can't take everything literally, how do we know what to believe and what not to believe?

Either way, the role of God as creator is up for debate.

Enter humanity.

To say that humankind was created presents another problem. Why was he created? Did God need a friend? Did God need someone to love or someone to worship him? Those explanations do not work because God should not need anything. God should be complete in and of himself. Otherwise, he is not perfect.[42] The introduction of man and all the dramas that will ensue as a result of his creation are pointless. It is folly for an all-knowing, all-powerful God to act out the whole play of humanity's creation, existence, and continuation in the afterlife, especially if God knows the outcome of everything in the first place. Here again, God's omniscience, a trait usually attributed to the idea of a personal God, gets in the way.

Regardless, humankind is created and soon after falls from grace.

The biblical account of it is interesting.

In Genesis 2:9, God creates the tree of life and the tree of knowledge of good and evil. In verse 17, God tells Adam that he should not eat from the tree of knowledge of good and evil. Adam is told that on the day he eats from it, he

---

42 "Be ye therefore perfect, even as your Father which is in heaven is perfect" (Matthew 5:48).

shall "surely die." You probably know the rest of the story, but it does not unfold exactly as it is often portrayed.

Adam and Eve were innocents. They did not know the difference between good and evil. They would have to eat from the tree to get that knowledge. The only way they knew that eating from the tree was something they should not do is because God told them so.

Not too long after, the snake told Eve that eating from the tree would not have the results that God said it would. "Ye shall not surely die," the snake said, "For God doth know that in the day ye eat thereof, then your eyes shall be opened, and ye shall be as gods, knowing good and evil" (Genesis 3:4–5).

Adam and Eve were, in a way, very much like children, who must sometimes learn from their mistakes. At some point, virtually all parents are faced with a situation where they tell a child to do something and the child disobeys. A good parent knows to discipline appropriately, forgive the child, and move on. Not so with God and the human race.

The first sin of humankind is met with harsh punishment that has little to do with the crime. In addition, the punishment is applied to future generations who did not commit the sin! God does this to Eve and all her descendants by causing childbirth to be painful. "Unto the woman he said, I will greatly multiply thy sorrow and thy conception; in sorrow thou shalt bring forth children" (Genesis 3:16).

God punishes man as well.

> "[C]ursed is the ground for thy sake; in sorrow shalt thou eat of it all the days of thy life; | Thorns also and thistles shall it bring forth to thee; and thou shalt eat the herb of the field; | In the sweat of thy face shalt thou eat bread, till thou return unto the ground; for out of it wast thou taken: for dust thou art, and unto dust shalt thou return" (Genesis 3:17–19).

Adam and Eve do not physically die on the day they eat the fruit of the tree of knowledge. Theologians will tell you the death that Adam and Eve died was a spiritual one. Because of this spiritual downfall, all future generations of humankind are in need of salvation.

This hardly seems fair, yet it is an "ethic" that is utilized by God throughout the Bible. The sins of the father become the sins of the son. We must suffer for what our parents and ancestors (many times removed) did, even though we never had any control over it.

This is the doctrine of original sin, reiterated by Paul in Romans 5:12: "Wherefore, as by one man sin entered into the world, and death by sin; and so death passed upon all men, for that all have sinned."

A God that punishes future generations for the crime of the parents is not a fair and just God. One argument against this states that any human in Adam and

Eve's place would have done the same. The actions of Adam and Eve, it is said, reveal the sinful nature of everyone. If that is true — if every person is destined by his or her nature to make the same kind of mistake — then free will, once again, becomes meaningless. We become victims of human nature, which God himself created.

If there is any validity to the notion of free will, then every human being should have a chance, as Adam and Eve did, to see if he or she can live without disobeying God. If none of the billions of human beings who have existed, or who will exist, are capable of doing so, then the flaw lies not with us individually but with our design, and therefore with the designer, God himself.

The fundamental premise of Christianity that humankind is in need of salvation is based on these events and these ideas. It fails miserably, thereby invalidating all that follows.

Even in regard to the idea that Adam and Eve's sin should have no effect on future generations, the Bible contradicts itself. In the book of Ezekiel, the prophet announces "the word of the Lord."

> "Yet say ye, Why? doth not the son bear the iniquity of the father? When the son hath done that which is lawful and right, and hath kept all my statutes, and hath done them, he shall surely live. | The soul that sinneth, it shall die. The son shall not bear the iniquity of the father, neither shall the father bear the iniquity of the son" (Ezekiel 18:19–20).

The book of Deuteronomy repeats this sentiment. In a list of commandments it says, "The fathers shall not be put to death for the children, neither shall the children be put to death for the fathers: every man shall be put to death for his own sin" (Deuteronomy 24:16).

There is no consistency.

An apologist might argue that the principle is different when God deals with humankind as opposed to when people are dealing with each other, but such logic is the result of a "God can do anything He wants" philosophy, which, as explained at the beginning of this chapter, is self contradictory.

Let's return to the story of humanity's "fall from grace." In most sermons, the following verses are glossed over:

> And the LORD God said, Behold, the man is become as one of us, to know good and evil: and now, lest he put forth his hand, and take also of the tree of life, and eat, and live for ever: | Therefore the LORD God sent him forth from the garden of Eden, to till the ground from whence he was taken. So he drove out the man; and he placed at the east of the garden of Eden Cherubims, and a flaming sword which turned every way, to keep the way of the tree of life (Genesis 3:23–24).

Hold on a minute! Are you telling me that if Adam and Eve had eaten from the tree of life before they ate from the tree of knowledge, they would have become immortal and like God himself? If that's the case, then Adam and Eve's big mistake wasn't so much eating the fruit, as it was a mistake of *when* they ate the fruit. They should have eaten the fruit of life *before* they ate from the tree of knowledge.

After reading this verse, it seems that the snake wasn't lying to Eve at all. If she had eaten of the tree of life, she would not have died. It is also apparent from this verse that the snake was right about the fact that God was afraid of Adam and Eve gaining the knowledge of good and evil *and* afraid of mankind becoming immortal like him. It says so, right there in verse 23. This changes everything!

In Sunday School I was taught that Adam and Eve were thrown out of the Garden of Eden for eating the fruit of the tree of the knowledge of good and evil, but the Bible reads differently. It does not say that Adam and Eve were thrown out of Eden for their disobedience. (The punishment for that was painful child-birth and having to till the ground for food.) Adam and Eve were thrown out because God did not want them to become immortal! That is a lot different from the reading we normally hear.

Metaphor or not, this whole introductory story — which is a basis for Christianity in that it tells us why mankind is in need of salvation — is inherently nonsensical.

So far, the Bible has told us that mankind was created by an unfathomable God for unfathomable reasons, and that mankind is sinful, which is the cause of all of his problems (a rather cynical conclusion). In addition to the punishment for sin that mankind must suffer on Earth, he must also suffer the punishment of Hell. According to Christianity, the solution to these problems is provided by Jesus Christ. Jesus is "God's son." He is, quite literally, God in human form walking the face of the planet.

The presentation of Jesus as God on Earth presents quite a predicament.

Surely this was not done so that God could understand what it was like to be a human being. Such an attempt would be doomed to failure. God, in human form, would know some of the physical sensations of being human and he could (as described in the gospels) feel the pain of a torturous death, but he could not know what it was like to feel and think like a human being because of his innate divinity. He could never know the doubt, uncertainty, confusion, and feeling of powerlessness that is part of the human condition. He could never demonstrate the faith that he demands of humankind because he always knows himself to exist!

The dilemma created by God taking on human form creates huge theological problems. We are given some insight into this through a dialogue between Jesus and the Pharisees as related in the Gospel of John.

> The Pharisees therefore said unto him, Thou bearest record of thyself; thy record is not true.
>
> Jesus answered and said unto them, Though I bear record of myself, yet my record is true: for I know whence I came, and whither I go; but ye cannot tell whence I come, and whither I go. | Ye judge after the flesh; I judge no man. And yet if I judge, my judgment is true: for I am not alone, but I and the Father that sent me.
>
> It is also written in your law, that the testimony of two men is true. | I am one that bear witness of myself, and the Father that sent me beareth witness of me.
>
> Then said they unto him, Where is thy Father? Jesus answered, Ye neither know me, nor my Father: if ye had known me, ye should have known my Father also (John 8:13-19).

The Pharisees have accused Jesus of invalidating his own words by bearing witness of himself. As I explained in the section "Fallacies and Critical Thinking," they are right; this is flawed logic. In John 5:31, Jesus himself agrees with this. He says, "If I bear witness of myself, my witness is not true."

So far, so good; but then Jesus does what he says is unacceptable. He tries to get around the issue by saying that God bears witness of him, but that is where it falls apart. Jesus claims to be the God that speaks in his defense, so in essence, Jesus is still testifying on his own behalf. It is quite the conundrum.

Jesus doesn't stop there. He poses the question that the Pharisees are most likely thinking. "Where is this God that speaks for you?"

"Right here," Jesus says in answer to his own question, "I am God [the Father]. If you had recognized me, you would have recognized God."

He has done nothing more than repeat the same argument, going around in circles to dizzying effect. Jesus himself is presented as giving a perfect example of how the undisciplined and irrational mind works.

He digs his hole deeper. In verses 54 and 55 of the same chapter, he repeats the same invalid argument, and for added effect, he sneaks in an insult and calls his accusers liars.

"If I honour myself, my honour is nothing: it is my Father that honoureth me; of whom ye say, that he is your God: | Yet ye have not known him; but I know him: and if I should say, I know him not, I shall be a liar like unto you: but I know him, and keep his saying" (John 8:54-55).

In John 12:49-50 Jesus says the following:

"For I have not spoken of myself; but the Father which sent me, he gave me a commandment, what I should say, and what I should speak. | And I know that his commandment is life everlasting: whatsoever I speak therefore, even as the Father said unto me, so I speak."

Given that Jesus is God the father, then in these verses Jesus is reporting that he tells himself what to say.

The concept of the Trinity has always been a problem for Biblical scholars and Biblical apologists alike. Frankly, it is confusing enough with the dual identity of God the Father and God the Son. We don't need the addition of the Holy Spirit to make it anymore so.

When Jesus is crucified, he says, "My God, my God, why hast thou forsaken me?" (Matthew 27:46)[43] It is a confusing statement. The pastor of one church I used to attend says that at the moment all of the sins of mankind were placed upon Jesus, God the Father turned away from him. No matter what interpretation you give it, it remains puzzling. Here you have God talking to himself while turning away from himself. He is also simultaneously everywhere at once while managing to sacrifice himself to himself. If you choose to believe that this actually happened and that it was part of a larger miracle, then you must not only leave rationality behind, but you must also reject it in regard to your philosophy.

I hope that it is now clear, for those who did not see it previously, that God taking human form presents some contradictions.

The reason for God coming to Earth and dying on the cross, and then being resurrected, was to solve the problem of mankind's sin and separation from God.

In the Old Testament, man atones for his sin by making blood offerings to God, sacrificing animals on an altar and then burning them, a primitive ritual not unlike those performed for gods of many other ancient religions. It's lucky for the people of those times that there weren't animal activists around.

I suspect that by the time that Jesus supposedly arrived, people were beginning to have doubts about these rituals. It was then that someone came up with a clever solution. Why not have one sacrifice that will make good for all the sacrifices? Wrap it up with a neat little theology, alter a few other rules that have become too restrictive and tiresome (like strict observance of the Sabbath), and you have New Testament Christianity.

In the New Testament, Christ is presented as the final and ultimate sacrifice for all of humanity's sins. One wonders why this wasn't just done in the beginning. It would have saved a lot of livestock.

What Jesus went through (especially if you accept the Mel Gibson account) was horrendous. The burden of all of humanity's wrongdoing being laid upon one's shoulders would not be easy to bear. But no matter how bad it was, the math does not add up. One day of the most extreme torture should not be able to pay a debt that would otherwise require billions of human souls to suffer an eternity. Something is out of balance in the equation.

---

43 See also Mark 15:34.

Supposedly, one weekend later, Jesus rose from the dead.

Christianity tells us that everyone is sinful and in danger of hellfire. To escape this fate, we need to believe all of the above. Depending upon whom you talk to, or which Bible verses you put the emphasis on, you may also need "works" (moral behavior) in order to make it to heaven. This "faith versus works" debate is the source of many a conflict between Christians. If you do not think this is an issue, visit several different churches and bring it up. You may even find fiercely different viewpoints within one congregation. Because of differing views of these doctrines, there are Christians who think that other Christians are going to Hell.

The idea of salvation through faith alone is primarily a Protestant idea and is one of the reasons why the teachings of Martin Luther, whose protests against the Catholic Church resulted in the creation of the Protestant Church, were so controversial. Incidentally, one of the initial complaints against the idea of salvation through faith alone is the same complaint lodged against atheism today. What reason do we have for acting morally, detractors ask, if acting morally is not obligatory?

The Catholic faith has many requirements for salvation in addition to faith, including baptism, the avoidance of mortal sins,[44] membership in the "one true church" (the Catholic Church), and confession of sins (via a priest). While some Christians in the United States may say that other Christians are going to Hell because of differing views of certain doctrines, in some parts of the world Catholics and Protestants kill each other because of differences over doctrines like these.

In addition to the "faith versus works" argument, there is the closely related issue of whether or not a person can lose salvation. The idea that you cannot lose your salvation is sometimes referred to as "Once Saved Always Saved" (OSAS) or "Magic Ticket" Christianity. The problem with it, as hinted at by the "Magic Ticket" label, is that if a terribly despicable criminal finds God at the last instant, he or she is saved. Meanwhile, someone who has led a good life, and whose main crime is to not believe in a religion that doesn't even sound plausible, is destined for Hell. Belief, the silliest of all requirements, is held as the primary requirement.

Christianity says that mankind needs salvation and the solution is belief in Jesus (and maybe moral behavior as well). What Christianity has managed to do is to create an imaginary problem and provide an imaginary solution.

---

44 Jesus said that there is only one unforgivable sin, blasphemy of the Holy Spirit. (See Matthew 12:31–32, Mark 3:28–29, and Luke 12:8–10.)

HEAVEN AND HELL

As a concept, Heaven is not unique to Christianity, but it is a basic tenet. The idea of a place where there is no cruelty, no physical pain, and where our bodies are immortal, is attractive. Heaven sounds great, but is it feasible?

Things get tricky right away if you say that Heaven is a place of eternal happiness.

In order for us to experience happiness, we must occasionally experience moments of sorrow and unhappiness. Many believers are fond of pointing this out in day-to-day life, but what about when it comes to eternity? It should be true there as well. Heaven is supposedly bereft of pain and sorrow, but if happiness cannot be had without occasionally experiencing them, then eternal constant bliss becomes impossible.

The idea of heavenly streets of gold[45] demonstrates this principle in a materialistic way. Gold is valuable on Earth because it is rare. If gold is so abundant in Heaven that the streets are lined with it, then the glamour of it is gone. If happiness is all there is, then it ceases to be happiness.

Maybe in Heaven there are various states of bliss that prevent us from become painfully bored, which is a potential problem given the Christian description of Heaven. Perhaps there is no sorrow in Heaven, but there are moments of melancholy and sadness mixed with larger periods of happiness. Possibly our psyches could be rewired so that happiness is not relative and can become a permanent state. That's a lot of maybes.

The idea of constant happiness presents more difficulties when you realize that loss and sadness are inevitable. They come with the passage of time. Even if all moments are good, we may hope for a better moment, or regret that a moment has passed. The only way to avoid this is stasis, where nothing changes, and that would be a prison.

Our individual personalities create a larger problem. If Heaven is filled with all the people who claim they are going there, it could not possibly be a good and pleasant place until many of those people first underwent a major personality change. Perhaps that is one of the first steps upon arrival at the pearly gates, that our psychologies are magically transformed. I think that might render many of us unrecognizable.

If we could be rewired in such a way, then it would not really be *us* who live forever, but us minus our flaws, which is an entirely different thing.

I have asked it before, and it comes up here again. If we can be changed instantly into better beings, then why go through all the rest of this drama in the

---

45 Revelation 21:21.

first place? We will all be far short of perfect at the time of our demise and supposed transformation. Why do all this work when, no matter how far we get and how far we have to go, the rest will be done for us?

That we could all get along together would be the biggest miracle of all.

Even with perfect personalities, there would still be plenty of room for conflict. Two beings, both in no way flawed, can want different things. As when a married couple wants to spend time together but does not want to spend that time engaged in the same activity, there is a conflict although neither party is in the wrong.

I often notice, when people are given the option to create anything they want in an artistic venue, that they not only create different things but, of their own choosing, they often create things that are dark and depressing. People choose to go to horror movies when they are showing in the same theater as a comedy. If we can have anything we want in Heaven, then here too is an aspect of being an individual that has the potential for conflict regardless of where we are.

Another problem presented by the conditions of Heaven is that one would think we would have free will there. If we still have free will, and we should, in an ideal state, then we must also be able to conceive of and do something against God's will. Satan was supposedly thrown out of Heaven for the sin of pride. There is nothing to prevent that from happening to any one of us on the other side of eternity.

Much of what makes us human, and what makes us so value our existence, is not possible in a place of constant happiness. As long as there is consciousness, individuality, and free will, there will always be conflict, sadness, and loss. It is a direct, unavoidable result of being aware.

The only way to escape it is oblivion. Just as most people are not in a rush to get to Heaven, I am certainly not in a rush to get to oblivion, but it is good to know that there is nothing more peaceful than nonexistence. Heaven is not possible. Eternal peace is.

Atheist friends of mine have expressed that coming to terms with the idea that "once you die, that's it," was the most difficult obstacle they had to overcome on their path to becoming nonbelievers. Once heaven, reincarnation, and any other form of continued individual consciousness are eliminated, each person must find his own way to deal with this. My solution is twofold, to realize that eternal consciousness might not be a good thing, and to realize that nonexistence is the only state of true peace that could ever be achieved. Once you are gone, it is not going to bother you in the least. As I implied in "The Soul," it also helps to get over yourself. A little humility is realistic in this case. It is not important that each and every consciousness continue for all eternity.

One of the best arguments against Heaven is its opposite, Hell. As long as there are suffering souls and we are aware of it, then if we are caring and considerate, we can never be truly happy.

There are a great number of beliefs about Hell and what it is like. Up for debate is the length of time it lasts, whether or not there is constant physical pain, and if there are worms that eat at your body forever. Are Satan and his demons there torturing people or are they so busy enduring their own pain that they are unable to inflict it on others? There are also gentler versions of Hell, where it is neither eternal nor a place of constant physical suffering. Some suggest that Hell is nothing but separation from God, which is so sorrowful, lonely, and hard to bear that no other suffering is needed.

Other doctrines have more than one Hell, some splitting it up into two places, one for Satan and his cohorts, another for the souls of humans. In some scenarios, a person may find himself in Hell immediately after death. In others, this doesn't happen until Judgment Day. Where souls spend the time between this world and the next also varies by belief system. It may or may not include Limbo or Abraham's Bosom.[46]

Anyway you have it, Hell is a terrible place and/or condition, to be avoided.

The following words about Hell come straight from Jesus:

> So shall it be at the end of the world: the angels shall come forth, and sever the wicked from among the just, | And shall cast them into the furnace of fire: there shall be wailing and gnashing of teeth (Matthew 13:49–50).[47]

> When the Son of man shall come in his glory, and all the holy angels with him, then shall he sit upon the throne of his glory.
> And before him shall be gathered all nations: and he shall separate them one from another, as a shepherd divideth his sheep from the goats.
> And he shall set the sheep on his right hand, but the goats on the left. [Verses 34–40 say why the "sheep" on the right are good.]
> Then shall he say also unto them on the left hand, Depart from me, ye cursed, into everlasting fire, prepared for the devil and his angels. [Verses 42–45 say why the "goats" on the left are bad.]
> And these shall go away into everlasting punishment: but the righteous into life eternal (Matthew 25:31–46).

> And if thy hand offend thee, cut it off: it is better for thee to enter into life maimed, than having two hands to go into hell, into the fire that never shall be quenched.
> Where their worm dieth not, and the fire is not quenched (Mark 9:43–44).

Jesus repeats the last verse two more times, but he substitutes feet and eyeballs for the hands, saying that it is better to be without them than to be in Hell (Mark 9:45–48). He makes it very clear that Hell is eternal (everlasting punish-

---

46 Luke 16:22.
47 See also Matthew 8:11–12, 13:41–42, and Luke 13:28.

ment!), very unpleasant, fiery, and filled with worms that do not die. We hope that Jesus is not being literal about the self-mutilation.

By the way, the phrase, "where *their* worm dieth not," as opposed to "where *the* worm dieth not," is correct. "Their" worm implies that the maggots belonging to the dead do not die (sorry, it wasn't my idea).

Another verse about Hell can be found in Revelations:

> And the sea gave up the dead that were in it, and death and hell delivered up the dead that were in them; and they were judged every man according to their works.
> And death and hell were cast into the lake of fire. This is the second death.
> And whosoever was not found written in the book of life was cast into the lake of fire (Revelations 20:13–15).

Hell is the destination of man if he fails to believe in the right thing. That a simple choice of belief alone should lead to the worst of all possible consequences seems to me, to be far too harsh and unforgiving.

Even if man did have free will (it is hard to see how he does, given the Christian doctrines of predestination and God's omniscience), then it is still an extreme punishment. Even the most vicious and terrible of criminals, name any example, would have paid for his or her crimes after several billion years. As an alternative, why not just wipe the evil soul from existence? Apparently, God has the same lust for vengeance that humankind does, and it cannot be sated. Hell, then, becomes a measure of God's cruelty. If it is eternal, then it is unjust, and the Christian God has proven to be an unjust God.

Even if it were not eternal, Hell would have to have levels (like Dante's inferno) for some justice to be served. That everyone should get the same punishment regardless of how he or she lived is unfair.

Incidentally, with Hell you run up against the same problem you encounter with Heaven. For the conscious being, constant misery is just as infeasible as constant happiness.

Another problem with using Hell as a consequence of sin, or the refusal to accept God, is that it minimizes the value of free will.

God could say, "Love me or don't love me. Do whatever you want." That would enable complete free will. But saying, "Love me or go to Hell," is like saying, "Do what I want or I'll shoot you." It's a choice, but not much of a choice. If I did believe in Hell, I would have a tough time loving a God who offered it as the only alternative.

I once believed in Heaven and Hell, but now I find it hard to look at these ideas and not see them as childhood fantasies. Like the ideas of reincarnation and karma, they feed on humankind's fear of death, the desire for justice, and the not-always-honorable desire for retribution. Simultaneously, the threat of Hell and the reward of Heaven provide both positive and negative reinforcement for a variety of belief systems. How very persuasive.

CREATION

Over the next few sections, I will provide commentary on quite a few quotations from the Bible. I'll begin with the biblical account of creation.

Day One (Genesis 1:2–5)

On day one, God created light, which he called day, and he separated the light from the darkness, which already existed. This darkness, which was now separated from day, he called night. We will return to this.

Day Two (Genesis 1:6–8)

On day two, God created a firmament to divide the water in the oceans from the water in the sky, and he called this firmament Heaven. If you're like me, you're probably wondering, what's a firmament? Well, the verse says that the firmament, this division between the waters, is Heaven.

"And God made the firmament, and divided the waters which were under the firmament from the waters which were above the firmament: and it was so. And God called the firmament Heaven."

You'll notice that this does not describe the Heaven we so often hear about, the place we are going to go to when we die. Nor are the clouds in our sky exactly separated from the water on the face of the planet by any sort of barrier. Some defenders of these passages state that a firmament is nothing more than an "expanse," but that does not really match up with the description given. What this image of a firmament does match is a picture of the world as understood in ancient times. In ancient times, it was thought that there were dome-like arcs over the planet where the stars or the clouds were placed. The situation in this verse fails even to match that model accurately, but is closer to that than what we know today to be true. In short, according to this verse, God spent a day creating something that does not exist.

If one is paying attention to the scriptures, it is evident by the time we have gotten to verse 7 that this must be a poetic rendering of how the planet came into being. The material presented is not accurate, scientific, or factual. The conservative fundamentalist has a lot to explain. The liberal Christian, while willing to accept this as a mythic story that signifies a greater truth — that God created the world in some manner (not matching the specific method described here) — has some problems as well. If portions of the Bible are mythical, then the liberal must evaluate which portions are to be taken at face value and what is to be taken as myth. They are stuck with the dilemma that all people of faith face — there are too few criteria for what is true and what is false.

Day Three (Genesis 1:9–13)

God separated the seas from the dry land. He commanded the earth to bring forth plant life, and it did.

Day Four (Genesis 1: 14–19)

God created the sun, the moon, and the stars. Here is how it reads:

> And God said, Let there be lights in the firmament of the heaven to divide the day from the night; and let them be for signs, and for seasons, and for days, and years:
>
> And let them be for lights in the firmament of the heaven to give light upon the earth: and it was so.
>
> And God made two great lights; the greater light to rule the day, and the lesser light to rule the night: he made the stars also.
>
> And God set them in the firmament of the heaven to give light upon the earth,
>
> And to rule over the day and over the night, and to divide the light from the darkness: and God saw that it was good.
>
> And the evening and the morning were the fourth day.

Do you see any problems? There are several. The first problem is that God puts the sun, the moon, and the stars in the firmament called Heaven. Unfortunately this firmament is described in verses 6 and 7 as being *between* the oceans and the atmosphere. If this description is to be believed, then above the ocean are the sun, the moon, and the stars, and above that there is a bunch of water, supposedly the clouds and the upper atmosphere.

This model now matches the ancient description of the heavens as dome-like arcs over the planet where stars, the sun, and the moon sit, a description we know does not match reality.

The next problem is that the stars and heavenly objects are described as being "for signs." This is sometimes used as a defense of astrology and horoscopes. For the conservative who thinks belief in astrology is a sin, there is a conflict.

Bigger problems await us. God created light on the first day, but he did not create the sun and the moon until the fourth. This would be fine except that, on the first day, "God called the light Day, and the darkness he called Night." Somehow, there was day and night without the sun and the moon. Moreover, there were mornings and evenings, which describe our normal days on a planet that revolves around the sun, without the existence of the sun. The events of every day in this chapter are punctuated with a sentence that reads, "And the evening and the morning were the [first through the seventh] day."

It gets worse. The moon is described as a light, when we know that it is not a light at all but simply an object that reflects the light of the sun.

To make it even more perplexing, the activities on Day Four seem to duplicate the activities on Day One. The light was already separated from the darkness. One was called day and the other night. Here it is Day Four and it's being done over again.

Day Five (Genesis 1:20–23)

God created fish and birds from the water.

Day Six (Genesis 1:24–31)

God created all of the land animals from the earth and created man in his image.

It is interesting that man would be made "in God's image." Why would God need hands, feet, elbows, knees, eyeballs, or an intestinal tract? If the passage is not referring to God's physical image, then we can only guess what it might mean.

Day Seven (Genesis 2:1–3)

God rested.

According to the Christian description of God, God should not need rest. The "resting" he did on the seventh day is often explained away as an act that God performed as an example for the benefit of humans, so that we would know to rest on the seventh day.

The explanation that this chapter was written back in a time when God was thought of as having attributes that are more human is a lot more believable. Thus, God is described throughout the early books of the Bible as jealous[48] and repentant[49] and in need of rest. He seems more like one of the ancient Greek gods than the God that Christians now claim to worship.

Chapter 2 of Genesis becomes confusing because starting at verse 4 we begin a second account of creation. This doesn't become obvious until one reads several verses into it. At first it just looks like more details are being given about creation.

In verse 19, though, God creates every beast of the field and every fowl of the air "out of the ground." This contradicts chapter 1, verse 21, where the fowls came from the water. The order is wrong, too. According to chapter 1, birds were created on day five before man. According to this new account, the birds were

---

48 Exodus 20:5, 34:14, Deuteronomy 4:24, 6:15, 29:20, Joshua 24:19, and Psalms 78:58 are some of the verses pertaining to this.
49 Genesis 6:7, I Samuel 15:11.

created at the same time as the rest of the animals, after man had already been created.

God brought all these animals to Adam in order for him to give names "to all cattle, and to the fowl of the air, and to every beast of the field" (Genesis 2:20).

Need I go into the logistical difficulties of this or ask why it is necessary for Adam to name all of these creatures? How long did this take? Is he going to see them all again? How are people going to know, remember, and use the names Adam gave the animals?

There are several points to be made at this juncture.

The first is recognized by biblical scholars but not acknowledged in most conservative Churches. It is that there are two accounts of creation here, put together side by side to form the narrative of creation. These two versions of the same story were taken from the verbal history of the Jewish people. If you put the chapter break between verses 3 and 4 of chapter 2, rather than where it is currently, it reads much more clearly.

The Biblical account of creation fails to accurately describe this galaxy as it exists or to describe events that actually happened. If these verses were dictated by God to man, then you would think that God would get a lot more of the details right. As I mentioned at the beginning of this chapter, the defense that God didn't tell the literal truth, because humankind would not have believed the truth, doesn't justify an untruth.

As you read through the rest of Genesis, and encounter the stories of Adam and Eve, Noah and the flood, and the Tower of Babel, it is easy to suspect (if not conclude) that much of Genesis was created as a series of stories to explain things such as the hardships of life, the pain that women suffer during childbirth,[50] and how the people of the world came to have different languages. They are like Aesop's fables. "How the tiger got its stripes" is not too far removed from "How the snake lost its legs."[51]

When no better explanations were available, men invented them. Verbal legend was later put down on paper. Yet I can walk into many a church on Sunday morning and hear these stories being reported as fact. If we respect truth and value honesty, we need to recognize that a literal interpretation does not work.

---

50 Genesis 2:16.
51 Genesis 3:14.

SOME PROBLEMS WITH THE TEN COMMANDMENTS

In a story that has been told many times, the Hebrews, under the leadership of Moses, were freed from slavery, crossed the Red Sea, and went out into the desert where they wandered as a nomadic tribe for forty years.

It was at the beginning of this time that they received the Ten Commandments. One interesting facet of the story is that Moses received the Ten Commandments twice. He broke the first set of tablets when he came down off Mount Sinai and saw the Hebrews worshipping an idol of a golden calf.[52]

At the time that this happened, Moses was angered by the behavior of his people, but God even more so. God was so angry that he ordered Moses to kill 3,000 of his own people.

> Then Moses stood in the gate of the camp, and said, Who is on the Lord's side? let him come unto me. And all the sons of Levi gathered themselves together unto him. | And he said unto them, Thus saith the Lord God of Israel, Put every man his sword by his side, and go in and out from gate to gate throughout the camp, and slay every man his brother, and every man his companion, and every man his neighbour. | And the children of Levi did according to the word of Moses: and there fell of the people that day about three thousand men (Exodus 32:26–28).

After this, Moses returned to Mount Sinai, where he again talked to God:

> And the Lord passed by before him, and proclaimed, The Lord, The Lord God, merciful and gracious, longsuffering, and abundant in goodness and truth, | Keeping mercy for thousands, forgiving iniquity and transgression and sin, and that will by no means clear the guilty; visiting the iniquity of the fathers upon the children, and upon the children's children, unto the third and to the fourth generation (Exodus 34:6–7).

In this passage, God begins by describing himself as "merciful and gracious, longsuffering, and abundant in goodness and truth." But he had just proven otherwise. Even the next sentence contradicts his claims. A God with the above mentioned qualities would not punish the children, great grandchildren, and great great grandchildren of those who sinned. (Here again we find the "original sin" mentality of the Old Testament that is central to Christian philosophy.)

Upon completing his mountaintop conference with God, Moses came down off the mountain with a second set of tablets and biblical history was made.

If you read the commandments[53] it is hard to tell exactly how they should be separated and numbered, which is why they are listed differently according to the Protestant, Catholic, and Jewish traditions.

There are a few more substantive problems with the commandments which should be mentioned.

---

52 Genesis 32:19.

53 Exodus 20:3–17. In the book of Deuteronomy, there is a recap of the history of the Hebrew people and the commandments are listed again in Deuteronomy 5:7–21.

The first and second commandments (according to Protestant tradition) are:

1) "Thou shalt have no other gods before me."

2) "Thou shalt not make unto thee any graven image, or any likeness of any thing that is in heaven above, or that is in the earth beneath, or that is in the water under the earth. Thou shalt not bow down thyself to them, nor serve them: for I the LORD thy God am a jealous God" (Exodus 20: 3–5).

Throughout the Old Testament we are given the sense that the biblical God feels threatened by, and is jealous of, other gods, as if they actually existed. Of course, the common interpretation is that it is a sin to worship other gods even if they do not really exist.

Those who advocate the posting of the Ten Commandments on publicly owned land and say that it is okay if other religious symbols are present should take into consideration that theirs is the only one that says, "any other God except ours must not be worshipped."

Following this is the commandment about the Sabbath.

> Remember the sabbath day, to keep it holy. | Six days shalt thou labour, and do all thy work: | But the seventh day is the sabbath of the LORD thy God: in it thou shalt not do any work, thou, nor thy son, nor thy daughter, thy manservant, nor thy maidservant, nor thy cattle, nor thy stranger that is within thy gates (Exodus 20: 8–10).

The commandment is clear. The Jews and the Seventh Day Adventists are right — the seventh day is the Sabbath. When I was a good Baptist boy, I thought about this and wondered if I was sinning every Saturday when I mowed the lawn. The day of worship changed from Saturday to Sunday in the fourth century when Emperor Constantine of Rome ordered the Christians to change it. To some people this is a big deal. Others say it does not matter when they worship and rest as long as they do it sometime.

The part that says "nor thy son, nor thy daughter, thy manservant, nor thy maidservant, nor thy cattle, nor thy stranger that is within thy gates, besides being a little redundant, also mentions servants. This does not mean butlers and maids. It is referring to slaves. This can be seen by reading many of the preceding passages. Right in the middle of a commandment telling us on which day we should rest, there is hidden a much greater moral problem, the question of whether we should have slaves. It would be far more beneficial to address this and all the pain, suffering, and death that slavery has caused rather than to tell people they should take a day off.

The next commandment says to "Honour thy father and thy mother." It is generally a good rule, except that it can all too easily come into conflict with other commandments and place one in a position where there is no choice but to sin. What do you do if your parents tell you to lie and will not take no for an answer? You are trapped. Either way, you sin.

Herein lies the problem with the so-called morality presented in the Bible. It is extraordinarily superficial. It doesn't take a genius, let alone a God, to come up with a list of "do's and don'ts." But what should we do when rules and principles come into conflict with each other? Do we obey the letter of the law or the spirit of the law? That is where we need significant guidance. Failure to address such issues results in tremendous difficulties. It often results in an unforgiving, black-and-white, right-or-wrong mentality.

You can see the depths of the dilemma when dealing with the commandment "Thou shalt not kill" (Exodus 20:13). This seems pretty straightforward until you realize that God had the Hebrews kill 3,000 of their own people, that he had just killed all the firstborn children of the Egyptians, and that the man carrying the commandments to the people had killed an Egyptian and buried him in the sand (See Exodus 2:11–12).

The meaning and importance of the commandment not to kill have already been highly diluted. Some people change the word "kill" to "murder" and provide justifications for the above incidents. Well then, if killing is not killing, this should be an important enough issue to call for a certain amount of clarification.

The Ten Commandments, as well as the situations surrounding them, demonstrate how flawed the Bible is and how futile it is to claim the Bible as a basis for morality. We can see such problems throughout all of the Old Testament. Let's do a spot check and see.

SEX AND VIOLENCE

The Old Testament is filled with sex and violence, the very two things that Christians often rally against and consider to be against "family values."

I think the violence of the Old Testament is often disregarded because it seems so distant and removed from us by time. If the events described took place in the present day and in our immediate vicinity, they would be taken much more seriously and would be seen as the atrocities they are.

For the record, the following is a partial listing of some of the Biblical accounts of sex, violence, and crassness in general. I encourage you to read not only the passages I have noted here, but also the rest of the Bible, especially the parts they avoid in church. Be sure to refer to the King James Version, as most fundamentalist Protestants do. Many other versions soften these passages and some even alter their meaning. I have heard several people say that reading the

Bible is what turned them against Christianity. These examples show what they are talking about.

Genesis 9:20–26

This is a brief story about Noah, the main person God opted to save when he killed off the rest of the population of planet Earth:

> And Noah began to be an husbandman, and he planted a vineyard: | And he drank of the wine, and was drunken; and he was uncovered within his tent. | And Ham, the father of Canaan, saw the nakedness of his father, and told his two brethren without. | And Shem and Japheth took a garment, and laid it upon both their shoulders, and went backward, and covered the nakedness of their father; and their faces were backward, and they saw not their father's nakedness.
>
> And Noah awoke from his wine, and knew what his younger son had done unto him. | And he said, Cursed be Canaan; a servant of servants shall he be unto his brethren. | And he said, Blessed be the LORD God of Shem; and Canaan shall be his servant (Genesis 9:20–26).

Apparently, Ham's great crime in the story is that he told his brothers that their father was drunk and naked. Maybe it was a disrespectful and maybe he should have kept it to himself, but the consequences for this error are severe. If it was bad for Ham to tell his brothers about Noah's nakedness, it is far worse for the Bible to report it to the whole entire world. "Noah was drunk and naked!" it announces to perpetual generations. One doesn't know whether to feel sorry for Noah, for Ham, or for all those who have to try to explain why such a thing, with all the details reported like a sensationalistic tabloid headline, appears in a book that was supposedly inspired by God.

Biblical historians say that its purpose is simply to explain the separation of the people of Canaan from the rest of Noah's descendants, but the manner in which it is done says otherwise. Why not just say, "There was a disagreement between Noah and his sons, and as a result the people of Canaan were exiled?"

Genesis 18:20–19:28

Lot and his family are living in the wicked city of Sodom and Gomorrah. Abraham and God bargain with each other, because Abraham does not want God to destroy the town if there are good people living there. After their bargaining session, God agrees not to destroy Sodom and Gomorrah if ten righteous people can be found there.

God sends two angels into town. They meet up with Lot and go to stay in his house. The townspeople of Sodom and Gomorrah demand that Lot release the two "men" to them so that the townspeople can have sex with them (this is where the term "sodomy" comes from). Lot refuses and asks the townspeople if they will take his daughters instead.

"Behold now, I have two daughters which have not known man; let me, I pray you, bring them out unto you, and do ye to them as is good in your eyes: only unto these men do nothing; for therefore came they under the shadow of my roof" (Genesis 19:8).

That's taking hospitality a little too far, if you ask me. Either way, God deems Lot and his family worthy enough to escape from Sodom and Gomorrah and then he destroys the town. On the way out of town, Lot's wife turns to look back at the city, as she has been told not to do, and is turned into a pillar of salt.

Lot's behavior of offering his daughters to the crowd is far from exemplary. If I were one of Lot's daughters, I would be inclined to think that he deserved to be killed with all the rest of the townspeople. Lot can get away with offering up his daughters to the people of the city with rape as the likely conclusion; he is allowed to live. His wife, on the other hand, is turned into a pillar of salt for what seems lie a minor infraction, looking back upon the city. It is both a sexist story and a senseless story. If we saw a story like this on TV we would say, "No way!" but many people believe it because it is in the Bible and because they have been told that it is true since childhood.

Genesis 19:30–36

The escapades of Lot and his daughters continue. Living in a cave with their father, the two girls get their father drunk and have sex with him. Their goal in doing this is to continue his lineage:

> And it came to pass on the morrow, that the firstborn said unto the younger, Behold, I lay yesternight with my father: let us make him drink wine this night also; and go thou in, and lie with him, that we may preserve seed of our father. | And they made their father drink wine that night also: and the younger arose, and lay with him; and he perceived not when she lay down, nor when she arose. | Thus were both the daughters of Lot with child by their father (Genesis 19:34–36).

I find it questionable that a man who was so drunk he could not recognize his own daughters would be able to perform sexually.

Genesis 38

Judah has several sons by a woman named Shua, two of whom are named Er and Onan. Er is wicked and so the Lord slays him. That's all that is explained about Er's death. Judah tells Onan, Er's brother, to go marry Tamar, his brother's former wife. He is instructed to give her a child so that Er's heritage is carried on. This was apparently customary at the time.

Onan goes in to have sex with Tamar, but knows that the child will be known as Er's heir and not his own, and so he ejaculates on the ground.[54] This makes God angry and so God kills him.

It is not clear if disobeying his father's wish is the sin or if ejaculating on the ground is the sin, but either way, Onan winds up dead.

The story continues. After mourning Onan, Tamar takes off her widow's garments, puts on a veil, and sits by the roadside. Judah (her father-in-law) sees Tamar wearing a veil, thinks she's a prostitute, and asks her to sleep with him. Tamar says she will if Judah will give her something. Judah offers to give her a goat.

Judah doesn't happen to be carrying a goat around with him, so Tamar asks for a pledge as insurance that she'll get the goat sometime in the future. Judah gives her a signet, some bracelets, and a staff. Tamar sleeps with Judah and she becomes pregnant with twins.

Several months later, Judah hears that Tamar has "played the harlot" and is pregnant. He says, "Bring her forth and let her be burned."

Tamar comes in, shows him his own signet, bracelets, and staff, and tells him that the man who gave them to her is the father of her children. Judah graciously decides not to kill her. The Bible specifically states that, after that, Judah never slept with her again, as if that redeems him. Notice that Tamar is treated poorly because of her sexual behavior but Judah is not.

Tamar gives birth to twin boys. The first one starts to come out of the womb and the midwife ties a red string around his arm. But then he withdraws his arm and the other boy is born first. Because of this, the midwife names the first born Pharez and the second born Zarah.

That is the end of the chapter and the Bible returns to the story of Joseph.

Exodus 15:3

Just in case there was any doubt about which kind of God we are dealing with, it is stated clearly in Exodus, "The LORD is a man of war: the LORD is his name."

Leviticus 20:10, 13, 15–16, & 18

The book of Leviticus is mainly a list of rules given to Moses by God. The majority of the rules deal with certain sins and the type of offerings that should be made in order to atone for these sins. Guidelines for the priests are also given, as well as methods for diagnosing and dealing with leprosy and the plague. (If God is going to go this far, I find myself wondering, why not provide some truly

---

54 Thereby providing the origin of the word, "onanism."

helpful medical advice instead of making humanity wait for its scientists to discover it centuries later?) Among the commandments listed in Leviticus are the
following:

> And the man that committeth adultery with another man's wife, even
> he that committeth adultery with his neighbour's wife, the adulterer and
> the adulteress shall surely be put to death (Leviticus 20:10).
>
> If a man also lie with mankind, as he lieth with a woman, both of them
> have committed an abomination: they shall surely be put to death; their
> blood shall be upon them (Leviticus 20:13).[55]
>
> And if a man lie with a beast, he shall surely be put to death: and ye
> shall slay the beast. | And if a woman approach unto any beast, and lie
> down thereto, thou shalt kill the woman, and the beast: they shall surely be
> put to death; their blood shall be upon them (Leviticus 20:15–16).

In short, the sin of adultery, as well as homosexuality and bestiality, are pun-
ishable by death. God does not only recommend it; he commands it. "They shall
surely be put to death," he says.

If we killed every man and woman who committed adultery, the world would
not have a population problem and there would be a lot fewer religious people
around, as well.

When it comes to homosexuality, another person's sexual preference is of no
concern to me. However, I do feel that it is morally reprehensible to recommend,
much less command, killing someone for homosexual behavior. I do not see how
someone who is gay can read verses like these and not realize that Christianity is
rife with intolerance and is not the religion for him.[56] We are only a few chapters
into the Bible and already in place is the invasive mindset that religion can tell
people what to do in their personal lives. Frankly, I find the attitude to be scary
and a bit too Big Brotherish for comfort.

Some people defend the third verse about having sex with animals by saying
that these (and other awkward verses in Leviticus) are in place for health reasons, using AIDS as an example. Yet, if the point was to protect people's health,
it is unlikely that the Law would recommend killing people.

The rules pile up in Leviticus. Leviticus 20:18 says, "And if a man shall lie
with a woman having her sickness (her period), and shall uncover her nakedness; he hath discovered her fountain, and she hath uncovered the fountain of her
blood: and both of them shall be cut off from among their people."

According to this verse, if a man and a woman have sex when a woman is
menstruating, then they should be exiled. It's not death, but it is awfully harsh.

---

55 See also Leviticus 18:22.
56 Paul speaks out against homosexuality in the New Testament in Romans 1–27.

Notice that the woman's time of the month is referred to as "her sickness." Sounds rather disparaging and chauvinistic, doesn't it? Check out chapter 15:19–30, where it details the strict regulations a woman who is menstruating should follow during that time. We might be able to disregard these rules as health measures if we did not keep reading. The women are then instructed to present a *sin* offering to God to make atonement for menstruating. It becomes obvious that health is not the only issue here in the eyes of the authors of the Bible.

Leviticus 24:11, 13–16, & 23

These verses, interspersed with the repetition of some rules, tell of a man who blasphemed and, upon God's command, is stoned to death for it.

> And the Israelitish woman's son blasphemed the name of the Lord, and cursed. And they brought him unto Moses (Leviticus 24:11).

> And the LORD spake unto Moses, saying, | Bring forth him that hath cursed without the camp; and let all that heard him lay their hands upon his head, and let all the congregation stone him. | And thou shalt speak unto the children of Israel, saying, Whosoever curseth his God shall bear his sin. | And he that blasphemeth the name of the LORD, he shall surely be put to death, and all the congregation shall certainly stone him: as well the stranger, as he that is born in the land, when he blasphemeth the name of the Lord, shall be put to death (Leviticus 24: 13–16).

> And Moses spake to the children of Israel, that they should bring forth him that had cursed out of the camp, and stone him with stones. And the children of Israel did as the LORD commanded Moses (Leviticus 24:23).

All this man did was blaspheme and he was killed for it by being pummeled with rocks. There are some who would defend such instances by saying, "If you don't like the punishment, then don't sin."

Here's what I'm talking about when I say the violence of the Old Testament is often disregarded because it seems so distant and removed from us by time. If someone were stoned to death before my eyes, or if I were asked to kill him or her for whatever sin — blasphemy, adultery, or homosexuality — I could not do it in good conscience. I would immediately think, *there's something wrong here. What I am being asked to do is even more immoral that the sin that was committed in the first place.*

Remember, as well, that the commandment "Thou shall not kill" had already been passed down.

Some will also say that the rules in Leviticus only applied to the people of Israel. But, if these rules were followed (and the Bible says they were), then the real issue is that terrible injustices have been done at the direct command of God. Ethically, it is irrelevant what nation acted them out.

Deuteronomy 2:31–35

> And the LORD said unto me, Behold, I have begun to give Sihon and his land before thee: begin to possess, that thou mayest inherit his land.
>
> Then Sihon came out against us, he and all his people, to fight at Jahaz.
>
> And the LORD our God delivered him before us; and we smote him, and his sons, and all his people.
>
> And we took all his cities at that time, and utterly destroyed the men, and the women, and the little ones, of every city, we left none to remain.
>
> Only the cattle we took for a prey unto ourselves, and the spoil of the cities which we took.

The Old Testament is filled with this kind of killing. If this is a historical document, then the stories are relevant. But as the story of a good and loving God, they communicate the opposite.

Deuteronomy 22:22–29

It is first explained that if a man and a woman sleep together, and the woman is either married or betrothed to another, then both the man and the woman will be stoned to death. The man's marital status is not mentioned as relevant. Then it gets more complicated.

If a man rapes a married woman, then he is to be killed and nothing bad should happen to her. Fair enough, I think. But here's the catch. If a man rapes an unmarried woman, the man has to give her father fifty shekels of silver and then marry her. So it is not rape that is viewed as bad, here. It is the act of doing it *to someone else's wife* that makes it a terrible crime. The woman is not the object of consideration. It's the pride of the men.

Deuteronomy 23:2

Following a verse saying that a person who has a testicular injury or who has had his "privy member" cut off cannot enter into the congregation of the LORD, we find this statement:

> A bastard shall not enter into the congregation of the LORD; even to his tenth generation shall he not enter into the congregation of the LORD.

As an illegitimate child, this verse has special significance to me. Sometimes when I am invited to go to someone's church, it is tempting to say, "Sorry, the Bible says I can't go."

The real problem with this verse is the idea behind it — the idea that an illegitimate child and his children are deserving of punishment because of their parent's sin.

Joshua 6:21

We hear a lot about Joshua and the Battle of Jericho, how they marched around the walls and blew their trumpets, and the walls fell in. This is reported as a great miracle and a testament to God's power, but how can we overlook what happens when Joshua's troops enter the city? "And they utterly destroyed all that was in the city, both man and woman, young and old, and ox, and sheep, and ass, with the edge of the sword" (Joshua 6:21).

To me, that's not such a great story.

Judges 11:30–39

Jephthah makes a promise to God that if God helps him to defeat the children of Ammon in war, that, upon returning, Jepthah will offer as a sacrifice whatever comes out of the doors of his house. Apparently, he was thinking a dog or some animal would greet him.

He fights the children of Ammon, destroying twenty cities with "a very great slaughter." When he returns, his daughter is the first one to come out of the house to greet him. He is sad, but does not renege on his promise. Jephthah tells his daughter of the promise he has made. She agrees to be sacrificed and then he allows her to go into the hills for two months to "bewail her virginity," mourning not that she will never get to live a full life, but that she'll never be married.

When Jephthah's daughter returns, he sacrifices her to God.

I presume that the lesson of this story is either that you should not make stupid promises or that you have to do what you promise, no matter how terrible it is. But there comes a time, I think, when breaking a promise is more honorable than killing your own daughter. Ultimately it shows that the Old Testament God is as barbaric as any other primitive icon of worship that accepts human sacrifices, like the gods of the Aztecs and Mayans.

I Samuel 15:2–33

God orders Saul to destroy the people of Amalek because they attacked the Israelites when they left Egypt. "Now go and smite Amalek, and utterly destroy all that they have, and spare them not; but slay both man and woman, infant and suckling, ox and sheep, camel and ass" (I Samuel 15:3).

Saul does as ordered, but the Israelites do not kill all the animals. They keep some of the sheep, oxen, fatlings, and lambs. God is angry because the people disobeyed him and Saul falls into disfavor with God for his disobedience.

Agag, the king of the Amalekites, is brought before the prophet Samuel. "And Samuel hewed Agag in pieces before the LORD in Gilgal" (I Samuel 15:32–33).

Samuel then goes to find another king for Israel because Saul has fallen out of God's favor.

The point of these verses, as relayed in church, is that if you disobey God or go against his people, you will pay for it. But it is terribly unjust! Innocents are slain — man and woman, infant and suckling, ox and sheep, camel and ass — and those who aren't innocent get chopped up into pieces in a manner more like that of Hannibal Lector than of a loving God.

It would be interesting to tally up a rough estimate of the number of people who were slain in the Old Testament, whether killed directly by God or at the hands of the Hebrews, including those of the Hebrew nation who were killed by their own people.

I Samuel 18:20–27

King Saul's daughter Michal falls in love with David. King Saul thinks that he can use the situation to get rid of David. Saul has his servants tell David that if he kills 100 Philistines and brings their foreskins to King Saul, David can marry Michal. How romantic! David does this one better by killing 200 Philistines and bringing all of their foreskins back to King David. King Saul allows David to marry his daughter.

I Kings 20:35–36

> And a certain man of the sons of the prophets said unto his neighbour in the word of the LORD, Smite me, I pray thee. And the man refused to smite him.
> Then said he unto him, Because thou hast not obeyed the voice of the LORD, behold, as soon as thou art departed from me, a lion shall slay thee. And as soon as he was departed from him, a lion found him, and slew him.

Do you see the flaws in this story? A prophet walks up to his neighbor and says, "God has asked you to smite me. Do it." The neighbor refuses and, because he refuses, is killed by a lion!

The only point of this story is that we should do anything God tells us to — or that some fellow tells us God is telling us to — even if it goes against what we know is right. Obey God at all costs or die. Rationality has nothing to do with it.

II Kings 2:23–24

> And he [the prophet Elisha] went up from thence unto Bethel: and as he was going up by the way, there came forth little children out of the city, and mocked him, and said unto him, Go up, thou bald head; go up, thou bald head.
> And he turned back, and looked on them, and cursed them in the name of the LORD. And there came forth two she bears out of the wood, and tare forty and two children of them.

Does the word "petty" or the phrase "passive aggressive" ring any bells? The one defense I have heard for this passage is that these were not children that were killed, but young adults. Supposedly the word "children" is a poor translation. Does that make it acceptable? Even if it was adults that were mauled by bears, what happens is unconscionable.

This story, like many of the stories in the Bible, appeals to our baser instincts. They appeal to the part of us that identifies with a vengeful God who can do whatever he wants whenever he wants. Someone calls you a name? Wipe 'em out. Someone behaves in a manner that you don't like? Have them executed. Such power is darkly attractive. I would venture to say that there are few among us who have not had moments when they wanted to be able to exact such retaliation. But is it fair? Is it just? Is it behavior worthy of a divine being? No.

II Kings 9:33–36

In first Kings, Jezebel forges letters so that men are slain and her idol-worshipping husband Ahab can take over a vineyard (thereby giving the name "Jezebel" a permanently negative connotation). At that time the Lord states that, "The dogs shall eat Jezebel by the wall of Jezreel" (I Kings 21:23).

It comes to pass in II Kings 9, when Jehu, now King of Israel, has her killed.

> And he said, Throw her down. So they threw her down: and some of her blood was sprinkled on the wall, and on the horses: and he trode her under foot.

Can you say, "gratuitous?"

> And when he was come in, he did eat and drink, and said, Go, see now this cursed woman, and bury her: for she is a king's daughter.

Of course now is the time to be respectful.

> And they went to bury her: but they found no more of her than the skull, and the feet, and the palms of her hands.
> Wherefore they came again, and told him. And he said, This is the word of the LORD, which he spake by his servant Elijah the Tishbite, saying, In the portion of Jezreel shall dogs eat the flesh of Jezebel.

Whew. Are you positive we're not talking about one of the Greek Gods instead of the Christian God we hear so many good things about? Maybe Zeus snuck into Israel for a while and was mistaken for him.

Song of Solomon

The Song of Solomon is a love poem told in both male and female voices. It is an embarrassing piece for the biblical apologist to explain. One of the most common defenses of it is that the Song of Solomon is a metaphor for Christ's love for his church. (So much for a literal interpretation, then.) It is a bit risqué, but sounds tame after what we have read so far. Here are a couple excerpts, the second expressing a concern I would not have expected to have found in the Bible:

> Thy navel is like a round goblet, which wanteth not liquor: thy belly is like an heap of wheat set about with lilies. | Thy two breasts are like two young roes that are twins (Song of Solomon 7: 2–3).

> We have a little sister, and she hath no breasts: what shall we do for our sister in the day when she shall be spoken for? (Song of Solomon 8: 8)

Isaiah 36:12

> But Rabshakeh said, Hath my master sent me to thy master and to thee to speak these words? hath he not sent me to the men that sit upon the wall, that they may eat their own dung, and drink their own piss with you?

Nice. We'll conclude with an excerpt that deserves a chapter all its own. It is perhaps one of the most gruesome and pointless stories of the Bible.

A HORRIFIC TALE

This story can be found in the book of Judges, chapters 19 through 21.

A man referred to as "a certain Levite," and not by name, has a concubine. The concubine leaves him and goes to her father's house. He goes to her father's house in Bethlehemjudah, gets her, and sets off to return home. On the way home he stops in the city of Gibeah, which belongs to the tribe of Benjamin. Another man sees him in the street and takes the Levite, his servant and his concubine in for the night.

At that point, the story turns into a flashback of the story of Lot and the two angels in Sodom and Gomorrah, but it takes a wicked turn.

> Now as they were making their hearts merry, behold, the men of the city, certain sons of Belial, beset the house round about, and beat at the door, and spake to the master of the house, the old man, saying, Bring forth the man that came into thine house, that we may know him.
>
> And the man, the master of the house, went out unto them, and said unto them, Nay, my brethren, nay, I pray you, do not so wickedly; seeing that this man is come into mine house, do not this folly. | Behold, here is my daughter a maiden, and his concubine; them I will bring out now, and humble ye them, and do with them what seemeth good unto you: but unto this man do not so vile a thing.
>
> But the men would not hearken to him: so the man took his concubine, and brought her forth unto them; and they knew her, and abused her all the night until the morning: and when the day began to spring, they let her go.
>
> Then came the woman in the dawning of the day, and fell down at the door of the man's house where her lord was, till it was light. | And her lord rose up in the morning, and opened the doors of the house, and went out to go his way: and, behold, the woman his concubine was fallen down at the door of the house, and her hands were upon the threshold.

And he said unto her, Up, and let us be going. But none answered. Then the man took her up upon an ass, and the man rose up, and gat him unto his place.

And when he was come into his house, he took a knife, and laid hold on his concubine, and divided her, together with her bones, into twelve pieces, and sent her into all the coasts of Israel.

And it was so, that all that saw it said, There was no such deed done nor seen from the day that the children of Israel came up out of the land of Egypt unto this day: consider of it, take advice, and speak your minds (Judges 19:22–30).

Let's review. The traveling man and his host turn the concubine out into the street to be raped. They do this in order to prevent the rape of the traveling man. The concubine is raped all night long and dies afterwards. Her owner wants everyone to know that this terrible thing has been done to her, so he cuts her up into twelve pieces, bones and all, and sends them out to the twelve tribes of Israel.

That's the story so far.

Because of this, the tribes of Israel have a big meeting. The Levite tells them what happened to his concubine, without seeming at all apologetic or embarrassed by his role in it. Eleven of the tribes of Israel unite against the tribe of Benjamin, go to the city of Gibeah, and demand that the men who raped the concubine be turned over to them. The children of Benjamin refuse, which results in a war.

The war lasts for three days and every night the people of Israel are upset because they are attacking one of their own tribes, but God tells them to keep fighting.

On day three, the fighting men of the tribe of Benjamin are lured out of their city and killed by the rest of the tribes of Israel. The final death toll is roughly 55,000. Of these, 30,000 are from the eleven tribes of Israel other than Benjamin, and 25,000 are from the tribe of Benjamin itself.

The people of Israel are distraught that the tribe of Benjamin is almost wiped out, even though it is they who have done it and their God who ordered it. Suddenly their concern shifts to finding wives for the surviving men of Benjamin. There's a big problem, though — everyone has sworn not to "give them [the people of Benjamin] of our daughters to wives."

They find a loophole when they discover that inhabitants of Jabeshgilead did not make this agreement. Do they go and ask the people of Jabeshgilead if any of their daughters want strong husbands from the tribe of Benjamin? No. Instead, they kill the people of Jabeshgilead except for the virgin women, whom they somehow manage to identify as virgins, and take them to be turned over to the men of the tribe of Benjamin.

> And the congregation sent thither twelve thousand men of the valiantest, and commanded them, saying, Go and smite the inhabitants of Jabeshgilead with the edge of the sword, with the women and the children. | And this is the thing that ye shall do, Ye shall utterly destroy every male, and every woman that hath lain by man. | And they found among the inhabitants of Jabeshgilead four hundred young virgins, that had known no man by lying with any male (Judges 21 10–12).

These women are given to the tribe of Benjamin as wives, but that still leaves them a couple hundred women short. So they tell the men of Benjamin that there is a feast of the Lord to be held at a place called Shiloh. The men are instructed to hide in the vineyards. When the women come out to dance at the feast, the men are supposed to catch the women and take them home as their wives.

> Therefore they commanded the children of Benjamin, saying, Go and lie in wait in the vineyards; And see, and, behold, if the daughters of Shiloh come out to dance in dances, then come ye out of the vineyards, | and catch you every man his wife of the daughters of Shiloh, and go to the land of Benjamin.
>
> And it shall be, when their fathers or their brethren come unto us to complain, that we will say unto them, Be favourable unto them for our sakes: because we reserved not to each man his wife in the war: for ye did not give unto them at this time, that ye should be guilty.
>
> And the children of Benjamin did so, and took them wives, according to their number, of them that danced, whom they caught: and they went and returned unto their inheritance, and repaired the cities, and dwelt in them (Judges 21:20–23).

The book of Judges ends with these words: "In those days there was no king in Israel: every man did that which was right in his own eyes." It seems difficult to imagine that these events occurred at the hands of men who were trying to do right in anyone's eyes. Moreover, God is right there. The people consult him. All of this craziness, raping, and killing occurs "on his watch." Much of the killing happens as a direct response to God's orders.

The excerpts I have covered here and in the previous section should serve to make my point. The morality presented in the Bible is contradictory and highly questionable. Some of the behaviors put on display and, more importantly, those that are directly commanded by God, do not fit any acceptable standard of morality, no matter what time period they are exercised in. Such things go against what Christians themselves consider moral, but these things are forgiven or overlooked because, well, they are in the Bible.

It seems to me that the writers of the Old Testament were very similar to the media moguls of today. They knew that sex and violence sell. Even as I examine the teachings of Jesus, it continues to be seen that the Bible is not as exemplary as it is made out to be.

JESUS IN THE BOOK OF MATTHEW

In comparison to the New Testament, the Old Testament receives treatment that is much more critical. It is easier to attack because of its antiquity, which makes it seem more removed from contemporary concerns. The New Testament, on the other hand, is regarded by modern day Christians as especially sacred. Many who criticize the Old Testament remain highly complimentary about the teachings of Jesus.

Jesus has a reputation for being kind and forgiving. New Testament Christianity, as exemplified by Jesus, is thought of as a religion of love, compassion, and fairness. By becoming the ultimate human sacrifice, Jesus also becomes a symbol of forgiveness. In some stories, Jesus is the personification of kindness and even passivity. He admonishes us to turn the other cheek.[57] He stops the crowd from killing a harlot by saying that he who is without sin should cast the first stone.[58] The little children surround him and he holds them in his arms.[59] He appears to be the kinder, gentler God of a new age.

No doubt, it was needed. What better way to save religion from having to continue the tired and embarrassing tradition of animal sacrifices than to say, "Jesus took care of it"? The Old Testament God, even then, must have seemed harsh to some. God needed an image change. Jesus was the solution. All he had to do was keep from slaughtering hundreds of thousands of people and he would look great in comparison.

Some will be surprised to hear that there is debate as to whether Jesus actually existed at all. It is, not surprisingly, a highly-charged debate and not one that I wish to take on. I intend to show in this section that even if Jesus did walk the face of this planet, and even if the gospels truly represent what he said, his teachings are highly overrated. He said little of great import and much that is either nonsensical or, quite simply, bad advice. At times, his teachings are completely irreconcilable with the practices of the Old Testament God. They often complicate issues, magnifying the moral ambiguity of the Bible rather than straightening it out. Nor was Jesus always kind, compassionate, or wise. As such, his teachings suggest that Jesus, if he existed, was just another human being and not God incarnate.

Early in the book of Matthew we hear the teachings of Jesus. Right off the bat, Jesus says that we should follow the commandments of the Old Testament, an idea we will revisit later.

---

57 Matthew 5:39, Luke 6:29.
58 John 8:07.
59 Mark 10:14, Luke 18:15–16.

"Think not that I am come to destroy the law, or the prophets: I am not come to destroy, but to fulfil. | For verily I say unto you, Till heaven and earth pass, one jot or one tittle shall in no wise pass from the law, till all be fulfilled. | Whosoever therefore shall break one of these least commandments, and shall teach men so, he shall be called the least in the kingdom of heaven: but whosoever shall do and teach them, the same shall be called great in the kingdom of heaven" (Matthew 5:17–19).[60]

Jesus continues.

"For I say unto you, That except your righteousness shall exceed the righteousness of the scribes and Pharisees, ye shall in no case enter into the kingdom of heaven. | Ye have heard that it was said of them of old time, Thou shalt not kill; and whosoever shall kill shall be in danger of the judgment: | But I say unto you, That whosoever is angry with his brother without a cause shall be in danger of the judgment: and whosoever shall say to his brother, Raca, shall be in danger of the council: but whosoever shall say, Thou fool, shall be in danger of hell fire." (Matthew 5:20–22).

First of all, I generally agree with the sentiment that people should be kind to each other (there are exceptions). We also should not go around calling each other names. What is odd is that the punishment Jesus ascribes to this crime is exceptionally harsh — worse, even, than the death penalty. He ascribes the penalty of eternal damnation for calling someone a fool.

Jesus covers himself by specifying that this applies only when dealing with your brother (presumably your spiritual brother). Had that qualification not been present, Jesus would be in danger of hell fire himself when he refers to the Scribes and Pharisees as fools in Matthew 23:17 and 23:19. The author of the Psalms, who claims that anyone who denies the existence of God is a fool, would also be in the same predicament.[61]

This verse is also the first in the New Testament to confirm Jesus' view that there is a physical place called Hell. He mentions it more than several times throughout the gospels, the implications of which we have already discussed.

Move ahead a few verses and you read this: "Ye have heard that it was said by them of old time, Thou shalt not commit adultery: But I say unto you, That whosoever looketh on a woman to lust after her hath committed adultery with her already in his heart" (Matthew 5:28).

It is because of this type of thinking, based often upon this very verse, that people feel guilty not only for what they do but also for what they think. It is because of this verse that people show up at confessionals and must say "Hail Marys" for impure thoughts. Here we have a principle that is both insidious and scary. With this verse, Jesus sets a precedent that allows the Church to get inside your head and tell you what it is okay to think and what it is not okay to think. He has unleashed the thought police.

---

60 See also Luke 16:16–17.
61 Psalms 14:11, Psalms 53:1.

People who accept the words of Jesus believe they are giving their minds up to God, but, in actuality, these people have given up their minds to priests, ministers, churches, and other authority figures. Nothing makes you more vulnerable to brainwashing and to becoming a victim than giving up the right to think for yourself.

In order to make decisions about what is right and what is wrong, we must first be able to consider the alternatives. If we cannot, we are mindless. Moreover, the person who considers the alternatives and makes a choice to act honorably has shown far more integrity than the person who is unable to consider the option. What is important is not what we think, but how we act.

"Thou shalt not commit adultery" is a hard enough commandment for people to follow. Jesus has made it even more difficult.

Jesus doesn't make it easy for anyone. While some Churches take the following literally, it is interesting to note how many Christians do not obey the next proclamation that Jesus makes.

> "It hath been said, Whosoever shall put away his wife, let him give her a writing of divorcement: | But I say unto you, That whosoever shall put away his wife, saving for the cause of fornication, causeth her to commit adultery: and whosoever shall marry her that is divorced committeth adultery" (Matthew 5:31–32).

In Matthew 5:38–39 Jesus says, "But I say unto you, That ye resist not evil: but whosoever shall smite thee on thy right cheek, turn to him the other also."

Isn't Jesus God? Doesn't he repeatedly state in the Gospel of John that he and the father are one? Well then, he has just contradicted himself, because it was God who issued the "eye for an eye" dictum.

All of the verses quoted so far from Matthew, chapter 5, are from the Sermon on the Mount. The following comes from it as well.

> "Therefore I say unto you, Take no thought for your life, what ye shall eat, or what ye shall drink; nor yet for your body, what ye shall put on. Is not the life more than meat, and the body than raiment? | Behold the fowls of the air: for they sow not, neither do they reap, nor gather into barns; yet your heavenly Father feedeth them. Are ye not much better than they? | Which of you by taking thought can add one cubit unto his stature?
>
> "And why take ye thought for raiment? Consider the lilies of the field, how they grow; they toil not, neither do they spin: | And yet I say unto you, That even Solomon in all his glory was not arrayed like one of these. | Wherefore, if God so clothe the grass of the field, which to day is, and to morrow is cast into the oven, shall he not much more clothe you, O ye of little faith? | Therefore take no thought, saying, What shall we eat? or, What shall we drink? or, Wherewithal shall we be clothed? | (For after all these things do the Gentiles seek:) for your heavenly Father knoweth that ye have need of all these things. | But seek ye first the kingdom of God, and

his righteousness; and all these things shall be added unto you" (Matthew 6:25–33).[62]

Don't worry about practicalities, Jesus says; focus all of your attention on God and the rest will follow. Don't worry about food or clothing. Don't worry about your job. Don't worry how much money you make or about your retirement plan or about whether you can pay the bills. God will take care of you. Jesus promises it in no uncertain terms. Try it, if you dare.

Before you do, however, you might want to take into consideration that this advice is delivered via flawed analogies and unclear thinking. In the section titled "Fallacies and Critical Thinking" I talked about the dangers of bad analogies and here Jesus delivers an excellent example. Jesus compares the activities and concerns of lilies and birds with those of humankind. We don't need to worry about clothes because the lilies don't worry about clothes. This fails to take into consideration that lilies don't worry because they don't have brains. And yes, they look good, but they are not clothed; they are naked. It's not even a valid comparison. Show me a field of lilies wearing shirts and slacks, and I'll think about reconsidering the analogy. Show me a lily that is consciously aware of the world around it, and I'll show you a lily that has some worries.

The fowls of the air, Jesus says, do not sow, reap, or gather food into barns. I'll grant you that, but they do gather sticks and grass to make nests; they do bring back worms and bugs for their babies, and they do spend much of their day looking for food. If they didn't do these things, they would die. They may not worry, but, like the lilies, if they had the mental capacity to worry, they would.

It is absurd to compare people with birds and lilies in respect to their concerns, and the arguments posed by Jesus are not worthy of someone claiming to be God.

Here's a great line: "Which of you by taking thought can add one cubit unto his stature?" (Matthew 6:27) The best interpretation of this is that in order to change reality, we need to take action. Finally, we have some practicality from Jesus, but it contradicts the previous statements he has made.

One verse from the Sermon on the Mount says, "Be ye therefore perfect, even as your Father which is in heaven is perfect" (Matthew 5:48).

The fundamentalist will tell you that this verse is not to be taken literally. This verse, we are told, means that we should become free from sin via belief in Jesus, and that we should *try* to live perfectly. As a Christian, this was a problem for me because it sounds a lot more like a commandment, and I wanted to follow the commandment. I had already sinned enough for one human being. Why not be perfect? Wouldn't God want that?

---

62 See also Luke 12:22–31.

Furthermore, it should be possible, because "With God all things are possible" (Matthew 19:26). Put those two things together and there is no reason a person shouldn't be able to be perfectly sinless after he or she becomes a Christian. As a youth, it had been made very clear to me that sin is a terrible thing. The consequences of it are eternal damnation. Jesus had to die on a cross to save humanity from the consequences of sin. So you would think that sin would be something God would give us the means to avoid.

I tried it. And failed. I tried it again. And failed. I asked my parents, my friends, as well as leaders in my church, and they said, "It's impossible, because we're human."

Listen to yourself! I wanted to shout. God can do anything! He doesn't want me to sin any more. I don't want to sin anymore. There is no need for it. What's the problem?

"We're human," was the only answer I received.

It seemed that everything was not possible to an omnipotent God. Even the most well-intentioned human is doomed to sin, even though he or she does not want to and even though sin is such a terrible thing.

***

Back in chapter 5 of Matthew, Jesus stressed the importance of the commandments. He said, "Whosoever therefore shall break one of these least commandments, and shall teach men so, he shall be called the least in the kingdom of heaven" (Matthew 5:19). In chapter 12, Jesus and his disciples break the commandment of keeping the Sabbath, and the Pharisees corner him on it.

> At that time Jesus went on the sabbath day through the corn; and his disciples were an hungred, and began to pluck the ears of corn and to eat. | But when the Pharisees saw it, they said unto him, Behold, thy disciples do that which is not lawful to do upon the sabbath day (Matthew 12:1–2).

Jesus explains to the Pharisees that he is breaking the Sabbath based on precedent. Others in the Old Testament, such as David and the Jewish priests had done it. Jesus then provides another reason.

> But I say unto you, That in this place is one greater than the temple. | But if ye had known what this meaneth, I will have mercy, and not sacrifice, ye would not have condemned the guiltless. | For the Son of man is Lord even of the sabbath day.
> And when he was departed thence, he went into their synagogue: | And, behold, there was a man which had his hand withered. And they asked him, saying, Is it lawful to heal on the sabbath days? that they might accuse him.
> And he said unto them, What man shall there be among you, that shall have one sheep, and if it fall into a pit on the sabbath day, will he not lay hold on it, and lift it out? | How much then is a man better than a sheep?

> Wherefore it is lawful to do well on the sabbath days. | Then saith he to
> the man, Stretch forth thine hand. And he stretched it forth; and it was
> restored whole, like as the other (Matthew 12:6 –14).[63]

In essence, Jesus has said that he is above the law, claiming that he is "Lord
even of the sabbath day." Mind you, this does not explain why the disciples
should break the Sabbath, too. He ends by saying that working on the Sabbath is
okay if you are doing good or necessary deeds.

More than anything, the reasons given by Jesus show that keeping the
Sabbath wasn't a very good rule in the first place. It's a rule Jesus continues to
break.[64]

I imagine that strict observance of the Sabbath over the years had become as
problematic as offering sacrifices. New Testament writings are conveniently designed to give Christians a way out of this dilemma. If it requires that God break
his own commandment and teach others to do so, most Christians are willing to
look the other way.

***

The faulty analogy is a chronic symptom of unclear and illogical thinking.
Jesus is not immune to it. When accused by the Pharisees of casting out demons
by the power of Satan, Jesus uses some incredibly flawed logic to explain to them
why he thinks such a thing should not be possible.

> But when the Pharisees heard it, they said, This fellow doth not cast
> out devils, but by Beelzebub the prince of the devils.
> And Jesus knew their thoughts, and said unto them, Every kingdom di-
> vided against itself is brought to desolation; and every city or house divided
> against itself shall not stand: | And if Satan cast out Satan, he is divided
> against himself; how shall then his kingdom stand? | And if I by Beelzebub
> cast out devils, by whom do your children cast them out? therefore they
> shall be your judges. | But if I cast out devils by the Spirit of God, then the
> kingdom of God is come unto you. | Or else how can one enter into a strong
> man's house, and spoil his goods, except he first bind the strong man? and
> then he will spoil his house (Matthew 12:24–29).[65]

What the Pharisees most likely meant by their accusation is that if Jesus
were Satan, then he could trick people by casting out demons occasionally. The
demons, knowing that it was Satan who was casting them out, would move on
to possess somebody else, laughing among themselves, saying, "Boy, we sure
tricked those humans." It's a common ploy used by con artists throughout the
ages, to have two people who are collaborating act as if they are on opposing
sides. All of Jesus' arguments state that this sort of thing is impossible when,
clearly, it is not.

---

63 See also Mark 2:23–3:5 and Luke 6:1–10.
64 See John 5:4–16 and John 9:1–16.
65 See also Mark 3:22–27 and Luke 11:15–20.

***

As we read the gospels without the preconceived notions that are often forced upon us in churches, the behaviors and words of Jesus become increasingly suspect. He answers questions glibly and sidesteps issues as if he were a modern-day politician. He postures; he obfuscates; he throws out rapid fire defenses that are more distracting than enlightening. These are not the behaviors of a messiah. These are either the actions and words of a charismatic man who was quick-witted but inconsistent, or, possibly, those of an imaginary character written for a religion that needed a figurehead.

Watch as he grandstands at the cost of his family's pride:

> While he yet talked to the people, behold, his mother and his brethren stood without, desiring to speak with him. | Then one said unto him, Behold, thy mother and thy brethren stand without, desiring to speak with thee.
>
> But he answered and said unto him that told him, Who is my mother? and who are my brethren? And he stretched forth his hand toward his disciples, and said, Behold my mother and my brethren! | For whosoever shall do the will of my Father which is in heaven, the same is my brother, and sister, and mother (Matthew 12:46–50).[66]

In Matthew 15, the Pharisees, always looking to find fault with Jesus and the disciples, point out that they do not wash their hands when they eat. Sure, it is unhygienic and unsavory, but during that time, it was also disrespectful and violated tradition.

> Then came to Jesus scribes and Pharisees, which were of Jerusalem, saying, Why do thy disciples transgress the tradition of the elders? for they wash not their hands when they eat bread.
>
> But he answered and said unto them, Why do ye also transgress the commandment of God by your tradition (Matthew 15:2–3).

Jesus wraps up the speech that this incident has provoked by saying, "For out of the heart proceed evil thoughts, murders, adulteries, fornications, thefts, false witness, blasphemies: | These are the things which defile a man: but to eat with unwashen hands defileth not a man" (Matthew 15:19–20).

Here again, Jesus acts like a politician. He answers a question with a question. He never answers the accusation made against him. We get his point, but it does not seem to be very insightful. The story is repeated in Mark 7:1–23 and Luke 11:37–39. In the verses from Luke, it is Jesus himself who does not wash his hands, and being questioned about it results in a tirade against Pharisees and lawyers. A good lecture, it seems, will make up for poor hygiene.

***

In chapter 19, Jesus has another interesting discussion with the Pharisees.

---

66 See also Luke 8:19–21.

> The Pharisees also came unto him, tempting him, and saying unto him, Is it lawful for a man to put away his wife for every cause?
>
> And he answered and said unto them, Have ye not read, that he which made them at the beginning made them male and female, | And said, For this cause shall a man leave father and mother, and shall cleave to his wife: and they twain shall be one flesh? | Wherefore they are no more twain, but one flesh. What therefore God hath joined together, let not man put asunder.
>
> They say unto him, Why did Moses then command to give a writing of divorcement, and to put her away?
>
> He saith unto them, Moses because of the hardness of your hearts suffered you to put away your wives: but from the beginning it was not so. | And I say unto you, Whosoever shall put away his wife, except it be for fornication, and shall marry another, committeth adultery: and whoso marrieth her which is put away doth commit adultery (Matthew 19: 3–9).[67]

Jesus repeats what he said earlier in Matthew, but with a suspicious catch. According to Jesus, Moses allowed a law regarding divorce that was immoral because of the "hardness" of men's hearts. Both the Pharisees and Jesus are in agreement that this was a commandment of Moses, but the Old Testament, as well as the modern day Church, indicates that this was a precept laid down by God. Moses merely delivered it. Either way, it seems unlikely that God the Father, who killed men for lesser offenses, would sanction an act of immorality against his wishes. Jesus again places himself in a position where his teachings are opposed to that of the Old Testament and to that of his counterpart, God the Father.

Now the disciples get into the discussion.

> His disciples say unto him, If the case of the man be so with his wife, it is not good to marry.
>
> But he said unto them, All men cannot receive this saying, save they to whom it is given. | For there are some eunuchs, which were so born from their mother's womb: and there are some eunuchs, which were made eunuchs of men: and there be eunuchs, which have made themselves eunuchs for the kingdom of heaven's sake. He that is able to receive it, let him receive it (Matthew 19:10–12).

Well, that's interesting. Jesus is encouraging men, at least those who are capable of it, of becoming "eunichs." This is usually accepted figuratively, meaning that men should go without sex rather than castrating themselves. In this passage, going without sex is promoted as "holy" behavior. We have seen the consequences of that in the Catholic priesthood as well as in the lives of the hundreds of thousands of people who feel guilty and ashamed about sex even within the confines of marriage.

***

Late in the book of Matthew we hear the following story about Jesus:

---

67 See also Mark 10:2–12 and Luke 16:18.

Now in the morning as he returned into the city, he hungered. | And when he saw a fig tree in the way, he came to it, and found nothing thereon, but leaves only, and said unto it, Let no fruit grow on thee henceforward for ever. And presently the fig tree withered away.

And when the disciples saw it, they marvelled, saying, How soon is the fig tree withered away!

Jesus answered and said unto them, Verily I say unto you, If ye have faith, and doubt not, ye shall not only do this which is done to the fig tree, but also if ye shall say unto this mountain, Be thou removed, and be thou cast into the sea; it shall be done. (Matthew 21:18–21).[68]

Another variation of this is given in Luke. "And the apostles said unto the Lord, Increase our faith. And the Lord said, If ye had faith as a grain of mustard seed, ye might say unto this sycamine tree, Be thou plucked up by the root, and be thou planted in the sea; and it should obey you" (Luke 17:5–6).

Presumably, Jesus wilts the fig tree to get the disciples' attention and teach them a lesson about faith, because otherwise it is a random act to kill a tree because it does not have any fruit on it. Either way, it is the lesson about faith and the promise of answered prayer that should cause people serious doubts. With faith, Jesus tells us, we can literally move mountains. Literally! The mountains will move!

Apparently, if you ask a religionist, the problem is that no one has enough faith to do this or that no one's faith is without doubt. Otherwise, there would be all kinds of terra-forming going on at the hands of the righteous. Bulldozers would no longer be in demand.

This is what I call, "the big faith trick." The problem with faith as a method of getting things done (or as a method of preventing one's self from going astray and sinning) is that faith is not quantifiable. It cannot be measured.

This puts anyone who questions the effectiveness of faith at the mercy of the believer. The believer can always say, "You don't have enough faith."

There is no way to prove it or disprove it, because you can't hold up a bottle of faith and say, "Yes I do! Look, I've got a quart of faith right here!"

This enables the believer to continually use the faith device against those who disagree with them.

Immediately after the above passage, Jesus says, "And all things, whatsoever ye shall ask in prayer, believing, ye shall receive" (Matthew 21:22).

If that's not clear enough, in Mark 11:24 Jesus says it this way, "Therefore I say unto you, What things soever ye desire, when ye pray, believe that ye receive them, and ye shall have them."

He expounds on this even further in Luke.

---

68 See also Mark 11:12–14 and 11:20–23.

"And I say unto you, Ask, and it shall be given you; seek, and ye shall find; knock, and it shall be opened unto you. | For every one that asketh receiveth; and he that seeketh findeth; and to him that knocketh it shall be opened.

"If a son shall ask bread of any of you that is a father, will he give him a stone? or if he ask a fish, will he for a fish give him a serpent? | Or if he shall ask an egg, will he offer him a scorpion?

"If ye then, being evil, know how to give good gifts unto your children: how much more shall your heavenly Father give the Holy Spirit to them that ask him?" (Luke 11:9–13)

The believer adds the caveat that whatever we ask must be in God's will, otherwise it will not be granted. But that is not what Jesus *says*. And we know there are many things that people ask for that they do not get, even when they are in God's good graces when they ask.

Still the religionist has arguments. Whatever was prayed for may seem innocuous, but God knows what is best and he is the ultimate decision-maker about whether prayer is answered. He may say "yes," "no," or "maybe."

That just happens to be the same exact results you would get if there was no one responding to your prayers at all and events just happened randomly. Some things will happen just they way you want. Some will not. Some will have unexpected results, for better or for worse. Jesus claims far more than this. He emphatically says that God will say yes!

Unfortunately, there's no definitive way to test prayer, because the second you pray with the intent of testing God, the elements of faith and trust are gone. The statements made by Jesus are impossible to prove or disprove. As such, they are insubstantial.

***

In chapter 23 of Matthew, Jesus rails against the scribes and the Pharisees for twenty verses, referring to them repeatedly as "blind," hypocrites, and fools. If one has the image of a passive Jesus in their head, this passage should dispel that. It is not a gentle God that says, "Ye serpents, ye generation of vipers, how can ye escape the damnation of hell?" (Matthew 23:13–33)

Talking in Circles — The Gospel of John

More so than any other of the gospels, John focuses on the theology of Christianity and places a special emphasis on belief. From John comes the term "born again."[69] The other three gospels come across as a serial account of miracles and events, but in John, Jesus is much more direct about who he is, and states that he is both the Son of God and God the Father.[70] He is clear about this, but on other

---

69 John 3:5–7.
70 John 10:36–37.

topics he becomes increasingly cryptic and verbose. He speaks in riddles and parables, much to the befuddlement of his disciples.

The attitude surrounding the Gospel of John can be found in a multitude of beliefs and in the teachings of many mystics. It is the attitude that profundity lies in vagaries and mysteries, not in straightforward statements of truth. If one thinks that profundity can only be hinted at or alluded to, then perhaps there is some credence to this attitude. The problem is that you could babble inanities and have the same effect. There are psychics, authors, and television personalities today who do exactly that. They make meaningless statements and are acclaimed for their wisdom. No doubt, you will make up your own mind as to whether Jesus was guilty of the same crime.

The book of John is unique in that many of the stories repeated in Matthew, Mark, and Luke are not repeated in it. The Jesus portrayed in the Gospel of John has a different tone and voice than the Jesus of the other gospels. Nowhere else does he say, "Verily, verily," but in the book of John he does it twenty-five times. In the Gospel of John, Jesus talks in circles. Phrases and words are repeated, sometimes with the purpose of justifying each other in a mode of circular reasoning that anticipates the teachings of Paul.

Given the fact that the narrative portions in the book of John are so similar in style to the parts that are spoken by Jesus, it is easy to infer that words of Jesus were not words spoken by an actual man, but rather by the storyteller himself. If this is the case, then the writer of John has made the mistake that many writers do. His characters talk like him.

Starting in chapter 1, verse 1, we get a sense of the style, "In the beginning was the Word, and the Word was with God, and the Word was God. | The same was in the beginning with God. | All things were made by him; and without him was not any thing made that was made" (John 1:1–3).

This is the narrator speaking, but it isn't long before Jesus talks the same way:

"That which is born of the flesh is flesh; and that which is born of the Spirit is spirit" (John 3:6).

"For as the Father hath life in himself; so hath he given to the Son to have life in himself" (John 5:26).

"He that is of God heareth God's words: ye therefore hear them not, because ye are not of God" (John 8:47).

Jesus answered, If I honour myself, my honour is nothing: it is my Father that honoureth me; of whom ye say, that he is your God: | Yet ye have not known him; but I know him: and if I should say, I know him not, I shall be a liar like unto you: but I know him, and keep his saying (John 8:54–55).

"But ye believe not, because ye are not of my sheep, as I said unto you. | My sheep hear my voice, and I know them, and they follow me" (John 10:26–27).

"If I do not the works of my Father, believe me not. | But if I do, though ye believe not me, believe the works: that ye may know, and believe, that the Father is in me, and I in him" (John 10:37–38).

"For I have not spoken of myself; but the Father which sent me, he gave me a commandment, what I should say, and what I should speak. | And I know that his commandment is life everlasting: whatsoever I speak therefore, even as the Father said unto me, so I speak" (John 12:49–50).

"I pray for them: I pray not for the world, but for them which thou hast given me; for they are thine. | And all mine are thine, and thine are mine; and I am glorified in them" (John 17:9–10).

"They are not of the world, even as I am not of the world" (John 17:16).

"That they all may be one; as thou, Father, art in me, and I in thee, that they also may be one in us: that the world may believe that thou hast sent me" (John 17:21).

"I in them, and thou in me, that they may be made perfect in one; and that the world may know that thou hast sent me, and hast loved them, as thou hast loved me" (John 17:23).

It is easy to get lost in this jumble of — "I am him; he is me; if you believe in him, you believe in me; if you don't believe in me, you don't believe in him" — craziness.

If you find the sayings of Jesus confusing, so did the disciples. In the book of John, however, their confusion is over the statements of Jesus that can be deciphered relatively easily. At one point they say, "What manner of saying is this that he said, Ye shall seek me, and shall not find me: and where I am, thither ye cannot come?" (John 7:36).

I love the expression "What manner of saying is this?" I can picture the disciples huddled around saying, "What did he just say? What does that *mean*?"

Of course, in this instance, Jesus is either saying that he is going to heaven and the disciples cannot immediately follow him, or he is talking about his death and resurrection.

A similar situation comes up in John 16:18. The disciples are again confused, "They said therefore, What is this that he saith, A little while? we cannot tell what he saith."

The author of John is using this as a literary device. Jesus had told them that he will be gone for a little while and they will not see him, but then he will return and they will see him (John 16:16). It's a variation on what he said in chapter 7.

"These things have I spoken unto you in proverbs:," Jesus says, "but the time cometh, when I shall no more speak unto you in proverbs, but I shall shew you plainly of the Father" (John 16:25). Then he rambles on for several more verses, and the disciples, wanting something comprehensible, make it known.

"His disciples said unto him, Lo, now speakest thou plainly, and speakest no proverb" (John 16:29).

They should have stopped there, but they go on to say, "Now are we sure that thou knowest all things, and needest not that any man should ask thee: by this we believe that thou camest forth from God" (John 16:30).

This gives Jesus his out. He says, "Do ye now believe?" (John 16:31) He has successfully avoided their plea to speak plainly and says, in effect, that the way he had communicated to them is just fine because they believe in him — although they still don't understand him. Yet, it is uncertain that his stories are what convinced the disciples. The miracles Jesus is reported to have performed are more likely to have been what convinced them. Jesus has justified his teachings by crediting them with a result that they did not cause. It is nonsensical from start to finish.

***

Let's return to chapter 6, where we meet up again with the troubling subject of predestination.

"But there are some of you that believe not. For Jesus knew from the beginning who they were that believed not, and who should betray him. | And he said, Therefore said I unto you, that no man can come unto me, except it were given unto him of my Father" (John 6:64–65).

This time it comes straight from Jesus — we do not have free will. Our salvation is predetermined by God. This shouldn't be surprising after Jesus' repeated insistence that the only ones who can hear and understand God's words are those to whom God has already given the ability to do so.

***

In chapter 9, before Jesus heals a blind man, there is a short conversation between Jesus and the disciples:

"And his disciples asked him, saying, Master, who did sin, this man, or his parents, that he was born blind?

"Jesus answered, Neither hath this man sinned, nor his parents: but that the works of God should be made manifest in him" (John 9:2–3).

There are two points of interest here. The first is that the disciples assume that the blind man is blind because someone, either his parents or the blind man himself, has sinned. The disciples hold the view that infirmities and sickness are the result of sin as opposed to being the result of diseases, viruses, etc. This belief is one of the central premises of Christian "Science." How wrong it is. It is unfair to add a burden of guilt to someone who is already in poor health or who is disabled. If there were a crowd of people with this attitude at a Special Olympics event, they would "tsk, tsk" the participants and wave their fingers in disapproval, rather than cheer the participants on.

Although it is not often expressed outwardly, this is similar to an underlying attitude that people of all sorts subscribe to, the attitude that if something is wrong in another person's life, regardless of what it is, that person is probably to blame. While we are responsible for things that happen as a result of our own poor choices, there are many things that are out of our hands, such as how we are born physically, events like natural disasters, as well as the many illnesses and tragedies that can easily come our way. Blaming the victim is a psychological defense that is often unconsciously employed so that people do not have to acknowledge that bad things could happen to them or so that they do not have to take any responsibility. It is another form of denial.

In the instance portrayed here in John, Jesus does nothing to point out to his disciples that they are suffering from a serious misconception that is injurious to people, nor does Jesus tell them that their attitude is not compassionate. Rather, Jesus says that the man has been made blind by God so that Jesus can heal him. This man suffered throughout his life to set the stage for a miracle. If Jesus had simply healed a blind man who was blind due to circumstances, this scenario would seem a lot more impressive. As it is, both the New Testament God and the Old Testament God come across as callous and insensitive.

***

Before Jesus is taken away to be crucified, he prays.

> "I have given them thy word; and the world hath hated them, because they are not of the world, even as I am not of the world. | I pray not that thou shouldest take them out of the world, but that thou shouldest keep them from the evil. | They are not of the world, even as I am not of the world" (John 17:14–16).

Being "not of this world" is a common Christian theme that takes advantage of the natural human feeling that we do not fit in or belong here. This feeling is natural for several reasons. We are surrounded by people who are different from us in thousands of ways. Our environment can be very confusing and/or hostile. Our thoughts and consciousness take place within our minds and, until we communicate with each other, none of us can know what is going on in the minds of other people. When we do communicate, it is not always easy, and there is no way to communicate all of what goes on inside us. Of course we feel like we are alone and like we don't belong.

However, this is our home, and it is the only home we will ever have. There is no *need* to feel distanced from our world and our philosophies should not make us feel removed from it either. When a religion does this, it does more harm than good.

BAD ADVICE

Throughout the rest of the New Testament we can find some very bad advice.

Early in Matthew, Jesus has the following conversation with Peter:

> Then came Peter to him, and said, Lord, how oft shall my brother sin against me, and I forgive him? till seven times?
> Jesus saith unto him, I say not unto thee, Until seven times: but, Until seventy times seven (Matthew 18:21–22).

That's 490 times, if you have done the math. Jesus expands upon this in Luke.

> "But I say unto you which hear, Love your enemies, do good to them which hate you, | Bless them that curse you, and pray for them which despitefully use you. | And unto him that smiteth thee on the one cheek offer also the other; and him that taketh away thy cloak forbid not to take thy coat also. | Give to every man that asketh of thee; and of him that taketh away thy goods ask them not again" (Luke 6:27–30).

If you take Jesus' words at face value, then here you have a recipe for extreme passivity. When I read these words, I think of the image of Jesus being led to the cross and being beaten mercilessly by the guards. If he's modeling the behavior we are supposed to emulate and his words are telling us how we should act, then it's not surprising that people have found other ways to interpret what Jesus has instructed. But do people truly believe that Jesus meant something else, or are they afraid to take him literally? Certainly what Jesus proscribes is not easy to do, but it may very well be that so many people have instinctively chosen not to do this because they know deep down inside that it's not a wise course of action. It is possible there are situations where turning the other cheek can communicate a message of love and tolerance to another human being. But to unnecessarily take abuse from our fellow man, even if we do so with dignity and love, reinforces the behaviors of those who would do ill unto us by letting them know they can get away with it. Despite the attitude in which it is done, turning the other cheek requires that one must suppress his or her self-interests, which, in the long term, can be psychologically (if not otherwise) detrimental, especially if done all the time. "Seventy times seven" is what Jesus said to Peter. The damage is magnified rather than lessened.

I would think that somehow we would want to strike a balance between "an eye for an eye" and turning the other check, but nowhere in the gospels is this mentioned.

Following this passage is the verse that says, "And as ye would that men should do to you, do ye also to them likewise" (Luke 6:31). This is known as the golden rule and is often referred to as one of Christ's greatest pieces of wisdom. Unfortunately, it is not even original. Great thinkers and figureheads of faiths other than Christianity said it a long time before Jesus did. In the Old Testament book of Leviticus it is said in this form: "thou shalt love thy neighbour as thyself" (Leviticus 19:18).

Although it is a nice principle, it doesn't always work well. In some cases, it is a recipe for trouble. People do not always want to be treated the way you want to be treated. Because of this some people recommend that we treat people the way *they* want to be treated. Unfortunately, that does not always work either. The way we treat people, and the way individuals want to be treated, depends on the individuals involved and the circumstances. There is no one generalized rule that will work for everyone, and to suggest one, as Jesus does here, is trite.

The intent of the verses following these, as described in many Sunday morning services, is that Jesus wants people to know that following him should be more important than anything else in the world, even family.

> And he said unto another, Follow me. But he said, Lord, suffer me first to go and bury my father. Jesus said unto him, Let the dead bury their dead: but go thou and preach the kingdom of God.
> And another also said, Lord, I will follow thee; but let me first go bid them farewell, which are at home at my house.
> And Jesus said unto him, No man, having put his hand to the plough, and looking back, is fit for the kingdom of God (Luke 9:59–62).

In addition to being rude and inconsiderate, this is in conflict with the above-cited golden rule and with the commandment to honor one's parents. A compassionate God would not put himself at odds with a person's loved ones, family, or their emotional need for closure, unless it was absolutely necessary. Those who are truly compassionate understand that it is no act of love to force others to choose between them and someone else. By making such a demand when it is unnecessary, a person (or in this case, someone claiming to be God) shows a lack of maturity, if nothing else.

Jesus finds an equally undiplomatic way of delivering the same message in Luke 14:26, "If any man come to me, and hate not his father, and mother, and wife, and children, and brethren, and sisters, yea, and his own life also, he cannot be my disciple."

If someone told me I wasn't allowed to bury my father, or that I couldn't say goodbye to my family, or that I had to "hate" my family, I would immediately see that this was not the kind of person that I wanted to follow. Even with the added explanation that what Jesus means is that he should be made first priority, he doesn't come off much better. This tyrannical demand for loyalty — at the expense of those we care for and even at the expense of those we are responsible for — is at odds with the image of Jesus that we are often force-fed. It is also at odds with the "family values" that Christianity is supposed to represent.

Note that these verses occur only in the Gospel of Luke. When I consider that each gospel was written by a different person with a slightly different take, I wonder if the writer of "Luke" might have been a tad less compassionate than the writers of the other gospels and, when doing his part in creating the Jesus myth, went a little overboard.

***

Throughout the Bible women are treated with disparagement. Paul adds his contribution to this in 1 Corinthians. Far too many times I have heard this particular verse written off as a result of "culture." During Paul's time, women were not out and about in the world, and because of the resulting lack of information and experience, they may not have had something to contribute to certain discussions. But when you read the words themselves, it becomes apparent that Paul was writing with a clearly chauvinistic mindset. Even with God at his side, he was unable to rise above his cultural surroundings, which is an important thing to do in a book supposedly written for the edification of all of humanity. Either the attitude of the modern feminist is wrong or the attitude of Paul and his predecessors is wrong.

> Let your women keep silence in the churches; for it is not permitted unto them to speak, but they are to be under obediance, as also saith the law.
>
> And if they will learn anything, let them ask their husbands at home; for it is a shame for women to speak in the church (1 Corinthians 14:34–35).

You can try to soften these words, but when you return to them and read them word by word, the attitude is clear. If that passage is not enough, in I Timothy, Paul expounds upon what the role and behavior of Christian women should be.

> In like manner also, that women adorn themselves in modest apparel, with shamefacedness and sobriety; not with broided hair, or gold, or pearls, or costly array; | But (which becometh women professing godliness) with good works.
>
> Let the woman learn in silence with all subjection.
>
> But I suffer not a woman to teach, nor to usurp authority over the man, but to be in silence.
>
> For Adam was first formed, then Eve. | And Adam was not deceived, but the woman being deceived was in the transgression. | Notwithstanding she shall be saved in childbearing, if they continue in faith and charity and holiness with sobriety (I Timothy 2:9–15).

Don't make yourselves look good, and don't wear jewelry, Paul says to the women. Since the very beginning of humankind, you were meant to be in second place. Be quiet, and if you are faithful and have children, you just might save yourself.

***

In James, we read the following:

> But above all things, my brethren, swear not, neither by heaven, neither by the earth, neither by any other oath: but let your yea be yea; and your nay, nay; lest ye fall into condemnation.
>
> Is any among you afflicted? let him pray. Is any merry? let him sing psalms.
>
> Is any sick among you? let him call for the elders of the church; and let them pray over him, anointing him with oil in the name of the Lord:
>
> And the prayer of faith shall save the sick, and the Lord shall raise him up; and if he have committed sins, they shall be forgiven him (James 5:12–15).

There are two pieces to this. The first is that we should not swear (it is clear that this means to make promises rather than to cuss), which is fine. But that means that, when we are in court, putting our hands on the Bible and taking an oath to promise to tell the whole truth, etc., is a sin. No one should be swearing on the Bible, not the atheist who doesn't believe in it, nor the Christian who does.

The second part of these verses presents a real, practical problem. If someone is sick, the advice is to pray over him or her. From these verses we get people who think that prayer can heal sickness and we get some of the doctrines of Christian Science. Sadly, there are real world headlines where people have chosen prayer over medical care, and the loved ones that they were trying to save have died. The "out" is to say that whatever happened was God's will. But if it is God's will that we take care of the sick with all earthly means we have at our disposal, or if God did not have a hand in the situation, or if God does not exist, then a senseless tragedy has occurred.

THE END TIMES

As a believer, one of the most difficult barriers I had to cross before I put Christianity behind me 100 percent was my fear that the world would turn out as predicted in the biblical book of Revelations. I envisioned myself wandering a planet that was torn by apocalyptic forces of good and evil, regretting all the while that I had made the wrong choices.

This fear was fueled by gloomy sermons and the works of authors like Hal Lindsay, whose vision of the "End Times" is not that far off from that of the more recent *Left Behind* series.

Christians will tell you that Jesus could return at any moment, and the events detailed in Revelation may already be in motion. I often wonder if, by the time humanity has made its way out through the solar system and taken up residence on other planets, there will still be Christians out there predicting that the return of Christ is imminent. The single most effective argument about prophecies of the future is the one thing that makes them so enduring: the fact that they have yet to come true. Like everything else in the world of belief, if it cannot be disproved, it continues to be believed. Yet the skeptic still has good reason to doubt.

Christ's return has been thought of as "just over the horizon" since the time of Christ himself. When describing the End Times, Jesus said, "Verily I say unto you, This generation shall not pass, till all these things be fulfilled" (Luke 24:34).[71] I was taught that Jesus meant "the generation of man," or "the generation of Christians," rather than the generation of people who were alive at the time he was speaking. The fundamentalist, who is willing to take everything else literally, is not willing to take this statement literally because then his whole belief system would be wrong. Yet many *did* think that Christ would return even back then.

Jesus describes the conditions that will exist at the time of his return.

> And ye shall hear of wars and rumours of wars: see that ye be not troubled: for all these things must come to pass, but the end is not yet.
> For nation shall rise against nation, and kingdom against kingdom: and there shall be famines, and pestilences, and earthquakes, in divers places.
> All these are the beginning of sorrows (Luke 24:6-7).[72]

With the exception of pestilence, which is often overlooked anyway, all of these have been happening since humankind has been around. There have always been famines, wars, and earthquakes at some place on the globe. When they occur, out come the same old verses and the cries of, "Look, it's the End Times!"

The number of the beast is a strong part of the apocalyptic vision as detailed in Revelation:

> And he had power to give life unto the image of the beast, that the image of the beast should both speak, and cause that as many as would not worship the image of the beast should be killed. | And he causeth all, both small and great, rich and poor, free and bond, to receive a mark in their right hand, or in their foreheads: | And that no man might buy or sell, save he that had the mark, or the name of the beast, or the number of his name.
> Here is wisdom. Let him that hath understanding count the number of the beast: for it is the number of a man; and his number is Six hundred threescore and six (Revelation 13:15-18).

There have been a slew of guesses as to who the beast is, what the number "666" actually means, and how it will be used. A common theory is that it signifies a number that will someday be assigned to each person and used for iden-

---

71 See also Mark 13:30.
72 See also Mark 13:17-8.

tification like a Social Security number or credit card number. At least such a description is in accordance with the words of Revelation.

However, it is quite possible that all this speculation centers around a riddle that was solved a long time ago and that was based on the premise that Jesus would return within the lifetimes of those who had known him as a human being.

John, the author of Revelations, spoke Hebrew as his native tongue. Michael Macrone, author of *Brush Up Your Bible*, makes the observation that Hebrews used letters to represent numbers.

> If you render the Hebrew name for Nero Caesar into Hebrew script, you get *nrwn qsr*. Each Hebrew character in turn has a numerical value, which, when summed up, yields the magic number, 666. (Try it yourself; n =50; r=200; w =6; q=100 and s = 60. Hebrews, like the Romans, used letters to represent numbers.) The trick works equally well in John's native language, Aramaic.[73]

There it is. We have been playing a pointless game ever since.

PROPHECIES FULFILLED?

Biblical apologists claim that many Old Testament prophecies were fulfilled by Jesus in the New Testament. This is often put forth as evidence of the legitimacy of the Bible.

Below I have provided a list of verses. The Old Testament verses are said to be prophecies, and the New Testament verses are reported to be the fulfillment of the prophecies. If you wish, you can compare them. You'll notice that the majority of the New Testament verses come from the book of Matthew. As he tells the story of Jesus, the author of Matthew often states, matter-of-factly, that what Jesus did was a fulfillment of prophecy as predicted in the Old Testament.

Subject	Old Testament Verses	New Testament Verses
Jesus born of a virgin	Isaiah 7:14	Matthew 1:18,24–25
"For unto us a child is born"	Isaiah 9:6	Matthew 1:18 –23
"Out of Egypt have I called my son"	Hosea 11:1	Matthew 2:13–15
"Rahel weeping for her children"	Jeremiah 31:15	Matthew 2:17–18
Jesus called a Nazarene	Isaiah 11:1	Matthew 2:23

---

73 Michael Macrone, *Brush Up Your Bible* (New York: Harper Collins, 1993), p. 316.

John the Baptist	Isaiah 40:3	Matthew 3:3, Matthew 11:10, Mark 1:2–4, Luke 7:26–29, Luke 3:4
People in darkness seeing light	Isaiah 42: 6–7	Matthew 4:14–16
Description of Jesus	Isaiah 42:1–4	Matthew 12:17–21
People won't understand Jesus	Deuteronomy 29:3–4	Matthew 13:14–15, John 12:37–40
Jesus will speak in parables	Psalms 78:2	Matthew 13:34–35
30 pieces of silver	Zechariah 11:12	Matthew 26:15, Matthew 27:9-10
Jesus not answering accusers	Isaiah 53:7	Matthew 27:12–19
Jesus crucified with thieves	Isaiah 53:12	Matthew 27:38
People would be hypocrites	Isaiah 29:13	Mark 7:6
Description of Jesus' actions	Isaiah 61:1–2	Luke 4:16–21
Jesus arrives on a donkey (Palm Sunday)	Zechariah 9:9	Luke 19:35–37, John 12–14:15
"The zeal of thine house"	Psalms 69:9	John 2:16–17
People will hate Jesus for no reason	Psalms 69:4	John 15:25
Jesus whipped and crucified for sinners	Isaiah 53:5–6	John 19:1,18
Soldiers casting lots for Jesus' clothes	Psalms 22:18	John 19:24
Jesus says, "I thirst."	Psalms 69:21	John 19:28
Jesus' bones will not be broken	Psalms 34:20	John 19:34–36
Jesus' side pierced with a spear	Zechariah 12:10	John 19:34–37

If you read the Old Testament passages noted in the list above, as well as the verses that surround them, you will see that the Old Testament passages are often long, vague, and filled with indefinite pronouns. It is not common for the focus to switch from one person to another without any identification of who is being talked about. The authors of the Old Testament frequently used the words "he" and "him" without antecedents. It makes you wonder what they had against proper nouns.

None of the Old Testament passages listed above refer to Jesus by name. They are not like the Old Testament prophecies, which are both "predicted and fulfilled" in the Old Testament and are quite specific, i.e., "The dogs shall eat Jezebel by the wall of Jezreel."[74] The Old Testament prophecies could be very specific because they were told as stories of something that happened in the past and were, therefore, easily subject to manipulation. Their reliability cannot be trusted.

Many of the Old Testament verses listed above are descriptions of something that happened in Old Testament times that you would not think of as a prophecy unless someone told you it was. The passages do not appear to have anything to do with the New Testament.

An example of this is the Old Testament reference of Hosea 11:1 that says, "When Israel was a child, then I loved him, and called my son out of Egypt." It is so obviously taken out of context that it is hard to accept that anyone could consider it a legitimate prophecy.

One explanation I have heard from the Christian camp is that the Old Testament passages are "dual prophecies," which are descriptive of what occurred in the past while being prophetic of what would happen with Jesus. I truly hope that you see how weak an argument like this is. If a prophecy is nothing more than words or situations from the past that are repeated in the future, then anything can become a prophecy and anyone can become a prophet.

Let's look at two more pairs of verses, Zechariah 11:12 as compared to Matthew 26:15 and then Isaiah 53:12 as compared with Matthew 27:38.

Zechariah 11:12 says, "And I said unto them, If ye think good, give me my price; and if not, forbear. So they weighed for my price thirty pieces of silver." Matthew 26:15 relates how Jesus was betrayed for thirty pieces of silver. Well, we've got a transaction and a matching dollar amount, but that is all we have. The verse in Zechariah does not even mention a betrayal. The rest of the surrounding passage is equally nondescript. It is even unclear who is supposed to be making this statement.

The second prophecy is said to indicate that Jesus was hung on the cross beside two thieves, but when you read the passage in Isaiah 53:12, all it says is, "He was numbered with the transgressors." There is a long way to go between the prophecy and the fulfillment. Again, who, exactly, is "he"?

The first verses from our list (Isaiah 7:14 and 9:6) are the ones that we hear so often repeated around Christmas time, which say, "Behold, a virgin shall conceive, and bear a son, and shall call his name Immanuel," as well as, "For unto us a child is born..."

---

74 I Kings 21:23.

The only proper noun that can be found anywhere around these verses are in Isaiah 8:1 where it says, "Moreover the LORD said unto me, Take thee a great roll, and write in it with a man's pen concerning Mahershalalhashbaz." This suggests that the verses are about Mahershalalhashbaz, but it's not clear who Mahershalalhashbaz is. Is he also called Immanuel? We do not know. It is such a jumbled mess that almost anything could be made of it.

Isaiah 11:1, the fifth verse from the list above, says, "And there shall come forth a rod out of the stem of Jesse, and a Branch shall grow out of his roots." Matthew 2:23, the verse that refers to it, says that Jesus shall be "called a Nazarene." To make any sense of this, one has to refer to the earlier Hebrew translation of the verse, where the phrase in question is "Yeshua Netzer." The phrase means that the savior will be a descendent of Jesse (and, therefore, David). For the prophecy in Matthew 2:23 to be accurate as it is stated, the word Netzer had to be mistranslated as "Nazer," which would then make it refer Nazareth. This is one of those errors that scholars recognize, but Biblical literalists refuse to acknowledge. It also implies that the phrase "Jesus of Nazareth" is the result of a mistranslation.

When one tries to take the Old Testament verses and correlate them with the New, it takes a bit of forcing, as if taking puzzle pieces from one puzzle and putting them into another.

The authors of the New Testament have used the generality trick. Matthew simply took Old Testament passages out of context and molded them to fit the situations surrounding the biblical Christ. It is not too difficult to imagine him doing so when the practice of reporting prophecies and their fulfillment was a standard literary motif in the Old Testament. Science fiction and fantasy authors of today do the same. Frank Herbert used the technique to great effect in his classic novel *Dune*. Christians will accuse me of trivializing the miraculous by saying this, but my conclusions come as a result of reading all the verses in their proper context.

There is little difference between what is happening here and how people interpret the prophecies of Nostradamus, except for the fact that a lot of people take the Bible more seriously. Biblical prophecies are convincing because of their reputation, not their content.

These are not all the verses that are sometimes identified as prophecies. A number of minor occurrences in the volumes of the Old Testament have been plucked out and transformed into a reference to Jesus. It is like a word game called, "Find the phrase in the Old Testament that matches the New Testament!" People have emulated the gospel authors without even thinking that what they were doing had no root in the predictive powers of the Bible.

These parallels hardly rank as prophecies, let alone as any sort of evidence or proof. At best, they are inconclusive.

SMART IS STUPID

After studying the Bible, I had many questions. Why didn't God provide us with useful medical cures rather than some generalized list of commandments? Why, if God were going to communicate to mankind through a book, did he not speak clearly? That could have prevented scores of debates, arguments, and deaths that occurred within the Christian community itself. If God had dictated portions of the Bible to the prophets, why wasn't he a better writer?

Responses are that I'm a fool for asking these questions, that I've committed the sin of pride and overestimated my own intelligence, and that God has his own way of doing things that is far wiser than I am ever capable of understanding. According to Christianity and the Bible, the wisdom of man is foolishness, at least in those instances where it does not agree with Christianity. If you recognize this as nothing more than contradiction, then you are correct. With this twisted logic, wisdom magically becomes foolishness and foolishness becomes wisdom. It has no more validity than the accusations of two children who shout back and forth at each other saying, "No I'm not!" and "Yes you are!" What this kind of thinking leads to is anti-intellectualism. The hidden message is that we should not think for ourselves, nor should we trust our own minds or reason. We should trust God, the Church, and the Bible to do our reasoning for us.

Here's how the Bible expresses it:

> Trust in the LORD with all thine heart; and lean not unto thine own understanding (Proverbs 3:5).

> For my thoughts are not your thoughts, neither are your ways my ways, saith the LORD. | For as the heavens are higher than the earth, so are my ways higher than your ways, and my thoughts than your thoughts (Isaiah 55:8–9).

> At that time Jesus answered and said, I thank thee, O Father, Lord of heaven and earth, because thou hast hid these things from the wise and prudent, and hast revealed them unto babes. | Even so, Father: for so it seemed good in thy sight (Matthew 11:25–26).

> For it is written, I will destroy the wisdom of the wise, and will bring to nothing the understanding of the prudent.
> Where is the wise? Where is the scribe? Where is the disputer of this world? Hath not God made foolish the wisdom of this world?
> For after that in the wisdom of God the world by wisdom knew not God, it pleased God by the foolishness of preaching to save them that believe (I Corinthians 1:19–21).

> Because the foolishness of God is wiser than men; and the weakness of God is stronger than men.

> For ye see your calling, brethren, how that not many wise men after the flesh, not many mighty, not many noble, are called:
>
> But God hath chosen the foolish things of the world to confound the wise; and God hath chosen the weak things of the world to confound the things which are mighty; | And base things of the world, and things which are despised, hath God chosen, yea, and things which are not, to bring to nought things that are (I Corinthians 1:25–28).
>
> Let no man deceive himself. If any man among you seemeth to be wise in this world, let him become a fool, that he may be wise.
>
> For the wisdom of this world is foolishness with God. For it is written, He taketh the wise in their own craftiness. | And again, The Lord knoweth the thoughts of the wise, that they are vain (I Corinthians 3:18–20).

Men are fools, says the Bible. We think we are smart, but we're not. This message stifles any independent thought that goes in a direction other than that which the Church would have us to believe. By redefining the word "wisdom," Christians not only convince themselves that they don't have any reason to listen to anyone else, but they embrace an attitude that says, "what you call knowledge is not useful."

It is no wonder that, as I grew up, I was suspicious of logic, reason, and science, and that I had to learn to trust and appreciate them, especially in regard to philosophical matters. Here again we see that the central battle over these issues comes down to what method we use to understand our world — faith or reason. It is no accident that many agnostics and atheists also refer to themselves as "freethinkers."

A Troubled History

As I wrap up this examination of Christianity and the Bible, it helps to gain a historical perspective on Christianity.

Biblical historians tell us that the four gospels of the Bible — Matthew, Mark, Luke, and John — were written in approximately AD 60 and later. That means that the earliest of the gospels was written thirty years after Christ's death. These were all written *after* the letters of Paul, which make up a great portion of the New Testament.

Some have suggested that the early theology of Christianity was mostly the creation of Paul. He developed it and spread it by visiting churches and sending letters. The gospels were written after the fact to back up what he said and to give a face to Jesus, the figurehead of Christianity.

C.S. Lewis, the well-known biblical apologist and Christian advocate, was well aware of the dates of these documents and the order in which they were created. Moreover, he was aware of what it implied, that Christianity could very well be "Paulianity." While acknowledging that Paul's writings came first, he manages to give it a different spin.

> The Resurrection is the central theme in every Christian sermon report-ed in the Acts. The Resurrection, and its consequences, were the "gospel" or good news which the Christians brought: what we call the "gospels," the narratives of Our Lord's life and death, were composed later for the benefit of those who had already accepted the *gospel*. They were in no sense the basis of Christianity: they were written for those already converted. The miracle of the Resurrection, and the theology of that miracle, comes first: the biography comes later as a comment on it.[75]

However, with the books written in this order, is quite conceivable that the events in the gospels were invented to complete the theology that Paul had al-ready devised.

Of the gospels, Mark was probably written first, with Matthew and Luke patterned after it. In church I was always given the impression that the gospels were first hand accounts, but this is not the case at all. The author of Luke con-firms that his book is not a firsthand account, in Luke 1:1–3.

> Forasmuch as many have taken in hand to set forth in order a declara-tion of those things which are most surely believed among us, | Even as they delivered them unto us, which from the beginning were eyewitnesses, and ministers of the word; | It seemed good to me also, having had perfect understanding of all things from the very first, to write unto thee in order, most excellent Theophilus.

Some of the material found in Matthew and Luke is the same, but cannot be found in Mark. This has caused some biblical scholars to speculate that Mat-thew and Luke took this material from another source that they refer to as "Q." A German author by the name of Christian Herman Weisse originated this idea. The "Q" represents the German word "Quelle," meaning source. A much sim-pler explanation would be that Luke borrowed passages from Matthew, or vice versa.

Here again, the conservative Christian account is different from the scholarly account. Some conservatives say that all the gospels were written independently and because the accounts confirm each other, the three gospels then serve as evidence of the historical existence of Jesus.

There is debate over who wrote the gospels as well. On one hand, some say that Matthew, Mark, Luke, and John were written by a Jewish tax collector, a missionary, a physician, and a fisherman respectively. On the other hand, some people say that we do not know who wrote them.

The history of how Christianity grew is also a bit murky. The Bible reports that the apostles of Jesus spread the word, creating many small independent churches. We do know that Christianity started as a small sect and that many

---

75 C.S. Lewis, *Miracles*, 2001 ed. (New York: HarperCollins, 2001), p. 234.

Christians were persecuted for their beliefs, forcing it to become an underground movement.

The Christian fish symbol with the letters IXOYE (an acronym that spells out the word for "fish" in Greek, but stands for "Jesus Christ, God's Son, Savior") was a secret symbol among the early Christians that they used to recognize each other.

The Christians were persecuted for their beliefs, tortured, crucified, and thrown to lions. Many of the early Christian leaders were targeted by the Roman Empire. Stephen was stoned to death, while Paul was incarcerated and eventually decapitated.

One of the weakest arguments for Christianity and the existence of Jesus as a historical figure, as put forth by C.S. Lewis and others, is that people would not have been willing to face persecution, willing to become martyrs, or have been so dedicated to spreading his teachings if Jesus had not existed. This completely disregards the fact that people can and do devote themselves fanatically (even to death) for ideas which are wrong. People die for cult leaders. It's terrible, it's frightening, and it proves nothing about the legitimacy of a belief.

(As a side note, I find it ironic that, while the ministers of the churches I attended as a youth told me that when I grew up I would be persecuted for my beliefs as a Christian, nearly the opposite is true. It is socially acceptable to be a Christian, but, more often than not, being an atheist is something that is looked down upon in America.)

As the years progressed, Christianity became increasingly mainstream. It worked its way up through the middle classes and into the upper classes. Church leaders accepted a hierarchical structure to the Church, patterned after those in use by the Roman Empire, and soon it was an organization. This helped it gain popularity and enabled it to grow, but one wonders what price Christianity paid for this. Did fundamental precepts of the religion have to be sacrificed in order for it to gain widespread approval? Years later, people like Martin Luther would argue that Christianity had lost something in the process, that important values had been lost along the way.

The Roman Emperor Constantine had a profound effect upon Christianity in many ways. At that time, the Roman Empire had been divided into regions ruled over by separate emperors. Constantine, who ruled out of York, England, far to the northwest, decided to take over. He waged a campaign, marched down through Europe and across to Rome, taking over the entire Roman Empire.

It is said that before he entered Rome to conquer it, he had a vision in which he saw a cross superimposed over the sun, and he heard a voice saying that he would conquer Rome under that sign. When he did so, Christianity had the backing of the emperor of the entire Roman Empire and, because of that, rose to become the predominant religion.

It is suggested that Constantine was a shrewd and cunning politician who knew that the religious masses were more pliable and were more likely to mindlessly follow a leader, so, with this in mind, he constructed the story of his vision. Although Constantine advocated Christianity, there was also a strong element of Paganism — another predominant religion that focused on the gods of nature such as the Sun God — in his beliefs.

In AD 311, Constantine issued the Edict of Milan, which ordered toleration for Christians so that they would no longer be persecuted.

The Christian Church, at that time, was the Catholic Church and was centered in Rome. Today's bumper sticker that says "Catholicism: the original Christianity" makes a good point. The Church that Paul established was not a Protestant Church. It became Catholicism. The Catholic Church was the dominant form of Christianity for hundreds of years.

By AD 325, the Catholic Church had become stronger, and it was then that another controversy occurred. A man by the name of Arius proposed the idea that since Jesus was conceived by God the Father, then Jesus must have had a beginning and was not the same as God the Father.

This idea, of course, was considered heresy. It caused a huge crisis, and Emperor Constantine called a meeting in which the issue was debated. This, the Council of Nicea, was to be the first of many Church councils. The result of this meeting was a document that clearly identified the ideas of Arius as heresy and officially established the idea of God as a Trinity (Father, Son, and Holy Spirit).

Emperor Constantine also commissioned the creation of fifty Bibles. Before that, different churches had different versions of the New Testament that included some books and did not include others. Some of the books that were present then, but that are not in the commonly accepted New Testament, include what are called the Gnostic Gospels and a book called "The Shepherd of Hermes."

At some point, it had to be decided which books would be kept and which books would be left out. There are several stories saying that the Council of Nicea voted on these books and that the Council also altered the Bible, doing various things such as removing verses that supported the idea of reincarnation.[76] Some Catholics claim that the Council argued about which books to include in the Bible, and when they could not come to a decision, an angel appeared and told them which books to use. Still others say that the Council had nothing to do with choosing what books were included in the Bible. Regardless, the decision was made somehow, and, in AD 367, the Church announced what the books of the New Testament would be. They have remained as such ever since.

The Council of Nicea did decide when Easter would be celebrated. The day chosen also coincided with the Pagan celebration of fertility and new life, which is why we have eggs and bunnies mixed in with the story of Jesus.

As one studies the history of Christianity, it becomes evident how great Emperor Constantine's influence was. Another thing he did was to force the Christians to move their day of worship from Saturday, the time-honored Hebrew Sabbath, to Sunday, which was a day dedicated to the pagan Sun God. Many Christians probably accepted this with the thought that it didn't matter when they worshipped as long as they *did* worship, but the conflict over this issue would rise again hundreds of years later as a force behind the Seventh Day Adventist Church. It cannot legitimately be denied that, when it comes down to the technicalities of this issue, they are right.

For years after Constantine, the Church was closely tied to the State. As the Roman Empire grew and fell, as barbarian hordes swept across Europe during the Dark Ages, and as King Charlemagne of France led his great campaigns, Christianity was a government-sponsored religion. This intertwining of Church and State made it clear that it is exceptionally dangerous to mix the two. It created political and religious divisions. It showed how the power and money associated with politics can corrupt a religion and the religious personages associated with it. When Church and State are not separate, any individual who does not accept the state's religion can then be considered a traitor and a state criminal. Hundreds of years later, America's founding fathers would take note of these problems when documenting the principles that America is based on.

During the first millennium, as King Charlemagne's troops took country after country under their control, people were converted to Christianity at the point of the sword. It is hard to imagine that such conversions would be conversions of the heart.

---

76 Shirley MacLaine's New Age potpourri of a book, *Out On A Limb*, is one of many places where this idea has been propagated.

The Catholic Church had been going strong for hundreds of years when, in 1517, Martin Luther, who had grown disillusioned with the Church and the abuses he had seen within it, posted his infamous 95 Theses. The Theses was a list of questions and complaints about the Catholic Church. With it, Martin began the Protestant Reformation, which would eventually result in the Protestant Church.

Sadly, it also led to religious wars and many people were killed, once again, over religious ideals. The Inquisition that followed, as well as the more recent witch hunts in America, reveal a much darker side of the Church, both Catholic and Protestant. Torture and killing done in God's name show Christianity, at times, to be no kinder than its Old Testament predecessor.

Today, the split between Luther and the Catholic Church is echoed a thousand times over, although not as markedly, as each new denomination splits off from an existing Church. It would be an interesting and lengthy book that detailed a complete history of all the denominations of the Christian Church. Whether these divisions are the result of flaws within Christianity itself or with the fallible humans who profess Christian beliefs is an ongoing debate. But it can clearly be seen that Christianity throughout the ages has not been guided by love and compassion, and it has not been the source of a consistent and respectable morality.

BRAINWASHED

Knowing all this about Christianity, I sometimes wonder how I once believed it all.

One answer suggests itself when I think about a discussion I had with an old friend. During our high school years, I succeeded in getting him to come to my church with me, but only once. He was not impressed at all. His main comment was that the congregation seemed brainwashed. I thought that assessment was a little harsh. It sounded paranoid to me. I had always considered brainwashing to be a process that involved strapping someone to a chair, showing him hypnotic images, and maybe injecting him with drugs. I asserted that my church was not as sinister as the images provoked by the term "brainwashing."

Over the years, I learned that brainwashing is a lot less complex and a lot subtler that I had envisioned it to be. Cult leaders (while not that subtle) use many techniques that involve little more than psychological influence. They repeat the same things over and over, appeal to their followers' respect for authority, stifle questions, make sure their followers don't start thinking for themselves, undermine self-esteem, keep people off balance, teach doublethink, offer false rewards and punishments, utilize peer pressure, and cut off outside influences.

I was startled when I realized that my church, at one point or another, had been guilty of all of these things.

***

Many ideas that are entirely wrong have been accepted as truth because they have been circulated in our society and repeated so often that we don't bother to think about them.

We learn many things through repetition, and undoing that kind of learning is sometimes difficult. Advertisers take advantage of this all the time. Infomercials and shopping channels provide perfect examples. About ten minutes into an infomercial, even the most rational of us can be tempted to think, Maybe there is something to this product. It would be easy to order it. What would it hurt? Sheer repetition gets to us.

Thinking back, I saw that, outside of two high school science classes, the only place I was getting any sort of information about how the universe worked was from church. The church's worldview had been pounded into my head every Sunday, with few exceptions, since I was an infant.

It began to get insidious when questions were stifled. By identifying doubt as a sin, by saying that mankind's wisdom is foolishness, and by teaching doublethink (which I will cover shortly), religion suppresses many questions that its followers might otherwise ask.

***

Telling people that they cannot trust their own minds is just one way of undermining self-esteem. Christianity excels at this. The more extreme the church, the worse it gets. The very premise of Christianity is aimed at self-doubt. It says that we, as humans, are all sinful and wretched, inherently terrible, and will continue to be that way until we turn to God. For the individual with low self-esteem, this is easy to believe and he or she can be sucked right into the Christian mythos. For the individual who knows at heart that he or she is not a bad person, it is far less attractive.

The church teaches the individual that he or she needs to be subservient to God, as well as sometimes to the leaders of the church. According to Christianity, God must always be more important than the individual.

A verse commonly used in churches to support this attitude can be found in John, where it says, "He must increase, but I must decrease" (John 3:30).

The Christian is supposed to be humble. But when that goes too far and individuality or self-esteem is squashed, it becomes slavery. Sadly, it happens all too often.

The individual who believes in his or her self is going to be less likely to believe in religion because the interests of the individual run contrary to the interests of religion.

***

One method of controlling people is to randomly praise and chasten them. A manager in the business world once confessed to me that he intentionally kept people off balance in order to keep them in line. People in a state of confusion are less likely to think for themselves or to be able to break free from oppression.

I remember a sermon that was preached in the fundamentalist church I belonged to (and that was repeated in revival meetings) in which the pastor caused everyone to question whether or not they had "really" been saved. They needed to make sure, he said. It got a great reaction, especially because it is hard to tell if you have been saved. When you are, nothing really happens. People were crying, praying, and scrambling to make sure they would not be eternally damned if they got in a car wreck on the way home.

There is a considerable amount of debate among churches as to whether a person can lose their salvation. For those who believe that they can, there is a constant state of anxiety. If they fall out of God's graces at the wrong time, then there may be Hell to pay, and not in a figurative sense. This whole aura of uncertainty keeps people under control.

***

I remember being told one Sunday that I never needed to fear danger because God would always protect me. The next Sunday I was told that I would be persecuted and have to undergo suffering because I was a Christian, and that I might someday have to even die for my belief in God.

I was told that the righteous are poor and that I should give my money to the poor, but it was also okay to be rich if it was because God was rewarding me for what I had done.

I was instructed that God is both cruel and loving.

Every time I turned around, there was another contradictory notion for me to ponder (many of which I have outlined in previous sections). In the world of religion, doublethink — the ability to entertain two contradictory ideas at one time — abounds. One cannot continue very long as a person of faith without this ability.

It is because of doublethink that the Christian has so much trouble recognizing contradictions. When you learn doublethink, you learn not to think. Your mind is in an illogical state, and you will believe anything that is told to you by those you trust, whether or not it makes sense or is consistent with what you have heard before.

***

Like a cult leader who told his followers that they would be taken from the planet by aliens to a better place, the religious leaders I trusted promised me the reward of Heaven. They also threatened me with Hell. The fact that I could never disprove the validity of these things was to their advantage.

The minister of a Pentecostal church I attended one Sunday told his congregation that if they tithed (gave ten percent of their income to the church), God would protect them from the devil. There was no vagueness about the promise. Fear is one of the most commonly used tools of those who try to control others.

One of the things that kept me from leaving Christianity for so long was my fear that the End Times would come, Jesus would return and leave me behind, and I would be left to face the Antichrist and all the terrible events of the Tribulation. It now seems ridiculous to me, but at the time, it was a very real fear.

***

Peer pressure is incredibly powerful. People do things they don't want to do and can do incredibly stupid things simply because of it. They don't want to stick out from the crowd, they don't want to be embarrassed in front of their friends, or they don't want to be ostracized by their families. There are many who are afraid to leave their religion because of what their friends and family will say. Some have taken this risk and found that the people they thought were their friends were not. When you combine peer pressure with the ideas of Heaven and Hell, you have a double-shot of positive and negative reinforcement. What is tragic is that this has prevented some people from following their better intentions.

***

I am also reminded of when my childhood church told me that I should avoid things that were "worldly." Movies and just about anything from pop culture were shunned. Instead, I was told to focus all my attention on the Bible, Christian literature, and to spend any free mental time in a constant inner dialogue with God. "Pray without ceasing,"[77] was the command.

What they were teaching me to do was to self-blind. I could go out anywhere in the world and not be influenced by, or learn from, what I saw there because I both consciously and unconsciously avoided anything that conflicted with my beliefs. I might as well have put my fingers in my ears and shouted "La. La. La. La. La. I can't hear you!" There is a natural tendency in humans to avoid and outright reject ideas they do not agree with, but when instructed to do it as a matter of faith, it becomes that much more powerful. The individual creates his own filter

---

77 I Thessalonians 5:17.

through which only those aspects of the world that correspond with his or her beliefs are seen.

∗∗∗

In retrospect, my church might as well have strapped me down, injected me with drugs, and ran electricity through my brain. My friend was right, perhaps there had been some brainwashing going on. No wonder it is so hard to put religion behind.

Chapter 7. Atheism and Beyond

Honeymoon

I came downstairs from the office where I had been working feverishly over a period of weeks — studying, learning, considering, and rewriting. I sat down at the kitchen table, had my wife sit down with me, and I announced to her that I had become an atheist.

In some households, that might cause a huge rift. I was lucky. My wife was not upset by this change in me, but she was concerned (because I have a tendency to pursue my interests wholeheartedly) that I might become an obnoxious atheist, one who went around ruining parties with philosophical arguments. At that time, I had no idea where I was going with my newfound worldview. I just knew I had reached an extremely hard-won conclusion.

It has been observed that when one adopts a new religion or a new worldview that there is often a honeymoon period, where one is filled with a freshness and vigor that comes as a result of seeing the world through new eyes. I had experienced it before, and I experienced it with atheism.

The world suddenly gained a sense of immediacy. Throughout my life and especially during those periods when I was religious, my focus was always on the future, on what I would someday accomplish and what it would be like then. As a Christian, the emphasis had been on the afterlife. Everything I did in the present was simply preparation for what was to come. The world directly around me at the moment did not get a lot of attention.

This changed when I became an atheist. I began to take in my immediate surroundings with new appreciation. I noticed with special intensity the taste of food and the shape of trees, buildings, everything, against the background of the sky. The sound of my footsteps on the pavement and gravel outside our apartment seemed crisper. Songs that had come to bore me regained their old vitality and were able to, again, send my adrenaline rushing. It was a religious experience without the religion.

The one thing that hit me, then, and that I have never lost since, was clarity about philosophical issues that had confused me for so long. It was a tremendous relief to escape the blurry indistinctness of mind I had once suffered from.

I also saw how superstition had permeated my life. I could list example upon example:

- I would go to Las Vegas and feel that my attitude or my state in life would affect whether or not I won.
- I wouldn't say certain things because I felt I could jinx whatever I was doing. Sometimes I joked about this, but often I half believed it.
- Now and then I would read my horoscope and think about it during the day, looking for situations that it might apply to. When those situations did occur and the advice helped me, I did not chalk it up to the stars, but I did chalk it up to some mysterious kind of divine guidance.
- I'd interpret coincidences, like the right song playing on the radio at the right time, to mean that I was on the right course in my life and that things were the way they were supposed to be.
- I would have experiences of Déjà vu and speculate that they signified that I had reached a landmark moment or a checkpoint in life. Or maybe, I thought, I had lived this whole life before.
- I would assign undue significance to certain days. What happened on New Year's, for example, was indicative of what would happen for the rest of the year.
- I seriously entertained the thought that a guardian angel was watching over me as I drove or that deceased loved ones were watching my actions and wishing me well.
- Although I no longer attended a particular church, I still prayed whenever things got rough, and I still thanked God for the good things as well.

When I gave up all of those kinds of thoughts, I felt freed. Sometimes I caught myself thinking these things and had to remind myself, Hey! I don't believe that anymore! Now that I no longer did, these types of thoughts were replaced by a growing sense of personal responsibility. Not only had I depended on God, fate, destiny, and a number of supernatural forces to guide me along the way, but when things did not go the way I wanted them to, I had been able to turn to the supernatural as a way out. "It must not have been meant to be," I'd say, and instantly I would have a cop-out. That cop-out was built into my belief systems.

No longer able to do that, I took full control over my life, knowing that it was my own persistence and willpower that would get me what I wanted. It did not look like anyone out there was eager to help me along, so I needed to make the effort myself. My sense of personal empowerment has grown ever since then, a side effect I would not have expected from discarding the notions of God and the soul.

Another sensation I experienced, that continues with me to this day, is that I felt, more than ever, that I belonged here on this planet. There is no need to feel alienated from it. This, rather than some distant Heaven or some remote and mysterious location that could never be found, is my home.

I also became more willing to forgive and appreciate others. It is a difficult, challenging, and sometimes incredibly unfair world that we live in, and because we have no one else to turn to, we are all in this together. Do you want equality? Get rid of God. Without God, there are no saints, no sinners. There are no saved and no damned. There are only people. And people, I saw, were just trying to get by.

I became fascinated with how people cope and interact with this crazy world. The approaches are so varied, innovative, and unique that the actions of humans around us are a never-ending source of interest. What I had gained was a true appreciation of the human condition — its futility, its hope, its struggles, and its rewards.

My writing began to take off. I poured words onto paper like never before. This happened because I finally felt that I *got it*. This world was no longer a mystery, and I understood the basis of the dramas that were taking place here. With this knowledge in hand, I could write about it, I could portray it, and I could see how what I wrote related to other human beings.

All of this increased my sense of confidence, which, in itself, can have a transforming effect. I became more outgoing as a result.

Decisions about my personal life and goals became more straightforward. I was no longer involved in an irresolvable guessing game of trying to figure what the universe wanted from me or what my place in the universe was. The questions became simpler. What is genuinely possible? What do I want to do?

I now knew I had a limited amount of time on this planet to do what I most wanted to do. My life span and situation were not designed to accommodate everything I wanted to fit into them, so I had to prioritize. In accordance with my long-held idea that everything was possible, I had once felt that somehow the powers that be would enable me to play every computer game, read every book, see every movie, and go to every place I wanted to. Now, I knew this wasn't true and with my new sense of personal responsibility, I was going to have to make intelligent choices about these things, using the criteria of what I most wanted to accomplish. Simply put, I became more realistic.

There was a trickle-down effect into tiny areas of my life. Issues as specific as money management came into sharper focus. I became less compulsive about things. I used to be the kind of guy who took the labels off sprinklers before I buried them in my yard. Behavior like that was tied into a personal ideology about perfection and how it meant something even if it could not be seen. My new philosophy helped free me from that (at least to some extent).

Being happily married, I was glad that I didn't have to worry about questions regarding relationships, but I saw how, without notions like destiny, fate, or the concept of "soulmates," making decisions regarding relationships could be a lot more straightforward. The questions became much simpler: Do you get along with the other person or not? Does the relationship work? There is your answer, then. You don't have to consult your horoscope. You don't have to review all the events that led up to the relationship in order to figure out if destiny had placed you together. The answers are in front of you.

When sitting in movies, reading books, and listening to people talk, it was now easy to identify common misunderstandings of the universe and our place in it. Ideas of God, the afterlife, numerous superstitions, misapplications of various principles, failure to make important distinctions, and many other errors and misconceptions leapt to the surface. The veil had been stripped away.

Years ago, I read the *Hitchhiker's Guide to the Galaxy* series by Douglas Adams, and in all their science fiction comedy, I detected a hidden knowledge. Douglas joked about the meaning of life, but it seemed like, underneath his mirth, there was something he wasn't telling us. It was as if he was intentionally dancing around a truth that only he saw. Upon finishing those books, I felt I had missed whatever it was that the author really wanted to tell me. Years later, after I became an atheist, I discovered that Douglas was one, as well. It was then that I understood what he was getting at.

People talk about clarity all the time in regard to their philosophies. Sometimes they say "it all became clear" when they discovered an explanation for a specific issue they had a question about. Sometimes they mean that they now have a vague sense of how their whole philosophy might piece together, but they can't put it into precise language. That is not clarity. That's the illusion of potential clarity. But the clarity I discovered was a groundbreaking, world-covering, ultra-sharp clarity that applied to just about every area of my life. Things weren't just falling into place with the soft and subtle click-click of puzzle pieces. They were locking into place with the metal clank of a vault door sealing shut.

UNDERSTANDING VERSUS DEALING

Many people have taken a path opposite to the one I took. One gentleman I know of became an atheist and felt that life as an atheist was "insipid," so he returned to a faith, albeit a different one from the one he had left.

Even if I found that I did not like life as an atheist, I had resolved that if I ever were to go back to an agnostic stance (or any other stance), there would have to be a good reason. I would not do it for an emotional reason or because of the way I felt. Logic had gotten me here. Logic would have to provide the way back. Either that or I would have to find a fatal flaw with reason.

Meanwhile, if I did not like what the answers I had found implied, I was not going to turn around and run the other way. The only way I could do that would be to consciously live in denial, if such a thing is possible.

I had come so far and solved some huge problems: How could I establish what was true and what was false? What was the meaning of life? Did I have a soul? Was there a God? These questions had all been answered to my satisfaction. That was quite an accomplishment!

But my honeymoon period with atheism was coming to an end. Now that I felt I understood the world, the big question was how would I deal with it? I could no longer turn to the spiritual answers I once had for this question. I could not find comfort in the idea that everything would be resolved in the afterlife. I could not claim that when things went wrong, it was because the universe was trying to teach me something or had better things in mind for me. How then was I going to deal with the inherent meaningless of life, existential angst, pain and suffering, the irrationality of the people and the world around me, the frustrations of unfairness and injustice, and the problem of unhappiness?

While reason was essential when it came to understanding the world, it was not up to the task of addressing these problems of everyday life. When it comes to dealing with the world, there is a much wider range of choices and many of them work perfectly well. I could use these options so long as I did not resort to deluding myself in the process. If I did that, then I would be back at square one.

This is the point where I come into conflict with those strict rationalists who say that, in addition to using reason as a means to understand the world, we should use reason as a guide for our behavior in daily life. Dealing with life requires an entirely different skill set than understanding the world. Once we discover that much about life is absurd — the random events, the inherent meaninglessness of what happens in it, and the behaviors of people — then sometimes the best response to those things is equally random or absurd. Because the chains of cause and effect that surround an action are so complex and can lead to results other than what you intend, sometimes the irrational or random action works just as well.

It is also true that we sometimes learn valuable lessons by doing stupid things. Here too, an illogical action can yield a positive result.

Laughter is one of my favorite ways of dealing with the difficulties of life, and it's not exactly a rational response. The creative process and its results are quite often illogical, but they bring a great deal of meaning and joy to my life. The happiness that I find in my relationships isn't based on logic and rationality either.

When dealing with people, if we react in a logical manner to what others say and do, we may find that we get absolutely nowhere. By reacting in a completely rational manner, we overlook the emotions and psychological needs of others, as well as the messages that they are sending us on a more subtle level. Human emotions and motivations are, quite frankly, not very rational, but a person without them is incomplete.

A friend told me of a pair of police officers, who, when dealing with domestic disputes, would go into a house and start rearranging the furniture instead of talking to the people who were fighting. One cop would say, "You know, I like that chair better over there," and the other would pick it up and move it.

The fighting couple would wonder what was going on and stop fighting. Having broken the couple's focus and relieved the tension of the situation, the cops could then better resolve it. Their actions were not logical in any strict sense of the word, but they were very practical.

With all this praise of irrationality, you might think I have changed positions entirely, which is why making the distinction between thinking rationally and acting rationally is so important.

Up to this point, I have stressed the value of reason. Now, I must draw a line that shows its true limits. In a paradox of sorts, reason provides a rational understanding of an irrational world. The world is not irrational in regard to the underlying rules of physics that govern it, but it can be crazy when it comes to the particulars of human behavior and chaotic circumstances.

Fortunately, along the way, I had already found some of the answers to dealing with such a world. Additional answers would come from Eastern thought, especially Buddhism. This did not mean I had given up the Western religions just to have them replaced by Eastern ones. Many principles of Buddhism are ideally suited to a philosophy that is atheistic, because Buddhism, as it was initially practiced, did not involve the concept of God. Several versions of Buddhism do not present the Buddha as a God, but rather as an enlightened human being. He did not ask to be worshipped. Rather he recommended a path that others could follow if they wanted to find what he had found.

In no way would I embrace the entirety of Buddhism or Eastern thought. It contained some fatal flaws. But what I could do was extract useful tidbits from Eastern thought, incorporate them into my philosophy, and utilize them to help solve some of the problems that I was faced with.

The solutions I discovered included adopting a more accepting attitude towards life and living in the moment. I have included cursory reviews of them because they have been incredibly helpful to me and because they tie in so neatly with the philosophy I had already established. In comparison to the philosophical topics I have discussed so far, these topics have more of a self-help flavor, but that's because I've moved from how to think about life to how to actively engage it. Personally, I sometimes find philosophical works frustrating because they give all kinds of information, but never deal with all the implications. Therefore, I have gone the extra mile in hopes that the knowledge is useful. By offering these solutions, I also show how to deal with life effectively without having to resort to a supernatural worldview.

The principles presented here allowed me to emerge from my philosophical quest with a balanced blend of Eastern and Western ideologies, as well as the answers I sought. By utilizing logic and the scientific rationality that is identified with Western thought in order to understand the world and by then adopting the practices of nonresistance, nonjudgmental thinking, and mindful awareness, I achieved an exceptionally practical synthesis. The resulting philosophy could be described as "Zen Atheism." While not entirely accurate, it does have a certain ring to it.

ANGST

The problem of meaninglessness presents huge difficulties for some people. For them, to say that life has no externally assigned meaning, or no intrinsic meaning, is to say that life is a joke. But to say that life does have such meaning unfairly places a label upon life. Life just is. It is not a joke, a tragedy, an exercise in vanity, nor a series of meaningless events. These things may describe aspects of life, or a feeling about life, but they do not accurately describe life as a whole.

Life consists of a multitude of things and is much bigger than any of these single descriptions.

As I explained in the section titled "Meaning," the meaninglessness of life in an ultimate sense enables it to be more meaningful in an immediate sense. When life has no externally assigned meaning, you gain freedom. You can then make of life what you wish. It's a fair trade.

If you want, you can spend your life sitting and meditating like a monk, albeit an enlightened monk, who has already realized how pointless striving can be and who meditates for that reason.

You are free to shoot for whatever goals you want. The very act of striving provides purpose and meaning. With the knowledge that striving may not be all that important in a universal sense, you can regain perspective when you need it, avoiding the trap of taking yourself or your endeavors too seriously. Finding meaning is not difficult at all, once you give up the idea that meaning has to come from somewhere outside yourself.

In my own life, I find that creativity, and the projects I am involved in, provide me with a great sense of purpose. Personal relationships give my life depth, making it that much more fulfilling and rich. Even if every thing I have done and said has no effect on the state of the universe a billion years from now, it still matters to me. I still want to have a good life.

Concerns about meaninglessness are similar to worries about death; one can be aware of them without dwelling on them or allowing them to ruin everyday experience. A cosmic perspective is difficult to maintain when the events of life are so immediate. It is a wonderful asset of the human mind that angst can be forgotten.

Still, people ask, "Why even bother, if there is no ultimate goal? Why try, if years from now nothing may come from it and all that we do will get washed away in the twirling, spinning atoms of the cosmos, where no one remembers and no one cares?"

Some who say this would insist upon being unhappy despite any assurances I offered. If their lives have no eternal consequence, then there is despair to be found and existential angst kicks in.

I say, only half jokingly, that such people are not cut out to be atheists. If the realities they are dealing with are harsh, it is easy to be sympathetic. However, it hould also be noted that anyone who chooses belief for the sole purpose of coping with life instantly justifies the sentiment that "religion is a crutch."

There are better ways to deal with reality than to hide from it. I think it is a triumph of the human spirit to go face-to-face with a universe that is indifferent to your fate and say, "Okay. Guess what? I am still going to do what I am going to do. I am still going to live. I am still going to be happy, or miserable, or whatever, but I am going to be! I am going to grieve when I must and then move on. I am going to accept my losses with dignity. I am going to fight the good fight, knowing that it may be fruitless. But I am also going to enjoy the good things that come my way and revel in what life has to offer."

When you do this, you become the best of what humankind can be. It takes a certain kind of bravery to acknowledge what life truly is. The reward for it is that you get to experience moments of joy, beauty, wonder, and intensity with a full awareness of just how precious they are. If existence were eternal then that preciousness would be lost. Yes, this knowledge may lend a taint of sadness to our experience, but it can be thought of as a melancholy to be savored, adding an almost indescribable richness.

The healthiest alternative is to understand life using reason, while dealing with it using attitudes that do not require self-delusion. This is the perfect separation.

In the next sections, I will put forth some attitudes that can be adopted when trying to handle the difficulties of life realistically.

PAIN AND SUFFERING

In addition to the many joys and wonders of life, there is also pain and sorrow.

Physical pain is easy enough to explain. It is simply a system whereby the body lets the brain know that something is wrong so that something can be done about it. There are people who suffer from a genetic disorder called CIPA,[78] in which there is a problem with the nerve endings that results in the inability to feel pain. It might not sound so bad at first, but people with the disease have to regularly do an inventory of their bodies to make sure that they are okay. They have to be careful not to burn themselves with hot foods and drinks, and have to be very cautious about what activities they engage in.

Due to natural selection, those creatures that were able to perceive that they were injured or in danger of being injured further were those that were more likely to survive. Pain is hard to ignore for good reason. Its constant insistence says, "Take care of me now!" If we did not, we would have some serious problems, especially those of us who tend to ignore things of importance so that we can do what we enjoy.

---

78 CIPA stands for Congenital Insensitivity to Pain with Anhidrosis. Anhidrosis is the inability to sweat, an associated effect of the genetic disorder.

Unfortunately, the body and brain never gained the ability to shut off pain once it was acknowledged. It would be nice if we could say, "I am aware of the anger. You don't have to keep reminding me," and then tell your body to shut off the pain, but such a mechanism is not available to us.

Emotional pain is a lot more complex. Both physical and emotional pain provoke us to ask, "Why do I have to suffer?" and quickly invoke philosophical questions. It is no wonder that many belief systems address the question of suffering immediately. Christianity proposes that pain and suffering are caused by sin. Suffering is man's fault, Christianity says, but the Eastern world has a different take on it. The First Noble Truth of Buddhism says that, "To live is to suffer — sorrow is the universal experience of mankind." According to Buddhism, suffering is caused by craving, attachment, and desire. This is the second of the Four Noble Truths.[79]

Ideas from Eastern thought may be foreign to many readers of this book, and parts of the Second Noble Truth deserve some exposition. What the Buddha said is that, if we don't want something, we are not going to be disappointed or saddened if we don't get it. If we don't become "attached" to the things we have, the people we feel close to, our possessions, or qualities we hold in the present that we wish would continue forever (like our youth), then we won't be sad and sorrowful when they are gone. The Buddha recognized that as long as we have the passage of time, we are going to have loss. It is a condition of existence. Buddhism tries to find a way to make us immune to this.

These ideas are hard for the Westerner to embrace because our lives are filled with striving, of working towards goals, and of trying to hang onto the things we treasure. "If we don't care," the Westerner asks, "then why bother?" We find ourselves, again, in an existential quandary.

Both Buddhism and Christianity suggest that a conscious entity can be free of emotional pain and suffering. This is unrealistic. As long as we have awareness, we can never be completely free from these things. Not only are they a part of existence, but they are, to a certain extent, an unavoidable part of existence.

The only escape from suffering is nonexistence. There is no conscious state, be it Heaven or Nirvana, where this can permanently be attained.

What Buddhism does manage to do is effectively identify some of the causes of suffering (judgments about reality, as well as desires and expectations). By identifying these, Buddhism provides something extremely valuable: a way to

---

79 The third states that if we want to get rid of suffering we must get rid of desire, and the fourth states that we can do this by following the Noble Eightfold path. The Noble Eightfold Path is, in turn, a list of ways in which we should act, talk, and speak in order to escape the suffering caused by desire.

reduce suffering and a way to make it tolerable in instances where it might otherwise not be.

When I first became an atheist, I wrote several pieces about how life was unfair. I was in the process of adjusting to the idea that there were some things we could not do anything about. Christianity provides a solution to the unfairness of life by saying that God will dispense justice. Some of the Eastern religions resolve the problem of injustice with karma. Both say that someday, somehow, everything will work out fairly, but not right now.

Anyone who thinks that justice will be dispensed and everything will come out fairly within the space of our lives is clearly not paying attention. The world is not a fair place. Many people suffer terrible things they do not deserve, while others enjoy pleasures and advantages they did nothing to earn. Still others get away with horrific deeds. The atheistic worldview recognizes that, because there is no afterworld or other lives in which these things can be resolved, all we can do is take action in the present. We should do whatever we can, but there are times when, no matter what we do, we cannot get the results we want.

This is not always an easy idea to get used to. It is difficult to face a world where there are no guarantees, where there are no rules saying everything has to work out right, where you may lose your battles despite your best efforts, and where justice does not happen automatically. A perfectly natural reaction to this is anger.

Anger is always the result of a judgment (or a series of judgments) that we have made about reality. The root cause of anger is the sentiment, "I don't like that." This is an important insight because, like many things I have discussed in this book, anger is often misunderstood or made out to be more mystical than it really is.

Because anger comes from the judgments we make, it is directly tied in to how we perceive the world. The things we get angry about, and even the amount of anger we feel, can be very closely connected to our philosophies. There are certain things that we feel we *should* get angry about and, quite possibly, that we would be wrong *not* to be angry about.

Those who make this kind of judgment often, and who constantly find themselves at odds with the world, are said to have entered a state called "resistance." This means, very simply, that they are resisting reality instead of adjusting to it. When this happens, people may become hypersensitive or antagonistic. Every judgment they make becomes amplified, and because judgments are the root of anger, anger is also amplified. Feelings of powerlessness and frustration may grow as well.

Fortunately, there is a solution to this.

The Serenity Prayer, which you may have seen posted on a cubicle wall or refrigerator near you, says, "God, give us grace to accept with serenity the things that cannot be changed, courage to change the things that should be changed, and the wisdom to distinguish the one from the other."[80]

The saying works just as well when you take God out of it and say, "May I have the grace to accept with serenity the things that cannot be changed..."

Therein lies our answer to the problem of resistance. The cure for resistance is to adopt an attitude of acceptance.

Once I discovered many of the beliefs I once had were wrong, I found myself getting angry with them. I felt lied to, deceived, and betrayed by those who had sold these ideas to me as "truths." I also began to feel that the big projects I was working on were too intimidating because I knew there was no guarantee they would be successful. Certain problems in life seemed to be endlessly frustrating. My honeymoon with atheism was over. I had gained an intellectual acceptance of how the world worked, but not an emotional one. That was the next big step.

What does it mean to accept what we cannot change? It means to acknowledge it, stop being angry about it, and stop fighting it. Acceptance is an attitude of openness, where one embraces the world for what it is. It means that whenever we catch ourselves making judgments about the world, we should ask if those judgments are necessary or helpful in any way. If not, giving them up can free us from anger and help us to be more satisfied with the world around us.

In no way should acceptance be thought of as surrender or compromise, as passive or as accepting defeat. There is nothing weak about it. To accept reality is not to relinquish power but to exercise a readily accessible, although often forgotten, power.

If we choose, we can even embrace moments of unpleasantness. If we only value those parts of our lives that are "good times," then we mentally identify the vast majority of our time on this planet as not as valuable. Moments of pain, misery, and unhappiness are a part of life. Experience them! Fun and enjoyment are not all there is, nor do they always have to be our goal. If we spend our time distancing ourselves from all the unpleasantness in life, then we spend our lives

---

80 The Serenity Prayer was originally written in 1943 by theologian Reinhold Niebuhr. It was later adopted by Alcoholics Anonymous and circulated though Hallmark Cards with his permission. The version quoted here (reportedly the original) comes from the book, *The Serenity Prayer*, by Niebuhr's daughter, Elisabeth Sifton.

avoiding life. Yet if we engage life in its entirety, our time can possess an undeniable immediacy.

When we resist pain and suffering, the only thing we often succeed at doing is making it worse. Accepting it can lessen the pain. It is like relaxing your muscles when you get a penicillin shot. It will hurt a lot less if you aren't tense.

With that example, we touch on an interesting point. In addition to helping us deal with suffering, nonresistance can help us with physical pain as well. Nonjudgmentally observing our own physical pain can be revealing. The first time I tried it was a moment when I had burnt my finger. Instead of fighting it and shouting, "Ow! Ow!" I stopped and tried to *experience* the pain, examining what it really felt like. The pain did not go away, but it immediately diminished and no longer seemed such a terrible thing. (This does not always work. I tried it with sinus headaches and it just made them worse, but there are times when it does help.)

A friend told me the story of when a loved one died and people were always trying to cheer her up and tell her it wasn't so bad. Her response was "Yes! It is that bad! Let me experience it. Let me grieve. This may be terrible and awful, but I'm not going to hide from it."

Exactly.

It is so much healthier to experience life for what it is. This change of approach gives us a way to deal with pain and suffering. We still know that the pain and suffering will someday end, but, in addition, we have something that we can do about it *now*.

In addition to resistance, Buddhism identifies its opposites — desires and expectations — as further causes of suffering. Resistance is called "aversion." Our desperate chokehold on our desires is called "clinging."

Understanding these attitudes can provide us with some insight into our mental states, as well as into that ever-pursued goal of happiness.

Many make happiness their measure of success. "Are you happy?" they will ask you, in an effort to judge your success by their criteria.

A tremendous pressure was removed from my life when I realized I did not have to try to be happy. Happiness did not need to be an objective. It is okay *not* to be happy all the time and it is okay to be happy for no reason. As far as I am concerned, that is the best reason to be happy. The seemingly contradictory result is that by not trying so hard to be happy, we can become happier.

I experience happiness often, and I experience sadness as well. But that's the way it should be. I know it is not necessary to fight the sadness. It will pass.

There are those out there who like to act like mood police. They are insistent that everyone around them be happy and always try to "fix it" when people are not. Not only is this a control issue, but it is also not healthy for anyone.

It is the desire for happiness that often causes people to say that we should look on the bright side. I have no problem doing that, provided it does not obscure reality. If there is a good side, a bad side, and a neutral side, we should look at them all. Again, I prefer to look at things as they are, rather than to play a game that involves tricking myself.

We should also be aware that satisfaction is a temporary state. Just as we cannot always be happy, we cannot be completely satisfied, at least not for long. This, too, is perfectly okay! The problem is not that we have not achieved these states, but that we have unrealistic expectations.

This is helpful information for anyone, but it is especially beneficial to the realist who must find his or her own way of coming to terms with a challenging world, a reality that is not always hospitable, and a universe that is indifferent to our fate.

In order to take full advantage of this knowledge (in addition to understanding and utilizing many of the other things I have talked about from the beginning of this book) we must first be aware of our own thoughts in the here and now.

Right Now

When I believed in an afterlife, my attention was aimed forward at what could be rather than on what is going on now. During my honeymoon period with atheism, I discovered an intensity of life that came from my immediate focus on the world around me. This focus made me happier and more productive. Inadvertently, I had begun living in the moment.

Eventually, not having made a conscious choice to keep my attention on the present, I stopped doing it. Later, it was suggested to me as a way of dealing with the world. I tried it again, but this time I was aware of what I was doing, and I was surprised at the quality of the results as well as the variety of benefits that living in the moment afforded.

The present moment is the most important moment there is because, even if we did live forever, it is the only moment that we have direct control over. As such, it makes sense to live in the moment regardless of your philosophy. We cannot change the past, and the only way we can affect the future is through what we do now. Living in the moment gives us an excellent way of dealing with the stresses and problems of life while, at the same time, adding to our enjoyment and appreciation of life. It does not require us to use supernatural aid or adopt a belief. It works for very straightforward reasons. Understanding our world provides us with clarity. Living in the moment makes that clarity crystal sharp.

Keeping our attention on the present automatically frees us from regret and worry. Because we are focused on what is going on now, our past mistakes no longer have much weight. Present moment awareness does not mean we should forget about the past altogether or that we shouldn't learn from our mistakes. What it does mean is that we should learn from the past and then move on. Repeatedly going over our past mistakes when there is nothing more to be gained helps no one. If we are living in the moment, we are also not going to be doing a lot of worrying about the future. Yes, we should plan for the future and think ahead when appropriate. But worrying about things that may never happen, or that we cannot do anything about now, only works against us.

If we are centered on the present, existential angst is out the door in no time. Our ultimate destination is not all that important in comparison to the present.

Living in the moment also means that we give up many of the expectations that we tend to impose upon our thoughts about the future. Most of us know how the anticipation of an event can ruin it or how, if we didn't expect much in the first place, our lack of expectations can make the event seem better than it otherwise might. Someone who is living in the moment is more likely to appreciate something for what it is, without having the experience altered by preconceptions. Birthdays and holidays always come to mind when talking about this. They can never live up to what I want them to be, but when I accept them without anticipation, I save myself a lot of disappointment.

There are two aspects of how we interact with the world in the here and now, the mental and the physical.

The mental aspect is perhaps the more difficult of the two to get a handle on, but it is well worth the effort involved. Being aware of our thoughts is vital if we are to accomplish certain things. In order to deal with anger effectively, as discussed in previous sections, we must pay attention to what is happening in our heads. The same goes for our ability to think critically as discussed throughout the earlier sections of this book.

While many of us think that we are in control of our own minds, it is easy to remain unaware of our thought processes and how random they are. Left unchecked, our minds tend to float from topic to topic in a stream of consciousness that affects our moods and behaviors. Random thoughts can control us rather than the other way around.

There are those of us who have had the experience of getting out of the shower or out of the car and finding that we are angry but do not know why. We may emerge from a daydream with the same kind of feelings. The reason for this is that our minds are busily working behind the scenes, regardless of whether we have consciously set them in motion.

If we want to maintain present moment awareness, our task is to keep our minds on the present and to bring them back whenever our thoughts stray from the present. A gentle reminder is all that is needed. Just a simple, "Oops, there I go again. I need to return to the now," will do the trick. It is a discipline, but it is not a strict discipline. It is a tool that you can use to make your life better, but it should not become a burden.

If you have never tried this before, you may find it surprising how often your mind wanders. It will probably be necessary to pull your mind back to the present repeatedly. Like everything you practice, you get better at it. The mind gets restless and bored, and you have to train it to recognize that there is plenty in the present to keep it busy and interested.

For the introvert, living in the moment will bring order to already familiar internal thought processes. For the extrovert, it may be quite a challenge to observe one's own thoughts, and he or she may discover a whole new unexplored territory.

The first few days that I started monitoring my own thoughts, I became aware of how much anger and unnecessary struggle I created for myself internally. Drummer and author Neil Peart describes an instance of such thinking this way: "I found myself having mental arguments about meaningless things with people who were thousands of miles away."[81]

There is no need for the arguments, worries, and other forms of negativity that take place nowhere else but in the spaces between our ears. If our minds venture into those danger areas that upset us and that don't help us to accomplish anything, we can draw our minds back into the present, allowing us to direct our thoughts in a more positive direction.

In my own case, I found that as I became increasingly aware of my thought patterns, I was able to catch my mind when it started to wander and prevent it from going astray. This awareness also gave me the objectivity to take what might once have been a fierce internal dialogue and turn it into fodder for a story. Either that, or I might find a positive solution to the situation that had come to mind.

Those who become familiar with their own habits of thought will quickly learn to recognize their own problem areas that ruin their mood and have the potential of destroying their day. The solution is to rein in the mind, and bring

---

81 Neil Peart, *Traveling Music* (ECW Press: Toronto, Ontario, Canada, 2004), p. 323.

it into the corral. When the wild horse of the mind is broken in, we can ride it wherever we like, knowing that it will follow our direction.

It is very important when practicing present moment awareness not to get aggravated with yourself. That defeats the purpose. The process should be as nonjudgmental as possible, and that goes for how you deal with yourself as well.

I emphasize the mental aspect of living in the moment because I am, by nature, an introvert. Present moment awareness also has a lot to do with how we interact with the world. The athlete who is "in the zone" knows exactly what it is to live in the moment and how empowering it can be. Anyone who is completely centered on what he or she is doing in the present can experience it — the way things are more vivid, the way time stands still and seems to fly at the same time.

There are plenty of things to keep us busy in the present. We can concentrate on what we are doing, examine our surroundings, focus on our breathing, or interact with others. The only "rule" is that we stay aware.

Driving on the freeway is one of the best times to remain in the moment. I swear that there are several times it has, quite literally, saved my life. How we survive on the freeways when we do so much on autopilot is amazing.

To live in the moment, and to do so with a nonjudgmental, accepting attitude (thereby incorporating the ideas and practices of the last several sections with this one) is what is referred to as "mindfulness." Mindfulness is an idea that has strong origins in Eastern thought. (I am told that in some educational circles, the term "mindfulness" is used in a different way that is not relevant to our discussion here.)

I find that when I practice mindfulness at work, rather than thinking about what I am going to be doing when I get home, my concentration is naturally better and the day zips by. I enjoy the day more because I do not bring an attitude of avoidance and resistance with me, and I do a better job in general.

With mindfulness comes a leveling of one's mood and a greater sense of equilibrium. When you are mindful, it becomes less of an issue when the present moment is not what you want or when you would rather be somewhere else. You can be in the middle of a crisis situation and say, "This stinks, but I'm okay with that, and I sure am handling it well." To be able to say that is a great feeling in itself. In contrast, good situations become that much better, especially when you are not missing out on them because you are so busy looking for something else.

By being mindful, instead of seizing the day you savor the day. The day becomes like a glass of expensive and precious wine that you experience to the fullest with every sip.

The principles I have discussed — an understanding of anger, nonjudgmental acceptance, being aware of our thoughts, and living in the moment — have special significance within the context of an atheistic worldview. If a full understanding of life comes with its own set of frustrations, then a way to deal with those frustrations is welcome, indeed. We need to be able to accept, both intellectually and emotionally, the implications of a world without God in order to cope effectively. Nonresistance contributes to our happiness and gives us tools to deal with pain and suffering. Awareness of our own thoughts helps us to think critically and to avoid unnecessary judgments that might otherwise make us miserable. If there is no afterlife and no ultimate goal for the universe, then the present moment becomes even more deserving of our full attention, and our daily lives become better for it.

These are ideas that fit together beautifully with each other as well as within the larger framework of the philosophy already established. The goal is to strip away the illusions, wake up, and pay attention to the world around us.

A related idea, called Right Understanding, is expressed in Buddhism as the first principle of The Eightfold Path to Enlightenment.

> Nurturing a sense of Right Understanding means viewing the world in its simplest form, as it immediately presents itself to the eye. To do this, we must restrain the urge to impose our preconceived notions upon the things around us. Ultimately, Buddhism challenges its students to experience everything with a clear, objective mind. Thus we are to overcome the temptation to categorize things too quickly, so we can keep our perceptions neutral and view events — and people — as they actually are.[82]

Throughout this book, I have been attempting to achieve Right Understanding. When talking about reason, I emphasized objectivity and was careful to avoid generalizations and incorrect categorizations. In talking about religion and the supernatural, I attempted to remove the layer upon layer of superstition that have been laid atop a straightforward reality. As I discussed acceptance and living in the moment, my goal has been to remove the expectations and labels that are habitually placed on things.

Understanding the world is not a matter of pulling back reality to see what is hidden beneath it, but rather a matter of pulling back preconceived notions of reality to reveal the straightforward truth in front of us — right here, right now.

CREATIVITY

The ability to imagine things works both for us and against us. Some of the problems our imaginations present are the problems we have had to address in the first six chapters of this book. We can come up with questions for which

---

82 Nicola Dixon, *The Little Book of Buddha* (Running Press: Philadelphia, 2003), pp. 42–43.

there are no answers, propose paradoxes for which there are no counterparts in reality, create problems when there are none, and invent answers that solve nothing at all. We imagine things that do not exist and mistake them for reality.

As long as we do not take the creations of our imaginations too seriously, imagination and creativity can be a wondrous asset. Books, movies, plays, games, art, and music all spring from creativity and are some of the things I immediately point to when asked where I find meaning in life.

While the products of creativity make life more fulfilling, being involved in the creative process gives life greater depth. Once we discover the creative spark within ourselves, we find that it adds to our appreciation of the artistry and creations of others. Creativity can transform a life from being boring to being vibrant, from being seemingly meaningless to being rich in meaning. Art and creativity can fill life with subtlety and inspiration. That spark is not far away, and I would encourage those who want more out of life and who claim they "do not have a creative bone in their body" to look for it despite that belief.

Artistic ability does not have to be mystical or magical, although it may feel that way. It is not required to be exceptional or amazing and does not demand that you have a special "talent." You do not have to meet anyone else's requirements. One's first artistic endeavors (and all of them, if you so desire) should be practiced nonjudgmentally. Creativity can be seen as just another way of interacting with the world that makes life better.

In my personal quest to find a group of people with whom I felt I belonged, I looked to many organizations. I found people who shared common interests and those who shared the same basic philosophical foundation as mine, but I did not find the warmth, the binding sense of unity, and the involvement in life that I was looking for.

It was not long after, that I attended a writers conference in Los Angeles and joined a local writers group. In the writers group there is a diversity of people, but these people share what I find to be most valuable. Even though we do not all agree on religious and philosophical issues, are not all interested in the same things, and are of varying degrees of education and intelligence, we are all involved in the creative process, which inevitably (especially when it comes to writing) causes us to examine, to some extent, the human condition.

In our writings, we often capture the details of life that we treasure and find interesting. We might pass them from person to person in the form of poetry, expressing a common delight or discovering a new one. In whatever form of writing it is, we take the experience of being a conscious and separate individual and enable others to participate in it. Art allows us to tear down the barriers of isolation that we feel as separate entities. Creativity allows us to share.

Even when we read about people with magical powers — the superheroes and the messiahs performing miracles — it is the human attributes of these characters that get our attention. It is what makes them, as well as you and me, the real heroes.

Whether our art truly reflects reality or is riddled with misperceptions, it always reflects some aspect of the human condition. The activities of interpreting life, trying to make sense of it, and trying to share it, make creativity valuable. The act of taking something and putting it on paper, canvas, screen, or photographic plate, of molding it with our hands, or of recording it as an audio track, grants importance to whatever element of life is involved. We decide it is important and so it becomes important. Suddenly, if it was not already there, we have meaning in our lives. If meaning already existed, it deepens.

Creativity also helps us to live in the moment. By focusing our attention on what we are doing artistically, or by trying to capture a moment in a picture or words, we effectively pull ourselves into the here and now.

I have read several descriptions of what it might be like to experience enlightenment, to have a transcendent experience as perceived by the Eastern mystics. After having read several of these, I sat down and wrote my own. Many years after writing the piece, I realized that such descriptions did not match any actual experience at all. They were flights of imagination. But they were fantastic flights of imagination that showed us how we could put ourselves in the place of other individuals and of other creatures, how we could see ourselves soaring through the cosmos, or how we could perceive ourselves to be an organism in a drop of rainwater. These visions came to us courtesy of our creative abilities. All of it is part of this amazing experience we share because we are conscious beings.

If I am ever accused of having a religion, I hope that my accusers identify that religion as creativity.

THE HUMAN CONDITION

It is in the consciousness of individuals that we find what it truly means to be human. In the grand mixture of suffering and joy, blandness and intensity, sadness and laughter that we experience, there are many emotions and thoughts that we share. These unite us.

For those of us who long for some form of immortality, it can be found in consciousness. As long as there is physical matter in motion in the universe, there is the possibility for awareness and thought that echoes our own. Wherever there is suffering and confusion, or happiness and clarity, a part of us exists as well.

Elements of our thoughts, experiences, and feelings are reflected, at this moment, in our fellow human beings.

In the eternity of time before, after, and even during the existence of our species, there may be other creatures in the universe who feel much the same as we do. Like humankind, they may also search for answers. They might have a completely different perspective than we do. Wherever and whenever they might exist, conscious entities who have a little bit of imagination may even think of us as we are thinking of them now. There, too, a part of us exists.

I often think about what the future of humankind will be, and I am glad that it is uncertain. I do not know if we will expand out into the galaxy in some Star Trekkian future, if we will meet an unexpected end, or if we will evolve into some higher life form. I think an unknown future is more exciting and interesting than any I have heard predicted.

It is often pointed out that we are greater than our origins, but it is not mentioned often enough that we are also greater than our future. Whatever will become of us does not change what we are now. It does not change the importance of our lives, or what we do, or how we live.

The human condition, like reality, simply is what it is. However, if we indulge ourselves and choose to romanticize it and assign values to it, we can see that, even from an atheistic perspective, the human condition is many things.

The human condition includes what is both bad and good about our experience. It involves the mistakes we make and our ability to carry on despite them. It involves the delusions we suffer from, as well as our ability to find clarity amidst the confusion. It includes our weakness and our triumphs. When we are good for no other reason but for the sake of it; when we show defiance in the face of death; when we find our own purpose; when we find unexpected joy and laughter; that, too, is a part of the human condition.

The human condition can never be fully described in a single sentence or paragraph because of the sheer extent of it. The full range of human experience will never be within our mental grasp and thus it must always possess an air of mystery.

While we cannot completely express the human condition in generalities such as the ones above, the artist knows that there is another way to express it. With a little poetry and vision, we can communicate what it means to be human in a manner far more eloquent that what adjectives and definitions portray. Because they evoke the emotions that we experience (which many consider to be one of our most human characteristics) and because they imply higher truths, individual scenes from our lives, like snapshots freezing moments in time, can sometimes best convey what it means to be human:

- A young girl staring out at the ocean, wondering at its immensity, while the waves splash upon her feet and hiss backwards down the shore
- A young mother admiring her sleeping baby, having spent the hours before in anger and frustration wondering how she was ever going to get the child to stop crying
- A couple celebrating their fiftieth anniversary, surrounded by family and friends
- A soldier in the trench still fighting while another lies motionless beside him
- A dancer spinning to music
- Tears streaming down the face of a woman in a funeral parlor
- A man kneeling at an altar, wondering why his prayers have not been answered
- A teenager in a wheelchair with his arms raised high, having won his first basketball game after a season of losses
- A veterinarian caring for an injured dog found on the road, and telling the boy who found it that the dog will be okay and that he can take it home
- Lovers holding hands, oblivious to the world around them
- A young girl waking from a terrifying dream to find that she is safe at home
- A young boy immersed in a computer game, learning problem solving skills he will use in everyday life
- An artist admiring his completed painting, finding things in it that are new even to him

This is the human condition. It is uncertain, complex, vast, and forever beyond the range of individual comprehension, yet wondrous nonetheless.

A New Approach

The priest, the nun, the minister, all go out into the ghetto and try to tell the gang member that God loves him. The gang member wants to believe them. He would like a better life than the one he leads. Maybe, once or twice, he attends church. The stories he hears there seem distant and removed from the life in which he lives. Moreover, they do not ring true.

When your father beats you and your mother shoots heroin, this image of a loving God is not an easy sell. While church figures try to portray a benevolent universe, the gang member finds that it simply does not correlate to reality. He goes back to the streets, not realizing that there were other alternatives.

There are times when the attempts of ministers and priests to help someone are successful, but, sadly, there are far more failures than successes.

We cannot do the best possible job of improving the world without first understanding it.

My wife, a schoolteacher, teaches in a lower income district, where sometimes the mothers of schoolchildren are prostitutes and the fathers are in jail. When her students come to her with problems, my wife doesn't lie to them. She never tells them that the world is not as bad a place as it seems. She never dismisses the harsh realities her students share with her. Instead, she acknowledges them. "Yes, it is difficult," she tells them. "It can be overwhelming at times."

"But guess what?" she adds. "You have choices. You are in control of what you do in school and how you act each day. You are in charge of your own ambitions and of your own plans to reach them." She ends by asking them what they want to change and what they can change.

If you are going to offer help, it should be real help, not a pie in the sky fantasy.

When New Testament Christianity came into being, the time was ripe for change. The Old Testament religions were not satisfying the needs of the people and were full of rules and rituals that were irrelevant. The time is ripe again. People want answers, but the answers given to them are often inadequate. An increasing number of religions and New Age groups pop up and pretend to offer solace, but they fail in the same way as their predecessors.

The recent period when science found alternative explanations for the origin of our world and the life upon it (and philosophers responded with existentialistic thoughts) is referred to as "The Enlightenment." I think it was aptly named, but unfortunately, it didn't catch on. The general public, at least in America, did not seem to realize the significance of the discoveries that were made, or their full philosophic implications.

They did not realize this because various belief systems were distracting them from answers that were more reliable. Religion pointed at the answers and declared them lies. In so doing, religion went from being helpful to being destructive. It was no longer a defender of the truth, but a defender of itself.

Humankind is again ready, just as it was at the time of the New Testament, for an improved way of looking at the world. Reason can help us achieve that, but in order for that to happen, reason must become a part of our lives and play a role in our communications with each other.

I long for a day when journalists would no longer ask questions that contain hidden assumptions or imply guilt. I would love to see politicians be called on it when they try to deflect questions by using faulty logic. I would like to see a barroom argument defused by the man who points out that personal attacks are irrelevant to the issue at hand. Critical thinking skills, especially knowledge of logical fallacies, could be taught as an elective in high schools and as a required general education course in colleges and universities. These things should become part of our collective knowledge as a society, part of what it means to be "civilized."

Reason deserves our respect and it needs to be utilized. The long-term reward for doing so is priceless — a greater understanding of the world. That, in turn, gives us the basis for much more.

It allows us to find genuine and realistic meaning in our own lives, rather than basing our lives on fantasy. It allows us to recognize suffering, injustice, and all the unpleasant aspects of reality for what they really are. Once that is accomplished, then we can deal with them in the best possible way. For those things that we cannot change, we can learn a nonpassive acceptance that leads to peace of mind. Reason brings our attention to the present, rather than to some unrealistic future. With our focus on the here and now, our lives are richer and can be enjoyed more fully. Reason can take us down the path towards living a life without illusions, clearly perceived. It helps us gain an appreciation for what it truly means to be human.

I think back, again, upon my own search for answers and it seems as if I have made it through a great maze with towering walls. The maze was full of twisted passages that circled back on themselves and side paths that led to dead ends. When I discovered the value of science, logic, and reason in general, it was as if I had found a compass, a map, and a ball of string — the tools I could use to finally escape. I emerged on the other side of the maze to a vast open plain. Beyond, there were dense forests, high mountains, and oceans of blue and green. Countless possibilities lay in store.

Bibliography

Armstrong, Karen. *A History of God*. New York: Ballantine Books, 1994.

Baggini, Julian and Peter S. Fosl. *The Philosopher's Toolkit*. United Kingdom: Blackwell Publishing Ltd., 2003.

Brogaard, Betty. *Dare to Think for Yourself*. Baltimore, MY: PublishAmerica, LLLP., 2004.

Brunvand, Jan Harold. *Curses! Broiled Again! The Hottest Urban Legends*. New York: Barnes & Noble, Inc., 2003.

Dawkins, Richard. *The Blind Watchmaker*. New York: W. W. Norton & Company, Inc., 1986.

Eller, David. *Natural Atheism*. Parsippany, NJ: American Atheist Press, 2004.

Macrone, Michael. *Brush Up Your Bible*. New York: Harper Collins, 1993.

Narciso, Dianna. *Like Rolling Uphill: Realizing the Honesty of Atheism*. Coral Springs, FL: Llumina Press, 2005.

Olson, Robert G. *An Introduction to Existentialism*. New York: Dover Publications, Inc., 1962.

Roach, Mary. *Spook: Science Tackles the Afterlife*. New York: W. W. Norton & Company, Inc., 2005.

Sagan, Carl. *The Demon-Haunted World: Science as a Candle in the Dark*. New York: Ballantine Books, 1997.

Shermer, Michael. *Why People Believe Weird Things*. New York: Henry Holt and Company, LLC., 1997.

Smith, George H. *Atheism: The Case Against God*. New York: Prometheus Books, 1989.

Walton, Douglas N. *Informal Logic: A Handbook for Critical Argumentation.* New York: Cambridge University Press, 1989.

Winell, Marlene, Ph.D. *Leaving the Fold.* Oakland, CA: New Harbinger Publications, Inc., 1993.

INDEX